SO WHAT'S
——— THE ———
DIFFERENCE?

FRITZ RIDENOUR

BETHANYHOUSE
a division of Baker Publishing Group
Minneapolis, Minnesota

Published by Bethany House Publishers
11400 Hampshire Avenue South
Bloomington, Minnesota 55438
www.bethanyhouse.com

Bethany House Publishers is a division of
Baker Publishing Group, Grand Rapids, Michigan

Bethany House edition published 2014
ISBN 978-0-7642-1564-3

Previously published by Regal Books

Printed in the United States of America

The Library of Congress has cataloged the original edition as follows:
Ridenour, Fritz.
    So what's the difference? / Fritz Ridenour.—[Rev. ed.].
        p. cm.
    Includes bibliographical references.
    ISBN 0-8307-1898-2 (trade)
    1. Christianity and other religions. 2. Christian sects. I. Title.
BR127 .R5   2001
261.2—dc21   00-066500

All Scripture quotations, unless otherwise indicated, are taken from the Holy Bible, New International Version®. NIV®. Copyright © 1973, 1978, 1984 by Biblica, Inc.™ Used by permission of Zondervan. All rights reserved worldwide. www.zondervan.com

Scripture quotations labeled KJV are from the King James Version of the Bible.

Scripture quotations labeled NASB are from the New American Standard Bible®, copyright © 1960, 1962, 1963, 1968, 1971, 1972, 1973, 1975, 1977, 1995 by The Lockman Foundation. Used by permission.

Scripture quotations labeled NLT are from the Holy Bible, New Living Translation, copyright © 1996, 2004, 2007 by Tyndale House Foundation. Used by permission of Tyndale House Publishers, Inc., Carol Stream, Illinois 60188. All rights reserved.

Scripture quotations labeled PHILLIPS are from The New Testament in Modern English, revised edition—J. B. Phillips, translator. © J. B. Phillips 1958, 1960, 1972. Used by permission of Macmillan Publishing Co., Inc.

Cover and Interior Design by Robert Williams

Edited by Kathi Macias, Bayard Taylor, David Webb, Deena Davis

14   15   16   17   18   19   20   7   6   5   4   3   2   1

CONTENTS

TODAY THE DIFFERENCE MATTERS MORE THAN EVER

The goal of this revised, updated and expanded edition of *So What's the Difference?* remains the same as it was when the first copies were printed 30 years ago: to spell out the differences between the historic Christian faith and other views represented in major religions, cults and ideologies that are vying for the hearts and minds of people today. And, to be sure, much in our society has changed since this book first appeared in the late 1960s.

The cultural center of America has shifted away from Christian, or at least Judeo-Christian, morals and attitudes, to post-Christian.

Relative thinking, the idea that there is no objective absolute truth and "what's true or right for you isn't necessarily true or right for me," has captured the imagination of vast numbers of people and has even infiltrated some Christian churches.[1]

There is increasing controversy in some denominations because some church leaders have abandoned Christian core teachings, including the incarnation of Christ, His redemptive work on the cross and His resurrection.[2]

School boards, other elected officials and the Supreme Court have sought to remove God from the classroom, making it difficult for Christian ministries and other Christian interests, by rulings and decisions of various kinds.

Increasing numbers of people have fled "organized religion" and are seeking "spirituality" in many "nontraditional" forms, particularly the New Age movement. Also, many new cults and ideologies have appeared on the scene, some claiming to be legitimate Christianity with newer and deeper insights. In addition to the "newer" views, the old cults and ideologies have developed more subtle approaches and more convincing arguments.

With a veritable smorgasbord of views and opinions now available, it is more important than ever for biblical Christians to be able to recognize and spell out the basic differences between a Christian worldview and the beliefs held by neighbors, coworkers and schoolmates.

DO YOU KNOW WHAT YOUR WORLDVIEW IS?

A common testimony binds all authentic believers in Christ together and distinguishes them from other worldviews. The term "worldview" may sound a bit abstract, but simply put, your worldview is the set of assumptions that make up your personal outlook on the nature of the world and how to live in that world day by day. It is your "set of beliefs about the most important issues in life."[3]

It is important to realize that everyone has a worldview whether or not he or she can recognize or state it. You may not think about your worldview when you make decisions or express opinions, but it influences your thoughts, feelings and actions. Your worldview is based on how you see answers to some rather important questions about life, which include: (1) Who or what is God? (2) Who am I and how do I operate in my world? (3) How can I tell right from wrong? (4) When it's all over, where do I go? (5) How can I know the truth; for that matter, how can I be sure that I know anything? (6) What does my life mean, and how do I fit into history, if at all?[4]

Today Christians face many nonbiblical worldviews, which can be broken down into several categories: naturalism, pantheism, polytheism and a possible fourth category, relativism, which in a characteristically postmodern way wants to avoid the straitjacket of categories.

Naturalism says that God does not exist and that physical matter is all there is. Charles Colson, prolific author and shaper of contemporary Christian thinking, believes that naturalism is by far the dominant worldview today and that it is responsible for creating our post-Christian and postmodern culture.[5] Linked closely to naturalism are other anti-Christian worldviews, such as secular humanism, empiricism and evolutionism.

The second major worldview category comes from the East. It is called pantheistic monism, which says, "All is one, one is all, and all is God." Hinduism and Buddhism share important elements of this worldview. The New Age movement is, in great part, a Western adaptation of Hindu and Buddhist religious and worldview thinking.

A third worldview that will come up from time to time is polytheism—the idea that there are many gods, goddesses and spirits that we must appease and please to have a reasonably good life. Some polytheists wear loincloths; others are dressed in business suits. Polytheism can be found in Hinduism and branches of the New Age, as well as among Mormons (although they would indignantly deny this—see chapter 10).

A fourth category is reserved for those who are reluctant to commit to any particular worldview. They would prefer to pick and choose what they like about different worldviews and aren't much bothered if the ideas contradict each other. The only thing that counts is "what works for you." These people will say things like, "I don't believe any one system contains all truth." Whatever else this worldview is, it is relativistic, and it is often a big part of the thinking found in secular humanism and postmodernism, as well as the New Age movement.

CAN YOU ARTICULATE YOUR BIBLICAL WORLDVIEW?

As this book presents the difference between Christianity and other worldviews, the goal is to sharpen your perspective on your own biblical worldview. Obviously, the Christian uses the Bible to answer all those worldview questions mentioned above: There is only *one* God, who is supreme and sovereign. And while He is transcendent—above and beyond us, He is also immanent—right here among us at the same time. He created it all—the universe and the world in which we live. Furthermore, He did it with *absolutely nothing*. He didn't rearrange or put together matter of some kind that was as eternal as He is.

His crowning creation was humankind—us. We are made in God's image; and when we die we will either go to be with Him or be separated from Him forever. There will be no coming back to "try to get it right." Because sin prevents us from getting it right, God sent His Son—part of Himself—to redeem and justify us (more on this in chapter 1).

As for knowledge, the Christian worldview doesn't agree with skeptics who say knowledge is simply unattainable. (By the way, if you want to ruin a skeptic's day, ask him how he *knows* knowledge is unattainable.) Because God is the all-knowing knower of everything, and because we are made in His image (see Gen. 1:27), we can know all we need to know as we work on our own Christian worldview. Obviously, the most important part of a Christian's worldview is knowing God. We can know God through two forms of revelation: the created order of His universe and special revelation—the Scriptures. (More on this also in chapter 1.)

Concerning right and wrong, the Christian does not cave in to secular humanist or postmodernist claims that there are no absolutes and that all truth is "relative"—that is, whatever is good for you is fine, and whatever is good for me is fine, too. Moral truth, in particular, is absolute because God has pronounced it so. The Ten Commandments are not the "ten suggestions." Not only do we need to learn God's commandments, but we also need His constant reminders of what is right and wrong because of our innate human capacity to be deceived, not only by other people but by Satan, who "masquerades as an angel of light" (2 Cor. 11:14; see also Eph. 6:12).

Surrounded as we are today with so many hostile, as well as subtly deceptive, viewpoints, we must always be aware that one of Satan's oldest and most diabolical strategies is to convince humans that God cannot be trusted (see Gen. 3:1-15). History is a record of how Satan has been all too successful in accomplishing his ends.

And speaking of history and its meaning for our lives, the Bible teaches us that history is linear. That is, history is headed somewhere in a straight line. It had a beginning, it's going toward a goal and it will come to an end planned by God. This is a much different view from that of Eastern pantheism, which sees history happening in cycles, going round and round, with time being rather meaningless.[6]

Because history is linear, it means that God has a plan for His Church. The Church has played a vital role in history for almost 2,000 years, but just what is the Church, and who is in it?

THE CHURCH IS VISIBLE—
AND INVISIBLE

From the very first church described in the early chapters of Acts until now, there has always been a core of genuine believers in Christ's atoning death on the cross and His resurrection, which guarantees life eternal. These genuine believers are identified in Scripture as the "Body of Christ," which Paul refers to in several of his epistles (see Rom. 12:5; 1 Cor. 12:27; Eph. 1:23; 4:12; Col. 1:24; 2:19).

Down through the centuries, this Body of Christ has met in local visible churches of all kinds. Theologian Wayne Grudem observes that the New Testament uses the word "church" when speaking of believers meeting in private homes (see Rom. 16:5; 1 Cor. 16:19), in an entire city (see 1 Cor. 1:2; 2 Cor. 1:1) or in a region (see Acts 9:31).[7]

Grudem acknowledges, however, that "the visible church . . . will always include some unbelievers . . . because we cannot see hearts as God sees them."[8] Grudem goes on to point out that the Church, while being visible, is also invisible. It is invisible "in its true spiritual reality as a fellowship of all genuine believers." Grudem cites the author of Hebrews who speaks of the "church of the firstborn, whose names are written in heaven" (Heb. 12:23). The invisible Church, then, is "the church as God sees it" (see 2 Tim. 2:19).[9]

This invisible Church—the Body of Christ—can be found today throughout the world, but it does not reside in any particular church or denomination.[10] Every year the *International Bulletin of Missionary Research* tracks the visible Church by gathering figures on seven major groups, including Roman Catholics, Eastern Orthodox and Protestants. According to the IBMR report for the year 2000, the estimated world population was 6,055,049,000. Of these, 1,888,441,000, or 33 percent, call themselves Christians.[11]

How many true Christians can be found among those claiming to be Christians? Because Scripture tells us that the wheat grows with the weeds (see Matt. 13:24-30), only God knows. However, He includes every sincere follower in the invisible Body of Christ as part of "the community of all true believers for all time . . . made of all those who are truly saved" (see Eph. 1:22,23; 5:25).[12]

BEING A CHRISTIAN IS A PERSONAL MATTER

Ironically and sadly enough, there are differences—some significant, some not so significant—among all of the branches or blocs of Christians throughout the world. So serious are some of these differences that members of one branch or bloc accuse members of another of not having full salvation (or having no salvation at all). But whatever ecclesiastical hoops you might be asked to jump through in your particular congregation, the real issue is personal faith in Jesus Christ as Savior and Lord—being justified by faith through the redemption that is through the blood of Christ Jesus (see Rom. 3:24).

We must be clear on one crucial point: Being a member of any one church or group does not guarantee automatic membership in the Body of Christ. To update a familiar cliché, going to church on a regular basis no more makes you a Christian than eating daily at McDonald's makes you a hamburger. You have to do personal business with Jesus Christ—put your trust in Him as Savior and Lord. Becoming a true Christian is a personal transaction between you and God. *No one else can do it for you.*

The reason you can take these very personal steps with confidence rests squarely on the major assumption of Christianity; namely, that the same God who created the heavens and the earth is able to communicate to His creation in ways that we can clearly understand. We will never completely comprehend the infinite God with our limited intellect, but that does not limit God's ability to communicate what He wants us to know.

The claim that God clearly communicates and reveals Himself to us is precisely what rubs so many people the wrong way. If this claim is true, we are all equally accountable and without any excuse before God. To say that God has communicated uniquely through inspired Scripture—the Old and New Testaments—denies the claim that all religions are equally valid. To say this also accuses some belief systems of being full of lies and falsehoods; it flies in the face of skeptics and agnostics who say no one can really know anything; it grinds at materialists who believe that the physical world is the only reality and everything else is just superstition; it denies the claim of mystics who label anything said about ultimate truth as inadequate and totally misleading; it offends those who have chosen pleasure or power as their gods.

So, what *is* it that God has revealed so clearly? The evidence for the biblical worldview is clearly written on the pages of the Bible. In chapter 1 we will review this evidence that forms the foundation of this book. The major question is how you want to treat the evidence, which is summed up quite well in 1 Corinthians 15:3,4: "Christ died for our sins according to the Scriptures, that he was buried, that he was raised on the third day according to the Scriptures."

PART ONE

THE IMPORTANCE OF A BIBLICAL WORLDVIEW

CHAPTER ONE

BIBLICAL CHRISTIANITY

A PLUMB LINE FOR COMPARING FAITHS

Biblical Christianity. What does that mean? Can you be a Christian and not be biblical? Are there brands of Christianity that are unbiblical? And what does it mean to have a plumb line for comparing faiths? Some defining of terms is definitely in order.

Biblical. Whatever their tradition or denomination, most who answer to the name of Christian claim in some sense to be biblical. For this book's purposes, "biblical" means that the Christian believer searches seriously and carefully for the meaning of the Bible on its own terms, not changing its meaning to fit the times. Biblical Christians approach the Bible with reverence and respect, because they believe it is true and authoritative—that it contains God's very words.

As early as the second century and even late in the first, Christians saw the need for separating right (true) Christian belief from various kinds of subtle heresies that began to creep in. Webster defines heresy as "an opinion held in opposition to the commonly received doctrine and tending to promote division or dissension." Christianity has always had its foes, but no enemy has been more dangerous than the heretics within who have held opinions in opposition to the commonly received truths on which Christianity was founded. These common truths are contained in the New Testament, the books and epistles that came to be recognized as God's inspired—and final—words on what Christianity really is.

From the gnosticism of the first and second centuries to the liberalism of the present day, biblical Christians—the Body of Christ—have had to guard against heresy as well as against being too quick to judge other Christians with differing viewpoints. Biblical Christianity is like a huge tent or canopy that covers a myriad of churches, denominations and groups, all of which have beliefs or interpretations of Scripture they prefer to emphasize. But what draws all of these groups together are basic biblical doctrines that center around this plain and simple teaching:

Christ died for our sins according to the Scriptures . . . he was buried . . . he was raised on the third day according to the Scriptures (1 Cor. 15:3,4).

Obviously, there is a lot more to Christianity than what is said in these two verses, but we find here a plumb line for measuring the difference between biblical Christianity and other faiths.

Plumb line. A plumb line—a string with a pointed weight on the end—is still used today by masons to make sure they lay a brick wall straight and true. In a short little book tucked among the minor prophets of the Old Testament, God told Amos, "Look, I am setting a plumb line among my people" (Amos 7:8).

As the Holy Spirit directed Amos's thoughts, the analogy of a plumb line came to his mind and he referred to this familiar tool to tell the Israelite people what God wanted them to know—that God would measure them by His standards, His Word, and no other.

In the same way, God's Word will be the plumb line used in this book to define the differences between the basic truths on which Christianity was founded and what other faiths believe. We will explore the teachings of the Bible on three key points, all contained in capsule form in 1 Corinthians 15:3,4:

- The person and work of Christ—who He is and what He did for us.
- Mankind's[1] major problem—all of us are sinners in rebellion against God and in need of a Savior.
- The truth and reliability of the Bible—divine inspiration of Scripture.

CHRIST DIED

By definition, the backbone of Christianity is Christ. There are two key issues concerning Jesus Christ: who He is and what He did.

1. Who is He? Only a man? God disguised as a man? Or was He someone uniquely different?
2. What did He do? Teach us how to live? Die for our sins? Both?

All biblical Christians subscribing to the Nicene Creed agree on Christ's deity. Following are some of the key questions that people often raise about Jesus Christ.

Was Jesus really God, or was He a great teacher and nothing more than that?

While the Bible does not use the exact words "Jesus is God," the biblical record clearly and frequently teaches that Jesus Christ is, in fact, God. For example, John 1:1 refers to Christ as the Word (Logos) and tells us that "in the beginning was the Word . . . and the Word was

God." John 1:14 testifies that "the Word [God] became flesh and made his dwelling among us. We have seen his glory, the glory of the One and Only, . . . full of grace and truth."

Of primary importance is what Jesus said about Himself. On several occasions, He claimed to be equal with God. See, for example, John 10:30: "I and the Father are one." On another occasion Jesus told Philip and some of the other disciples that because they had seen Him they had seen the Father (see John 14:9).

In addition, Jesus frequently referred to Himself as God. In John 8:58, Jesus told the Pharisees, "I tell you the truth, before Abraham was born, I am!" The Pharisees, being excellent Bible students, knew that in Exodus 3:14 God had said to Moses, "This is what you are to say to the Israelites: 'I AM has sent me to you.'" The Pharisees knew that Jesus was claiming to be the God of Israel.[2] They picked up stones and would have tried to kill Him, but He slipped away.

Jesus also claimed to be God in important conversations with His own disciples. For example, before being arrested on the night of the Last Supper, Jesus told His disciples, "I am the way and the truth and the life. No one comes to the Father except through me. If you really knew me, you would know my Father as well."

Philip then asked, "Lord, show us the Father and that will be enough for us." Jesus' reply was a clear claim of divinity and equality with God: "Anyone who has seen me has seen the Father" (see John 14:5-9; see also 20:24-29).

In summary, if Jesus Christ was not who He claimed to be (God), but only a man, then Christianity is a fraud and Jesus would have to be a liar or a lunatic. As C. S. Lewis said, "He leaves us no other alternative. He did not intend to."[3]

Did Jesus' virgin birth actually happen?

According to the Bible, the virgin Mary gave birth to Jesus. People with an atheistic or naturalistic worldview scoff at this story because they cannot accept miracles or the supernatural. Other people object to the doctrine of the virgin birth on the grounds that it is similar to another legend, like pagan (polytheistic) stories of heroes who were half god, half man. But there is an enormous difference between the pagan worldview and the biblical. In all pagan stories of this kind, there is gross physical cohabitation of a god with a human being. In the Scripture account, Mary is simply informed, "The Holy Spirit will come upon you, and the power of the Most High will overshadow you. So the holy one to be born will be called the Son of God" (Luke 1:35). There is no suggestion that Jesus is half God and half man.

According to theologian Wayne Grudem, "The virgin birth made possible the uniting of full deity and full humanity in one person."[4] Jesus could have descended from heaven as a fully grown man, but that would have made it very hard for us to see how He could be just as human as we are. Or, He could have been born of two human parents, but that would have made it hard for us to see that He was truly God.

Instead, writes Grudem, "God, in His wisdom, ordained a combination of human and divine influence in the birth of Christ, so that His full humanity would be evident to us from the fact of His ordinary human birth from a human mother, and His full deity would be evident from the fact of His conception in Mary's womb by the powerful work of the Holy Spirit."[5]

Does the Trinity make three gods?

Even though the Bible never uses the word "trinity," Christians teach the doctrine of the Trinity, namely, the one eternal and living God, always existing as God the Father, God the Son and God the Holy Spirit. This leads some religions to reject the Trinity on the grounds that it sounds like Christians worship three gods, not one. It is true that Deuteronomy 6:4 states, "The LORD our God, the LORD is one." But it is also true that the Old Testament uses the plural form elohim for the word "God" 2,346 times.[6] (See, for example, Gen. 1:26; 11:7.)

The New Testament also clearly states that "God is one" (see Gal. 3:20), yet here again is abundant evidence that the unity of God, His oneness, involves three "persons." For example, as Matthew describes Jesus' baptism, He speaks of Jesus coming up out of the water, the heavens opening, the Spirit of God descending like a dove and a voice from heaven (God the Father) saying, "This is my Son, whom I love" (see Matt. 3:13-17).[7]

One of the strongest reasons that many critics reject the doctrine of the Trinity is that it makes Christ co-equal with God the Father. The Trinity is the particular target of critics in religions like Judaism and Islam, and in cults such as Unitarianism, Jehovah's Witnesses and Mormonism. All of these groups reduce Christ to a created being who is "second-in-command" at best or just another teacher on the same par with Buddha, Krishna or Moses.

But we have already seen that Jesus frequently referred to Himself as God. In addition, the rest of the New Testament fully concurs that the Son, Jesus Christ, is the God-man who was perfectly human and perfectly divine. He was one person having two distinct and separate natures. (See, for example, John 1:1-4 and Phil. 2:5-7.)

As for the Holy Spirit, Scripture clearly teaches that He enjoys the same interrelationship with the Father that Jesus does. In Matthew 28:19, the Holy Spirit is clearly made equal with the Father and the Son when Jesus commands the disciples to go and teach all nations "baptizing them in the name of the Father and of the Son and of the Holy Spirit."

When Jesus was preparing His disciples for His death and resurrection, He told them He was going to send a Comforter, whom he identified as the Holy Spirit, the Spirit of Truth who would live with them and be in them (see John 14:15-26). Also, Jesus' continued activity after His ascension, through the promised Holy Spirit, is the central theme of the entire book of Acts.[8]

Despite the many Scripture passages that clearly describe how the oneness of God includes three Persons—the Father, the Son and the Holy

Spirit—the Trinity remains one of the most difficult concepts for Christians to understand or explain to other people. How three persons can be one God called the Trinity is a puzzle to natural reasoning. If you try to see God your creator in natural or creaturelike terms, then you want to believe He is some kind of infinitely powerful person who is THE BOSS. If He is such a gigantic, all-powerful person, then how in the world could He be three big persons or even three smaller persons at once?

However, one question we might ask is, *If God is supernatural—beyond nature—why must He be understood only in natural terms?* The biblical believer accepts the mystery of God's greatness, realizing that the real point is that God is not the "Big Fella" upstairs. As Wayne Grudem points out, "The Trinity is a kind of existence far different from anything we have experienced."[9] We should not be surprised, then, that in the Trinity there is an element of mystery that defies any human analysis or understanding, because we are only human and God is God.[10]

Did Christ actually rise from the dead?

Biblical Christians say He did. The significance of this event in the biblical, historic Christian faith cannot be overestimated. It is absolutely nonnegotiable. Biblical Christians claim that by conquering death, Jesus Christ proved He was God. Furthermore, He ensured that all who believe in Him will have eternal life (see John 11:25,26), and He lives today as our mediator (see 1 Tim. 2:5) and our high priest (see Heb. 4:14-16). For Resurrection accounts, see Matthew 28:1-10; Mark 16:1-8; Luke 24:1-42; John 20 and 21.

The doctrine of the Resurrection is the foundation on which Christianity rests. As Paul wrote, "And if Christ has not been raised, your faith is futile; you are still in your sins" (1 Cor. 15:17).

Dr. Wilbur M. Smith, well-known American Bible scholar, comments in *Baker's Dictionary of Theology* that the Resurrection doctrine teaches "the absolute uniqueness and the supernaturalness of the person of Jesus Christ, and the particular hope which he has brought to men. . . . Remove the truth of resurrection from the New Testament and its whole doctrinal structure collapses, and hope vanishes."[11]

If the Christian's hope is in a dead Christ who was martyred because He threatened the existing religious establishment, then the Christian is in the same boat with the Muslim, the Buddhist and the follower of Confucius. Mohammed is dead. Buddha is dead. Confucius is dead. But the Bible affirms that Christ is alive; and because He lives, the Christian will live also, eternally.[12]

Because the Resurrection falls into the same supernatural category as the Trinity, many doubt that Christ actually did rise from the dead. Some theorize that He never really died but that He just passed out and was awakened later by His disciples. Or possibly the women went to the wrong tomb and found it empty. Another theory says that either His friends or His enemies stole the body.

As one Bible scholar has said, none of the "standard" explanations can account for the total change that occurred in Jesus' followers after they found the empty tomb. And as for His postresurrection appearances—to as many as 500 people at a time (see 1 Cor. 15:6)—they were far more than just a spiritual presence or apparition. Instead, "history, theology, and experience combine to show that the glorious fact is that Christ *did* rise from the dead" (see 1 Cor. 15:20, *Phillips*).[13]

So far we have looked at what it means when 1 Corinthians 15:3 says, "Christ died and was raised." Next we will see that Christ died for a good reason: our sin.

CHRIST DIED FOR OUR SINS

People often ask, "Who is Christ?" but they are equally puzzled over the question "Who are we?" Or perhaps more to the point "What does it mean to be human?" Following are biblical Christianity's answers to these questions.

Are we all good, all bad or in between?

Most people wouldn't want to say that we are all good; neither do they want to admit that we are all bad. They prefer the little-bit-of-both approach. Most of us like to think we're bad enough to be fun (i.e., a regular type—not dull or holier than thou). But of course we like to think we're also good enough to do the right thing when it counts.

The typical eulogy at many a person's funeral says, in effect, "He was a great guy," when he may have hated his mother-in-law, nursed a 20-year grudge against his neighbor, cheated on his income tax, padded his expense account, chased (and possibly caught) several other women besides his wife and blasphemed God daily in speech and actions.

The Bible teaches that all human beings are born with a crucial flaw in their natures, and that flaw is sin. In Ephesians 2:1 Paul tells us, "You were dead in your transgressions and sins." The reason for our spiritually dead condition is the sin of the first man, Adam. According to Genesis 1:26, Adam was made in the image of God. He was a free moral agent. Of his own choice, Adam sinned (disobeyed God), and the entire human race was plunged into sin. (See Gen. 3 and Rom. 5:12-21 for the account and the implications of what is commonly known as the Fall.)

How could Adam's disobedience plunge all of us into sin? Theologians from all the major branches of the Christian Church agree that Adam acted as "federal head of the human race."[14] That is, he represented all of us, and his initial act of sin had consequences for everyone, for all time. In his letter to the Romans, Paul sums it up by saying, "Sin entered the world through one man, and death through sin, and in this way death came to all men, because all sinned" (Rom. 5:12). Because Adam was our representative, God counted us guilty because of his sin.[15]

At first glance, Romans 5:12 sounds like an unfair judgment on everyone who lived after Adam. But is it? All of us know by experience that we do not live up to all that we know we should do (or not do) in relationship to God and our fellowman. Scripture teaches that we are all descended from Adam, and because we are part of Adam's family (the entire human race), we all have Adam's nature—a sinful heart. "The heart," writes Jeremiah, "is deceitful above all things and beyond cure. Who can understand it?" (Jer. 17:9).

While all of us are created in the image of God, just as Adam was, Adam's sin led us into a state that theologians call 'total depravity.' As Wayne Grudem points out, "Every part of our being is affected by sin—our intellects, our emotions . . . our hearts (the center of our desires in decision-making processes), our goals and motives, and even our physical bodies."[16]

Yes, unbelievers can do good on a social or human level. But Scripture clearly teaches that we *totally lack spiritual good before God.* Furthermore, we have no ability in ourselves to do anything in our own strength to please God or even come to Him to have a relationship. Only when God moves toward us in His grace and love through Jesus Christ can our total depravity be overcome. Total depravity is a serious condition, but *we are redeemable.* God does not give up on us. Although we are far from what He intended us to be, He loved us and sent His Son to die for us (see John 3:16). Adam's act of rebellion plunged all of us into sin, but Christ's act of obedience made it possible for us to be made righteous (see Rom. 5:17-21).

Just what is sin? Who decides what is or isn't sin?

In our culture it has become generally accepted that truth and morals are relative, that there are no objective or absolute truths and morals. All questions of right and wrong are seen as relative to the situation or to the culture or to each individual personal opinion. Since no one's opinion is more valuable than anyone else's, each of us must personally decide what is right and wrong—for us. To claim there are absolute truths about right and wrong is viewed as being intolerant, bigoted or judgmental—the three great "sins" of our postmodern secular culture.

Interestingly enough, those who take the "all truth is relative" approach, constantly find themselves having to make judgments about what is true, what is right and what is good. As they do this, they cannot help but judge other people with whom they disagree. With no absolute measuring stick about right and wrong, the ultimate result is moral chaos. (For where postmodernism is leading us, see chapter 12.)

According to the Bible, God has clearly shown us how to know what is objectively and absolutely right and wrong. In other words, God has defined sin for us and He has done it in two ways: general revelation (the moral law planted within each one of us) and special revelation (the Scriptures).

Paul describes the universal moral law (general revelation) in Romans 1: "For since the creation of the world God's invisible qualities—his eternal power and divine nature—have been clearly seen, being understood from what has been made, so that men are without excuse" (v. 20). Paul goes on to say that men knew God through nature and the very world around them, but they neither glorified God nor thanked Him and instead plunged into idolatry—serving created things rather than their creator (see vv. 21-25).

As for special revelation, Scripture is full of definitions for sin, which all boil down to breaking God's laws or going against God's will. Summed up, these definitions might be stated: *Sin is proud, independent rebellion against God in active or passive form.*

To put it in scriptural terms, "Everyone who sins breaks the law; in fact, sin is lawlessness" (1 John 3:4). Also, "all wrongdoing is sin" (1 John 5:17).

Examples of actively breaking God's laws or doing wrong can be summed up quite well in reviewing the Ten Commandments. Active sin includes such things as lying, stealing, murder and adultery. Passive sin is subtler, because it may not involve actions but may instead be a matter of attitude or thought. We can passively sin as our thoughts draw us into lust, selfishness, greed, jealousy, pride, indifference and lack of love.

James describes passive sin when he says, "Anyone, then, who knows the good he ought to do and doesn't do it, sins" (Jas. 4:17). Passive sin is summed up in the attitude that says to God or others, "Get lost, you're cramping my style. I'm too busy for you."

All of us sin actively and passively. As John puts it, "If we claim to be without sin, we deceive ourselves and the truth is not in us" (1 John 1:8). Isaiah zeros in on our basic nature this way: "We all, like sheep, have gone astray, each of us has turned to his own way; and the LORD has laid on him the iniquity of us all" (Isa. 53:6).

The laying of our iniquity (the guilt of our sin) on Christ is another puzzler for many people. They wonder:

How could Jesus Christ die for everyone's sins? Isn't every person responsible for his own sins?

Many religions and cults admit the problem of sin, but their answer is to seek salvation from sin through good works or by keeping rules and laws. The Christian's Bible teaches that Jesus Christ redeemed us from sin by dying on the cross. Nowhere is this more clearly stated than by the apostle Paul: "For all have sinned and fall short of the glory of God, and are justified freely by his grace through the redemption that came by Christ Jesus" (Rom. 3:23,24).

Justification by faith is the doctrinal pillar of biblical Christianity. When we place our faith and trust in the fact that Christ died to pay the penalty for our sins, we are justified, meaning that God's justice has been satisfied through the substitutionary death of His Son Jesus Christ, and we have been brought into a correct relationship with God. When Paul spoke of the redemption that came by Christ Jesus, he was saying that Christ paid the penalty for our sin by removing our guilt.

To illustrate, suppose you have to go to court for speeding, but you do not end up paying the fine. You learn that it has been paid by someone else—possibly good old Dad or rich Uncle Charley. Getting your fine paid by someone else partially illustrates justification, but God goes one important step further. While your traffic ticket is taken care of, it doesn't alter the fact that you are guilty. But when you, as a sinner, turn to God through Christ, amazingly (and inexplicably), *your guilt is wiped out as well.*

Paul went on to say, "God presented Him [Christ] as a sacrifice of atonement, through faith in his blood" (Rom. 3:25). When the Bible speaks of atonement, God's justice and His love are both involved. When Jesus Christ—God incarnate—died on the cross, He rendered satisfaction to God's holy standard and paid the penalty for the sin of all mankind (see John 3:16,17).

How can Scripture say that Christ's single death is adequate payment for the sins of the entire world? It is adequate because *Christ is God.* No one less than God could make payment for the sins of everyone. God is the one who set the holy standard. Who could fulfill its requirements but God Himself?

The Bible also teaches that we can do nothing to earn our justification. The Christian is saved by grace—God's unmerited favor, mercy and love. "For it is by grace you have been saved, through faith—and this not from yourselves, it is the gift of God—not by works, so that no one can boast" (Eph. 2:8,9).

Many people, however, have difficulty accepting the concept that they cannot earn God's favor. Deep down, they believe they can earn salvation by being "good enough." Also at work is the popular and widespread idea that "Somebody else shouldn't be punished for my mistakes." That kind of thinking sounds noble, humble and honest. Actually this reasoning stems from pride, from not wanting to admit that no one can attain the standard of a holy God. For any of us to say that we can earn our own salvation is to say that God is something less than perfectly holy, and this is to say that God is less than God. Not only has Christ provided salvation by dying for our sins, but He will also return to Earth to judge the living and the dead (see John 5:22,27; Acts 10:42).

CHRIST DIED FOR OUR SINS ACCORDING TO THE SCRIPTURES

For Christians, the Scriptures are the Old and New Testaments of the Bible. Christians view these writings as the God-given basis for their faith.

Inspiration of the Bible is a main watershed between Christianity and other faiths. If the Bible cannot be trusted to be the inspired Word of God, then its claims concerning the deity of Christ, our sinful state and our need for salvation through faith in Christ's death and resurrection have no force. The biblical Christian recognizes the Old and New Testaments as the only words that come from God Himself—the final authority for faith and practice. For biblical Christians, all claims to authority must be judged according to Scripture. Following are answers to common questions concerning the Scriptures.

Is the Bible actually "inspired by God"? Why is the Bible supposed to be superior to other books?

The favorite verse for claiming the Bible's superiority to other books is 2 Timothy 3:16. The most familiar translation of the verse reads: "All Scripture is given by inspiration of God" (*KJV*). A better translation of the Greek word here is found in the *NIV*, which says, "All Scripture is God-breathed." In other words, God the Holy Spirit guided or acted on the minds of the authors of Scripture, revealing to them what He wanted written (see also 2 Pet. 1:21).

As you read the pages of Scripture, particularly the New Testament, there is an unmistakable tone of authority and accuracy. This is because the writing was done either by eyewitnesses or by people very close to those who actually knew and lived with Jesus. No wonder J. B. Phillips, the gifted translator of the New Testament, said that again and again he "felt rather like an electrician rewiring an ancient house without being able to 'turn the mains off.'"[17]

What kind of proof can Christians offer for the Bible's inspiration and accuracy?

As we have already seen, there is first of all the Bible's own claim to be the inspired Word of God. But can the biblical Christian prove this claim? There is plenty of historical and scientific evidence for the Bible's validity and evidence in the form of fulfilled prophecy. The Old Testament contains over 300 references to the Messiah that were fulfilled in Jesus Christ. Computations using the science of probability on just 8 of these prophecies show the chance that someone could have fulfilled all 8 prophecies is 10^{17} power, or 1 in 100 quadrillion.[18]

As for scientific evidence, archaeologists have proved again and again the accuracy of Scripture accounts, the names of peoples, places and dates. Nelson Glueck, eminent Jewish archaeologist, has categorically stated that "no archaeological discovery has ever controverted a biblical reference."[19] William F. Albright, recognized as one of the greatest of archaeologists, testified that there is no doubt that archaeology "has confirmed the substantial historicity of Old Testament tradition."[20]

Another piece of evidence for the Bible's inspiration is its unity. The Bible was written by 40 authors over a period of 1,600 years. Most of these writers never knew the others. When J. B. Phillips began work on his *New Testament in Modern English*, he was not predisposed to regard the Bible as verbally inspired (that the very words were God-breathed). But as the work progressed, Phillips was increasingly impressed and amazed at the unity that existed throughout the books of the Bible. He said, "In their different ways and from their different angles, these writers are all talking about the same thing and talking with a certainty as to bring a wonderful envy into a modern heart."[21]

How was the canon formed?

In the Early Church, apostolic authorship (or at least close association with a recognized apostle) was one of the chief criteria for deciding what books should be included in the New Testament canon ("group of authoritative books"). The apostles were men who had served and lived with Christ. They actually had known Him or had experienced Him in a unique way, as did Paul who was converted on the road to Damascus. The apostles suffered incredible persecution; most, if not all, died horrible deaths for the Christian cause. The only plausible explanation for their zeal was that they had actually seen, talked and eaten with the resurrected Lord Jesus Christ. If Christ had not risen and appeared to the apostles, it's unimaginable that they all would have died for a lie.

Even more powerful than the claims of those who wrote the different books of the Bible is the testimony of Jesus Christ Himself concerning the inspiration and authority of Scripture.

Christians believe that Christ is God incarnate (in the flesh). The most important claim to inspiration for the Bible is what Christ Himself said about Scripture (the Old Testament at that time, because the New Testament was not yet written). Jesus believed that all of Scripture is sacred; that's why He said, "The Scripture cannot be broken" (John 10:35). In the final days and weeks before He went to the cross, Jesus mentioned what He had to do in order that the Scriptures be fulfilled (see Luke 18:31; Matt. 26:54).[22]

To claim anything less than God-breathed inspiration for Scripture is to claim that Jesus is mistaken or lying; if He is either, He is something far less than God. And if He is less than God, His work of atonement on the cross for our sins is insufficient.

Throughout history, attacks have been made on the Bible's accuracy and inspiration, but the Bible still stands. Critics may disagree with or reject the Scriptures, but they cannot conclusively prove that the Bible is not what it claims to be: the inspired Word of God. As the psalmist said, "Your word, O LORD, is eternal; it stands firm in the heavens" (Ps. 119:89).

IS BIBLICAL CHRISTIANITY RIGHT?

Holding a biblical worldview based on the absolute truth of Scripture can sound like Christians believe they have all the truth. Christians do not claim to possess all the truth because only God knows all the truth perfectly and exhaustively. At best, we can know truth only partially as 1 Corinthians 13:12 clearly teaches. Neither do Christians claim that there is absolutely no truth in non-Christian religions and other worldviews. There are many truths that are common to all people. Nor do Christians claim that they alone are immune from cultural blinders or other errors. Error and foolishness is a common human problem, even among Christians.

This chapter is built around 1 Corinthians 15:3,4, which centers on the person and work of Christ, the nature of man and the inspiration of Scripture. Obviously, there are many other doctrines to the Christian faith, but we will make these three crucial areas our plumb line as we study other faiths in the rest of this book.

Admittedly, this plumb line is based on a Protestant, evangelical, conservative point of view. Not all Christian bodies would agree with it at every point, particularly Roman Catholics or Eastern Orthodox, who believe that Tradition is equally as important as Scripture. More on that later, but for now we proceed with the assumption that biblical Christians from all points of the theological compass can agree with Paul's words in 1 Corinthians 15:3,4:

> For what I received I passed on to you as of first importance: that Christ died for our sins according to the Scriptures, that he was buried, that he was raised on the third day according to the Scriptures.

These verses are the touchstone for the Christian who wants to be biblical. Biblical Christians believe that Christ is God and that He died for our sins. Biblical Christians believe that by nature they are sinners, spiritually dead, and that their only hope of salvation from sin is faith in Christ's death and resurrection. Biblical Christians believe they have a Bible that is inspired by the living God, and it is the only infallible rule of faith and practice.

In order to make intelligent comparisons with other faiths, Christians must know what their own faith teaches—what their own Bible says. These teachings are not to be revised, watered down or "demythologized." Biblical Christianity stands in faith and assurance upon the evidence "that was once for all entrusted to the saints" (Jude 3). Only God can provide saving faith to a person, and that happens only when that person is open to what God has to say. In Paul's words in 1 Corinthians 12:3, "No one can say, 'Jesus is Lord,' except by the Holy Spirit."

Why is Christendom so splintered?

Throughout the history of the Church—A.D. 30 until the present—the biblical truths discussed in this chapter have been challenged and denied by all kinds of groups, some within the Church and some without. The story of how the Church has dealt with everything from heresy to holy war is inspiring as well as saddening. From the very beginning, Christians have fought a battle to believe the faith once delivered to the saints.

In the first century, Christ's apostles founded the Church, which spread quickly from Jerusalem out into the entire Mediterranean world despite persecution from (1) the Jews who did not accept Christ as the Messiah and (2) the Roman government, which branded Christians outlaws because they insisted that Jesus, not Caesar, was Lord.

Many Christians were martyred, but their blood became the seed that spread the Church even more. As the Church grew, however, an even greater threat came from within its ranks in the form of heresy, particularly Gnosticism, which threatened to corrupt and twist the gospel into just another pagan religion or philosophy. But the Church fought off this threat as well, particularly through the work of men called apologists who wrote and spoke for the truth.

By the second century, the Church founded by the apostles developed into the Catholic (universal) church; and early in the fourth century persecution of Christianity was ended by Constantine who became

emperor of the western Roman Empire after winning a battle in which
he believed Christ gave him special help. Christianity soon became the
dominant religion of the Roman Empire, and eventually the Church
included five patriarchates—four in the East (Constantinople, Jerusalem,
Alexandria and Caesarea) and Rome in the West. Distance, different languages and culture, and conflicting theological opinions were all reasons
for serious disagreement between the East and the West; but the chief
cause of division was a continuing insistence by the Church at Rome on
supreme power and authority over all of Christendom. The rift came to
a head in 1054 when a major split created the Roman Catholic Church
in the West and the Orthodox Church in the East.

After the split, the Roman Catholic Church gained even more
power and continued to add doctrines not found in Scripture. In addition, the Roman Church became more and more corrupt, which finally led to the Protestant Reformation, started by a Catholic monk
named Martin Luther. In the beginning, Luther intended to reform the
Roman Church by making the Bible the only authority. But Church
leaders, particularly the pope, rejected his views and he was forced out.

The Reformation spread throughout Europe, and those who
protested against the teachings of Rome came to be recognized as a
new form of Christianity called Protestant. From one Christian
Church, then, came three major branches or trunks: Roman Catholic,
Eastern Orthodox and Protestant, which further divided into many
different denominations.

How did the simple gospel taught by Paul and other writers of the
New Testament develop into scores of viewpoints that all call themselves
Christian but who cannot agree, often on very crucial issues? Why do
these disagreements persist to this day? Can the gaps ever be bridged?

To begin seeking answers to these challenging questions, we will
begin with a look at the differences between the evangelical Protestant
view presented in this chapter and the Roman Catholic view being
taught by the Vatican as the second millennium ended and the twenty-
first century began.

PART TWO

OTHER TRUNKS OF THE CHRISTIAN TREE

CHAPTER TWO

ROMAN CATHOLICISM

THE ONE TRUE CHURCH?

To compare specific or particular differences between the Catholic Church and the many Protestant churches that came out of the Reformation would be a hopeless task.[1] For our purposes, we will compare the plumb line of biblical Christianity to the Roman Catholic Church regarding *authority* (Rome's claim to be the only "true church," with the exclusive right and ability to interpret the Word of God for believers) and *salvation* (how a person finds justification from his sins).

SOLA SCRIPTURA OR THE BIBLE PLUS TRADITION?

One of the major battle cries of the Protestant Reformation was *sola scriptura*—"Scripture alone." The reformers rejected many Roman Catholic

traditions and practices and argued for a Church that would base its doctrines and practice strictly on what the Bible teaches. But at the Council
of Trent (1545-1563), the Roman Catholic Church rebuffed this teaching and retained the right and power to interpret the Holy Scriptures
according to what it believed the Bible says.[2]

During Vatican Council II (1962-1965), the claims of Trent were
simply upheld in a little different form. Among the Vatican Council II
documents is the "Dogmatic Constitution on Divine Revelation" (*Dei
Verbum*). A careful reading of the *Dei Verbum* shows that the Roman
Catholic Church believes that the apostles passed on their authority to
succeeding bishops in the churches of the first century and the centuries that followed. As the years went by, the Church added certain
teachings based on what it calls Sacred Tradition.[3] Because the bishops
supposedly possessed the same apostolic insight and wisdom as the
apostles, the traditions they began to pass on were given equal weight
with Scripture. Instead of *sola scriptura* (the Bible alone), the Catholic
Church assumed and claimed the correct approach to be Scripture *plus*
tradition.[4]

WHY IS SOLA SCRIPTURA
SO IMPORTANT?

The evangelical Protestant, a direct spiritual descendant of the
Reformers of the sixteenth century, should understand that *sola scriptura* is not just an unfamiliar Latin phrase. *Sola scriptura* is a direct contradiction of the Roman Catholic claim that Scripture and Sacred
Tradition are equal sources of spiritual authority. Following are basic
reasons why Protestants stand on *sola scriptura* as their only basis for
authority.

Sola scriptura means the Bible alone is all we need for our spiritual
authority. All the things we need to know, believe and practice are clearly stated in the Scriptures, which are given by inspiration of God.

Anyone with common sense can understand what the Bible says in order to believe in Christ and be saved.

At the same time, the Bible is not a catalogue containing all knowledge of everything—including religion. Some Roman Catholic apologists claim that because the Bible does not include the many other things that Jesus did (see John 21:25), it is incomplete as the rule of faith. Protestants reply that the Bible is complete enough (sufficient) to teach the truth about redemption from sin. Scripture plainly says that if you confess with your mouth that Jesus is Lord and believe in your heart that God raised Him from the dead you shall be saved (see Rom. 10:9). It does not mention the need to know all the other things that Jesus did.

Nor does *sola scriptura* mean that anyone can believe whatever he likes and interpret the Bible as he sees it. The Church is commissioned to teach the truth, but the Church must remain subservient to the truth. The Protestant believer can trust his church only to the extent that it stays true to Scripture.

Also, to believe in *sola scriptura* does not deny that the Word of God was communicated for a time by word of mouth. Obviously, the gospel was passed on orally with amazing accuracy during the first 20 or 30 years of the Church's existence, before any of Paul's letters were written or any of the Gospels penned. But the point is, what was put down on paper as Scripture was essentially the spoken gospel message.

Roman Catholics maintain that the Bible is a "church-based book" because the Church wrote or at least determined what comprised the New Testament. Evangelical Protestants say the Church *discovered* the New Testament as the Holy Spirit made clear which writings were authoritative and inspired. And never was the Church without the Scriptures. It had the Old Testament, which clearly pointed to the New, and it might be noted as well that New Testament writers often quoted from the Old Testament as they wrote under the guidance and inspiration of the Holy Spirit (see 2 Pet. 1:20,21).[5]

READ SCRIPTURE, YES—
INTERPRET IT, NO

Contrary to what some Protestants have thought over the years, Catholics are encouraged to read the Bible; however, they are not encouraged to interpret it for themselves. The *Dei Verbum* document confirms this idea when it says, "All that has been said about the manner of interpreting Scripture is ultimately subject to the judgment of the Church which exercises the divinely conferred commission and ministry of watching over and interpreting the Word of God."[6] Evangelical Protestants, however, believe that the Holy Spirit guides individuals in learning what God has to tell them; believers are to search the Scriptures themselves (see John 16:13; Acts 17:11).

A key example of Roman Catholicism's insistence that it is the only accurate and authoritative source of interpretation of Scripture is Matthew 16:13-20. In this passage, Jesus paused to ask His disciples, "Who do you say I am?" Peter tells Him that He is the Christ, the Son of the Living God. Jesus tells Peter that only His Father in heaven could have revealed this truth to him and then adds the famous lines,

> And I tell you that you are Peter, and on this rock I will build my church, and the gates of Hades will not overcome it. I will give you the keys of the kingdom of heaven; whatever you bind on earth will be bound in heaven, and whatever you loose on earth will be loosed in heaven (vv. 18,19).

According to the *Catechism of the Catholic Church*, Jesus named Peter the "rock" of his Church, gave him the keys and made him shepherd of the whole flock. "This pastoral office of Peter and the other apostles belongs to the Church's very foundation and is continued by the bishops under the primacy of the Pope" who "as Vicar of Christ and as pastor of the entire Church has full, supreme and universal power over the whole Church, a power which he can always exercise unhindered."[7]

Evangelicals do not agree with Rome's interpretation. First, Jesus does not say directly that He will build his Church upon Peter himself, but upon "this rock." The Greek text clearly refers to Peter as *Petros* (meaning a small stone) and to "this rock" as *petra* (meaning a very large Gibraltar-size rock).

At Vatican Council I (adjourned in 1870), in addition to the doctrine of papal infallibility, Catholic bishops proclaimed that the "Peter is the Rock" interpretation of Matthew 16 was the "clear doctrine of Holy Scripture as it has been ever understood by the Roman Catholic Church." On the contrary, many of the Church fathers believed that the rock mentioned by Jesus in Matthew 16 was the *confession of faith* made by Peter and not Peter himself.[8]

The point is, down through the centuries, there has been no unanimous interpretation that Christ planned to make Peter the foundational rock on which the Church would be built. When the New Testament speaks of the Church's foundation, it always clearly identifies Christ as that foundation, and no one else (see 1 Cor. 3:11; Eph. 2:20; 1 Pet. 2:4-8). In his own letters to the Church, Peter never assumed the title or authority of anything like a pope. He was an elder who urged his fellow elders to "be shepherds of God's flock" (1 Pet. 5:2).

As evangelical Protestants comb the pages of the New Testament, they do not find convincing proof for the claims of Rome regarding Peter.[9] Conclusive evidence simply is not there, but Rome explains this by saying that tradition is to account for its interpretation of passages referring to Peter.

Building on its claim to be the only infallible authority as to what Scripture really means, the Catholic Church has understandably been rather subjective in interpreting various passages of Scripture to make the Bible fit or support its traditions. It is incorrect to say Roman Catholics have no scriptural base for their teachings. They find scriptural base either by directly interpreting certain passages to mean what they believe the passages mean or by finding their doctrines to be *implicitly* taught in Scripture. In other words, dogmas such as the

Immaculate Conception, the bodily assumption of Mary, and papal infallibility are implied in Scripture and, when viewed according to the teachings of the papacy, they make perfectly good sense to Roman Catholics.

Another important doctrine held by Roman Catholics (and the Eastern Orthodox Church) is apostolic succession. This view grew out of the Church's move toward an episcopal type of government in the first and second centuries due to its fear of heresy and other concerns. Bishops became the most important officials in the Church and by the late second century were considered the supposed successors to the apostles, complete with their powers, authority and wisdom.

Evangelical Protestant scholars refuse to accept the principle of apostolic succession, a term that is not found in the New Testament. They find no "clear unbroken line of succession" reaching all the way back to the apostle Peter. (For more on apostolic succession, see chapter 3.)

SAVED BY FAITH OR FAITH PLUS "WORKS"?

Just as Protestants rely on *sola scriptura* (the Bible alone) for a source of final authority and truth, they rely on *sola fide* (faith alone) for their source of salvation. The Catholic, however, believes that the Christian must rely on faith *plus* "good works" and God's grace mediated through the Seven Sacraments. These are:

- *Baptism* (see Matt. 28:19), for infants or adults, imparts sanctifying grace and erases original sin. The Catholic believer keeps sanctifying grace only through "spiritual battle" (following the program of good works).[10]
- *Confirmation* (see John 14:26) is the completion of baptism, the giving of the Holy Spirit in a fuller outpouring. Children who have been baptized are confirmed at age 12.

- *The Holy Eucharist* (see Matt. 26:26-28; John 6:35-58) is also called Holy Communion and is the most important sacrament of the Catholic Church. During Mass, through the miracle of *transubstantiation,* Christ is re-presented as an unbloody sacrifice for sins.
- *Penance (confession or reconciliation)* (see John 20:19-23) is how a Roman Catholic is forgiven by God—through the ministry of a priest—for the sins he commits after baptism.
- *Anointing of the Sick* (see Jas. 5:14,15) was formerly called *Extreme Unction.* In performing this sacrament, the priest lays hands on the sick or dying believer, prays over him or her in the faith of the Church, and anoints the believer with oil blessed, if possible, by the bishop.[11]
- *Holy Orders* (see 1 Tim. 3:1; 2 Tim. 1:6; Titus 2:15) is the sacrament through which Catholic ministers are ordained at three levels: bishops, presbyters (priests) and deacons. Only bishops can confer the Sacrament of Holy Orders.[12]
- *Matrimony* (see Gen. 2:18, 21-25; Eph. 5:22,33) is the sacrament in which Christ joins a Christian man and woman in a grace-giving, lifelong union. Divorce and remarriage cut the Catholic off from eucharistic communion but not from the Church.

Of the Seven Sacraments, the two most significant concerning doctrinal differences with Protestants are the Holy Eucharist and Penance. Roman Catholics believe that when the priest consecrates the bread and wine during the Mass, these elements are transformed into the actual body and blood of Christ. Catholics call this transubstantiation.[13]

Mass is offered daily in every Catholic parish, and many Catholics take part daily or several times a week. The *Catechism* states that the Eucharist is a memorial of Christ's passover but also a sacrifice. Christ gives participants in Eucharist the very body that He gave up for mankind on the cross and the very blood that He poured out for the forgiveness of sins. "The Eucharist is thus a sacrifice because it re-presents [makes present] the sacrifice of the Cross . . . in this divine sacrifice which is celebrated in the Mass, the same Christ Who offered Himself once in a bloody manner on the altar of the Cross is contained and is offered in an unbloody manner."[14]

When the *Catechism* speaks of Christ being "offered in an unbloody manner," it means that during the Mass, Christ is not suffering and dying again. As one Paulist priest has written, "There are millions of Masses, but only one sacrifice of Christ."[15] Instead, His great moment of sacrifice is *re*-presented so that Catholic believers can be part of it.

Evangelical Protestants reason that there is no need for repeatedly re-presenting Christ's sacrifice. There is no need for believers to become part of that sacrifice. Christ's death has made us righteous. We have no need for more forgiveness because Christ's one and only offering of Himself gained us all the forgiveness we could ever possibly need (see Heb. 9:27–10:14). To continue to offer the Mass as a propitiatory sacrifice is unnecessary and a contradiction of the true gospel.

Penance (confession) is another key sacrament because it involves "acts" or "penances" which the Roman Catholic must do to be forgiven for his or her sins. Catholics differentiate between "mortal" and "venial" sin. Mortal sins are grave offenses committed "with full knowledge and deliberate consent" and result in loss of sanctifying grace. If mortal sin is not confessed and forgiven, "it causes exclusion from Christ's kingdom and the eternal death of hell."[16]

According to one Catholic writer, examples of mortal sin would include adultery, fornication, stealing, lying or drunkenness. Mortal sins also include blasphemy, refusing to help someone in serious need, religious discrimination or segregation that does serious harm, dwelling on lustful or hateful thoughts, seriously neglecting duty to family, job, country and the underprivileged.[17]

Venial ("easily forgiven") sins are less serious offenses that can weaken the believer's faith and moral fiber but which do not result in the loss of sanctifying grace.[18] Venial sins can include white lies, overeating or immoderate drinking, going a few miles over the speed limit, etc. While venial sins are less serious, they can weaken one's love for God and neighbor.[19] Catholics are urged to confess venial as well as mortal sins, particularly the kind of venial sins that might accumulate. As the *Catechism* says, "Deliberate and unrepented venial sin disposes us little by little to commit mortal sin."[20]

Before asking forgiveness for mortal or venial sin, it is important to have sorrow or contrition brought on by examining the conscience. When confession is made to the priest, the Catholic believer's sins are absolved, but absolution does not remedy all the disorders sin has caused. To recover full spiritual health, the sinner must do something more to make amends or make satisfaction for his sins (do "penance").[21]

The confessor (priest) assigns a penance that fits the gravity of the sin committed.[22] Doing penance might involve repeating a certain number of prayers; acts of self-discipline, such as fasting; doing prescribed "works of love," which could be anything from a kind word to patiently listening to someone.[23]

Protestants would agree that all of these acts are good, but they should not be thought of or done as a means of earning or securing salvation. Protestants would also agree that confessing sins to one another is a beneficial practice (see Jas. 5:16) that is too often ignored, and that a wise Christian can give a person a framework for accountability and spiritual growth. However, Protestants would insist that one believer cannot absolve another believer's sins. The believer's connection to God need not be mediated by a priest or anyone else, since Christ is the "one mediator" between God and man (1 Tim. 2:5).

CATHOLICS ARE SAVED BY MORE THAN "WORKS"

While Roman Catholics place high value on their liturgy and sacramental system, it is incorrect to say that they believe they are "saved by works." Roman Catholicism teaches that Christ's blood "has become the instrument of atonement for the sins of all men."[24] At the same time, they insist that faith in what Christ did on the cross in and of itself is not enough.[25]

Today the Catholic Church teaches what was reemphasized at the Council of Trent: For Catholic theologians, to "justify" means to *make righteous and holy*; therefore, justification and sanctification are considered to be the same process. For the Catholic, faith in Christ is the *beginning* of salvation and lays the foundation for justification. Then the Catholic builds on that with good works, because "man has to merit God's grace of justification and eternal salvation."[26] Catholics believe that as they do good works, righteousness is *infused* into them, sin is eradicated and the soul merits heaven.[27]

Protestants do not see justification in this way. Being justified doesn't mean that you have to be *made* righteous and holy but, instead, you already *are declared* righteous and holy even though you still have a sinful nature. Evangelical Protestants teach that people are declared righteous in God's sight for only one reason—their faith in what Christ did for them on the cross (see Rom. 3:21–5:21; 10:4; 1 Cor. 1:30; Phil. 3:9). Evangelical scholars believe that God's righteousness is *imputed* to Christians: "The righteous work of Christ manifested in His death on the Cross is reckoned to the account of the believer as a gift of righteousness apart from human merit or works."[28]

SANCTIFICATION: A SEPARATE, LIFELONG PROCESS

After being justified by faith, evangelical Protestants believe they enter the process of sanctification, the progressive work of growing in Christ and becoming a mature Christian (see John 17:15-19; 1 Cor. 1:1,2). Sanctification begins the moment we are saved (washed by regeneration and renewed in the Holy Spirit—see Titus 3:5).[29] The New Testament is full of admonitions, commands and instructions on how Christians are to live and grow in Christ. Most branches of evangelical Protestants believe that sanctification is "a process that continues throughout our Christian lives"[30] as we work out our salvation while God works within (see Phil. 2:12-13).

Works, then, are very important to the evangelical Protestant and to the Roman Catholic, but each views works differently. Evangelical Protestants believe they are fully justified through faith in Christ and that this naturally leads to the fruit of good works, as they grow in the Christian life as God has planned for them to do (see Eph. 2:8-10). Catholics, however, do not believe that faith alone provides justification but that they must work for justification all their lives. Catholics, in effect, blend justification and sanctification together as one *process*.

PURGATORY TAKES CARE OF "UNPAID-FOR" SINS

But even when Catholic believers do all the works required of them throughout their lives, to the best of their ability, they still are not assured of immediate entrance into heaven and into the presence of Christ at death. Except for certain exceptions, such as sainthood or martyrdom, Roman Catholics believe they do not pay sufficiently the temporal punishment for their sins through their acts of penance. They still expect to face punishment for sins in purgatory, a special place of cleansing where payment for sins is completed and believers are made fit for heaven.

Part of the Catholic reasoning for purgatory is that, because sinners have failed to make themselves perfect, they could not be happy with an all-perfect God (see Rev. 21:27, which describes heaven by saying: "Nothing impure will ever enter it"). Purgatory, however, is not to be confused with being in hell for a short time. Nor is it a torture chamber where God gets revenge on those who didn't work hard enough on

Earth to prepare their souls for heaven. Purgatory is, instead, a para-
dox—a state of joy and yet of suffering. As the soul submits to the burn-
ing, purifying love of God, it sheds itself of immature self-love, and the
"real self then emerges, perfected, totally absorbed in God."[31]

INDULGENCES LESSEN TIME
SPENT IN PURGATORY

Catholics believe that those in purgatory cannot help themselves, but
Catholics left back on Earth can enable them to obtain heaven more
quickly by praying for them, offering Mass for them and doing forms
of good works, which includes gaining indulgences. According to the
Catechism, those seeking indulgences want to shorten their own or
someone else's time in purgatory.[32]

Prayers and good deeds are two acts that can be endowed with the
privilege of indulgences. According to the *Catechism*, the Church uses
the power originally given to Peter to bind and loose sins (see Matt.
16:19) and can intervene in favor of individual Christians by opening
for them a "treasury" of the merits of Christ and the saints (the spiritual treasury of the Church). So, in effect, when we speak of indulgences
we are speaking of God "indulging" (being kind to) a believer by giving
to the believer from an inexhaustible supply of spiritual merits that
have accumulated in the Church's treasury through the work of Christ
and the prayers and good works of the Virgin Mary and the saints.[33]
These merits are then used to cover the temporal punishment for venial
or mortal sins that the believer did not finish paying for before death.

An indulgence is a kind of "pardon for sin" that can be partial or
plenary (complete). A plenary indulgence can be granted only by the
pope for the remission of a believer's entire temporal punishment.
Much more common are partial indulgences, which can be granted by
bishops, archbishops and cardinals. These partial indulgences are usually expressed in units of time—so many days or even years.

An indulgence of, say, 100 days, applied to a soul in purgatory means that the temporal punishment of that soul is reduced from what it would have been by 100 days, through penitence performed according to the Church's penitential system.[34]

MARY: BLESSED AMONG WOMEN OR "CO-MEDIATOR"?

Scripture calls the virgin Mary highly favored and blessed among women,[35] but to Roman Catholics Mary is much more. Special honor and veneration for the Virgin began in the early centuries of the Church and turned into what many evangelical Protestants believe is the pure and simple worship of Mary, which has finally reached the point of saying her role in redemption is of equal importance with Christ's.

Catholics, however, have an answer for the "you worship Mary" charge by pointing out the different levels of worship used in the Catholic church: *latria*, adoration for the triune God alone; *dulia*, veneration due the angels and canonized saints; and *hyperdulia*, a category reserved for Mary alone in which she is given "superveneration."[36]

Protestants note that the superveneration has grown through the centuries, beginning with tradition taught as early as the fourth century that Mary's virginity continued after the birth of Jesus and that she never had any more children.[37] Other doctrines that grew out of tradition include the Immaculate Conception (she was conceived without sin and lived a sinless life), proclaimed dogma in 1854 by Pope Pius IX, and the doctrine of the Assumption (that she was taken up body and soul directly to heaven), proclaimed dogma in 1950 by Pope Pius XII.

Beginning in the late nineteenth and continuing into the twentieth century, several papal encyclicals referred to Mary in different ways, as "Mediatrix"—co-mediator with Christ between God and man—and

"Redemptrix," Christ's "associate in the redemption." Most explicit, perhaps, were the words of Pope Leo XIII in 1891: "[A]s no man goeth to the Father but by the Son, so no man goeth to Christ but by His mother."[38]

Vatican II documents claim that special titles for Mary neither take away nor add anything "to the dignity and efficacy of Christ the One Mediator."[39] But for Protestants, Pope Leo's statement definitely obscures Christ's function as unique mediator and encourages Catholics to put Mary on too high a pedestal.

PROTESTANTS AND CATHOLICS CONTINUE TO DIALOGUE

As the third millennium dawned, efforts continued to be made to bridge the gap between Protestantism and Roman Catholicism. Getting much attention during the final decade of the twentieth century was the work of Evangelicals and Catholics Together (ECT), which issued a statement in March 1994 entitled, "Evangelicals and Catholics Together: The Christian Commission in the Third Millennium." ECT does not officially represent denominations or churches. It is made up of pastors, priests, theologians and other leaders from Protestant and Roman Catholic ranks who have come together with "no official church sanctioning" but still seeking to find common ground for discussions that could produce unity at some level.

The ECT statement drew fire from some evangelicals who believed it had "sold out the Reformation" by asserting, "Evangelicals and Catholics are brothers and sisters in Christ."[40] It is not enough, said ECT's critics, to claim that Catholics and evangelicals can both subscribe to the same Nicene or Apostles' Creed. The major issues— authority and salvation, or how one truly is saved—are still there. The ECT critics believe that to speak of Catholics and evangelicals as "brothers and sisters in Christ" was to confuse their entirely different ways of looking at just what it means to be saved and justified before God.

In late 1997, participators in ECT from both sides came together to draft what appeared to be a groundbreaking statement called "The Gift of Salvation." In this statement, signed by leading evangelicals and Catholics alike, are the following quotations:

1. We agree that justification is not earned by any good works or merits of our own; it is entirely God's gift, conferred through the Father's sheer graciousness, out of the love that He bears us in his Son, Who suffered on our behalf and rose from the dead for our justification.
2. In justification, God, on the basis of Christ's righteousness alone, declares us to be no longer His rebellious enemies but His forgiven friends.
3. We understand that what we here affirm is in agreement with what the Reformation traditions have meant by justification by faith alone (*sola fide*).[41]

While the above statements seem to say that at least some Roman Catholics now agree with Reformation thinking about justification by faith, it must be pointed out that the statement was drafted by men who "speak from and to, but not for, their different church communities." This is not an official statement from Rome nor is it endorsed by official Protestant denominations. The Gift of Salvation statement goes on to point out that, while those who drafted it rejoice in their unity, they also recognize that many questions remain for urgent exploration, including:

· The meaning of baptismal generation, the Eucharist and sacramental grace.
· Historic uses of the language of justification as it relates to imputed and transformative righteousness.

- The assertion that while justification is by faith alone, the faith that receives salvation is never alone.
- Diverse understandings of merit, reward, purgatory and indulgences.
- Marian devotion and the assistance of the saints in the life of salvation.[42]

Whether or not the work of ECT will finally reach the official halls of the Roman papacy or the council tables of leading Protestant denominations and churches is hard to predict. Some evangelical critics of ECT and The Gift of Salvation statement point out that, because the issues listed above remain to be discussed, there is not any real agreement between Catholics and evangelicals on justification by faith.

The same kind of criticism has also been leveled at a Joint Declaration on the Doctrine of Justification, signed on October 31, 1999, by the Roman Catholic Church and the Lutheran World Federation, which represents 58.1 million Lutherans worldwide. The result of years of work, the Joint Declaration is filled with vague language and still ignores many areas of real difference, "such as indulgences, penance, and purgatory (to name only a few)."[43]

Not all Lutherans signed the Joint Declaration. Notable in its dissent was the Lutheran Church-Missouri Synod, which issued a statement calling the declaration "A Betrayal of the Gospel."

Other conservatives also considered the declaration a denial of the gospel, calling it a "cleverly worded document, which defends the false Catholic sacramental gospel in every point."[44]

While ecumenical efforts made slow and cautious headway at the beginning of the third millennium, there still appeared to be thinkers on both sides who could agree that at the heart of Christianity is simple trust in Jesus Christ as personal Savior and Lord, no matter what kind of theological matrix may be insisted upon by one church or another. A key to any real progress in the twenty-first century will be how willing both sides are to make Scripture—and only Scripture—the final word on the matter, for Scripture clearly teaches that no one has to live under the burden of the law and depend on works of any kind to be saved. As Luther discovered so very long ago, those who are justified by Christ's saving work can and do live by faith alone.

SUMMING UP MAJOR DIFFERENCES BETWEEN ROMAN CATHOLICS AND EVANGELICAL PROTESTANTS

Regarding authority: Catholics claim that Scripture and "Sacred Tradition" are equal in authority.[45] Protestants say the Bible is the sole guide for faith and practice (see 2 Tim. 3:16,17; 1 John 5:13). Rome says the magisterium (teaching authority of the Roman Church) has been entrusted to interpret the Bible for Catholics, who are not to interpret it for themselves.[46] Protestants say that individual Christians can trust the Holy Spirit for guidance as they read and interpret the Bible for themselves (see John 5:39; 14:26). Catholicism teaches that Peter was the first pope, and that through apostolic succession other popes have succeeded him, each serving as "vicar of Christ"; Protestants insist the apostles had equal authority and there was no "pope," a word not found in the New Testament (see Matt. 18:18; John 20:23). Catholics teach that the pope is infallible when he speaks "ex cathedra" (lit. "from the chair" or with authority) on matters of faith and morals; Protestants reply that no human being is infallible, and only Christ is head of the Church (see Eph. 1:22; Col. 1:18).

Regarding salvation: Catholics claim that salvation is secured by faith in Christ plus good works and grace conferred through the seven sacraments of the Church; Protestants reply that salvation is secured through *sola fide* (faith alone) in Jesus Christ's atoning sacrifice on the cross (see Rom. 3:24; Eph. 2:8,9). Catholics blend justification and sanctification into one process as the believer must work to merit eternal life; Protestants believe God justifies the believer by declaring him or her righteous, and that sanctification is a lifelong process of becoming holy as God works within (see John 17:15-19; Phil. 2:12,13). Catholics believe they cannot pay for all their sins in this life, and at death they go to purgatory for an undetermined time to be made totally fit for heaven; Protestants, believing they are justified by faith in Christ and nothing else, trust that they will go straight to heaven where sanctification is completed in Christ's presence (see 2 Cor. 5:6-10; 1 John 2:28–3:2).

CHAPTER THREE

EASTERN ORTHODOXY

JUST LIKE THE CATHOLICS EXCEPT FOR THE POPE?

Despite the substantial number of members of Orthodox churches* in the United States—some estimates go as high as 6 million[1]—few evangelicals or other Protestants know much about Orthodox Christianity. They are, indeed, a "best kept secret" as far as other parts of Christendom are concerned.

The first thing to understand is that the Orthodox are not just like the Roman Catholics but without a pope. While there are many similarities between Orthodoxy and Roman Catholicism, there are some very key differences.

Nor is Orthodoxy one big church that split away from the church at Rome in 1054 and now has its main headquarters at a certain city.

---

* Because Eastern Orthodoxy has spread to the West as well as remaining strong in the East, we will refer to it as Orthodoxy throughout this chapter.

There are at least 13 autocephalous (independent and self-governing) churches, including the four ancient patriarchates that still exist in the Middle East: Constantinople, Alexandria, Antioch and Jerusalem.[2] The current number of Orthodox believers worldwide exceeds 200 million.[3]

Most of those who are heads of Orthodox churches are called patriarchs; some go by the title "archbishop" or "metropolitan." For historical reasons, the Orthodox Church at Constantinople and its patriarch enjoy a certain "primacy of honor" but have no power to interfere in the internal affairs of the other Orthodox churches.[4]

ORTHODOXY: "CORRECT BELIEF AND CORRECT WORSHIP"

Those who are Orthodox dispute Rome's claim to be the one true Church. According to Timothy Ware, "Orthodoxy, believing that the Church on Earth has remained and must remain visibly one, naturally also believes itself to be that one visible church."[5] Ware goes on to say that the Orthodox Church guards and teaches the true belief about God, glorifying Him with right worship as it preserves the original apostolic faith.

When Constantinople and Rome parted ways in 1054, Eastern and Western ends of the Catholic (universal) Church went on with their respective worship and practices of Christianity, with one major difference: Orthodox Christians in the East sought only to preserve the faith as they had understood it for 1,000 years, sticking closely to the decisions of the first seven General Councils of the Church, held between 325 and 787.

The Orthodox Church maintains that down through the centuries the East has kept the faith, while the West (Rome) strayed into heresy through the development of the papacy and claims to absolute primacy (supremacy) over all other churches. Also heretical, say the Orthodox, is Rome's *filioque* doctrine, which was put into the Nicene Creed arbitrarily, without the decision of a General Council.[6]

The following brief look at Orthodox doctrine will examine the same major issues that separate evangelical Protestants and Catholics. The Orthodox see certain points of doctrine in the same way as do the Roman Catholics, but on other points they differ substantially.

ORTHODOXY'S VIEW OF APOSTOLIC SUCCESSION

Like Roman Catholics, the Orthodox place much stock in apostolic succession, but their viewpoint of the role of bishops differs. According to Rome, bishops of the Catholic (universal) Church have descended from Peter, the first pope. The Orthodox believe that bishops continued in apostolic succession; but while they give Peter (and even today's pope) a certain primacy, they do not grant the pope supremacy. Instead, all bishops "share equally in the apostolic succession."[7]

Evangelical Protestants do not agree with the teaching of the Roman Catholics or the Orthodox concerning apostolic succession, bcause they do not believe apostolic succession occurred. Protestants agree that the very foundation of the Church is "the apostles and the prophets, with Christ Jesus himself as the chief cornerstone" (Eph. 2:20), but they see the work of the apostles as unique and their powers as incommunicable. Protestants see the message of the New Testament itself as what "succeeded" the apostles (see Acts 6:7; Titus 1:1-4; 2 Pet. 1:19, Jude 3).

Scripture is silent concerning anyone succeeding the original apostles by being endowed with their supernatural power and divine capabilities. The "apostolic age" ceased with the death of the last apostle, John, around the end of the first century. The apostles appointed pastors (bishops) and deacons to lead local congregations that sprang up, but they could not give these men the power to be apostles; only God could do that, and there is no biblical evidence that this happened.

Pastors, bishops and deacons only had authority inasmuch as they held true to the proclamation of the gospel as given by the original apostles.[8]

ORTHODOXY ADDS
TRADITION TO SCRIPTURE

Protestants believe that only the Scriptures are authoritative, and all believers have the right and responsibility to examine Scripture for themselves, rather than depend on the Church to explain its meaning. For the Orthodox, the Church is authoritative; in fact, the Church is everything. Believers are to listen to and obey the Church's interpretation of Scripture.

Protestants put the Scripture above everything else as the supreme authority over the Church. The Orthodox put the Church over Scripture, saying that Scripture is only part of a larger tradition that makes for a complete organic whole—the "fullness of the Christian faith." In this regard, they agree with the Roman Catholics, but not completely.

The Orthodox have no objective, clear and formally definable criteria of truth, such as papal authority (Roman Catholics) or *sola scriptura* (Protestants). Instead, the Orthodox speak of an "internal norm" for determining authority—the Spirit of God living within the Church.[9] A record of the Holy Spirit's work in the Church can be found in Christian Tradition, which Orthodoxy believes includes the books of the Bible, the Nicea/Constantinople Creed, the Decrees of the Seven Ecumenical Councils, the writings of the Fathers, the canons of the Church, the service books (liturgy) and holy icons.

Timothy Ware, an Englishman who became an Orthodox priest in 1966 and a bishop in 1982, explains that according to Orthodox belief, "The Bible is not something set up *over* the Church; it is something that lives and is understood *within* the Church."[10] A standard Orthodox view is that the Bible gets its authority from the Church, not vice versa.

According to Orthodox theologians, the Church existed and flourished before any of the New Testament books were ever written. The Orthodox stress that the Church originally decided which books would be in Holy Scripture; therefore, only the Church can interpret Holy Scripture with authority.[11]

The Protestant view of the Bible is much different. The Bible does not get its authority from the Church; in fact, as John Calvin put it, the Word of God gave birth to the Church.[12] The Bible gets its authority from being the inspired ("God-breathed") writings of men who were led by the Holy Spirit (see 2 Tim. 3:16; 2 Pet. 1:20,21). The Church did not "decide" which books would be in Holy Scripture; the Church took approximately 200 years to recognize which writings had "divine authority" and belonged in the canon of Scripture.

ORTHODOXY BELIEVES THE REFORMERS WERE WRONG

The Orthodox believe the Reformers' mistake was dividing and separating the "organic whole" of Scripture and tradition. The Reformers said that Scripture is over and above the Church, that it has no need to be confirmed by the authority of the Church, that it speaks directly to the individual heart and mind. Putting the Bible above the Church and tradition is what one Orthodox theologian calls "the sin of the Reformation," because it allows subjective interpretation of Scripture.[13]

One of the standard criticisms of Protestantism by Orthodox theologians, as well as Roman Catholics, is to point to the "hopeless mess" that has been caused by the many Protestant denominations that have sprung up, because Protestants have so much freedom to interpret the Bible under what they believe is the Holy Spirit's guidance.

There is no denying that Protestant churches have many different viewpoints on certain doctrines. At the same time, in an in-depth analysis of Eastern Orthodoxy, missionary and Bible scholar Don Fairbairn stated, "Evangelicals have never affirmed that all interpretations of Scripture are equally valid." Fairbairn goes on to say that evangelical Protestants have definite standards of what constitutes correct interpretation of the Bible. In fact, Protestant "insistence on the responsibility of individual believers to seek truth in the Bible themselves serves as a check on potential misuses of Scriptures by a person or group of people. If a group proclaims a false interpretation, other Christians who have access to the Bible can recognize the error and correct it."[14]

The "weakness" of Protestantism—its diversity and many denominations—is really its great strength, because no one church, pope or church council is in total control of interpreting Scripture.

HOW THE ORTHODOX VIEW THE SEVEN SACRAMENTS

The Orthodox observe the same seven sacraments practiced by the Roman Catholic Church but differ at certain points regarding interpretation and emphasis. Preeminent among the seven in Orthodoxy are baptism and the Eucharist (Divine Liturgy). For the Orthodox, everything starts with baptism—it is the foundation of the believer's life in the Church. Orthodox baptism, which is administered to infants as well as adult converts, is a "bath of regeneration" through which the person is born again and cleansed from original and actual sins.

The other most important sacrament—the Eucharist—is so central to all Orthodox belief and practice that it is another name for the Divine Liturgy itself. The Eucharist is considered "the center of the life of the Church and the principal means of spiritual development, both for the individual Christian and the Church as a whole."[15]

The Orthodox believe that the very body and blood of Christ are present in the elements of the bread and wine (both of which are served to all participants), but they hesitate to use the Roman Catholic term "transubstantiation." They prefer to say that the reality of the changing of the bread and wine into the body and blood of Christ is there, but it cannot be explained.

A key line of the liturgy during the serving of the Eucharist is, "Your own from Your own we offer You, in all and for all." The Orthodox consider the Eucharist a propitiatory sacrifice "offered on behalf of both the living and the dead."[16] According to Timothy Ware, the Eucharist is not a new sacrifice or a repetition of the sacrifice on Calvary, because the Lamb was sacrificed only once and for all time. Instead, during the Eucharist, the events of Christ's sacrifice—Last Supper, Crucifixion and Resurrection—are made present even though they are not repeated.[17]

Regarding sins committed following baptism, the Orthodox deal with this through their sacrament of confession or repentance. They do not, however, confess in a closed area with a grill separating the priest and the one confessing. It is done in the open, sometimes in a special room set apart for confession. Both parties stand or sit, the priest to one side to emphasize that during confession the priest is not the judge but God Himself is. After hearing the confession, the priest often gives advice and occasionally assigns a penance, but this is not essential and is often omitted.[18]

Because of the Orthodox emphasis on *theosis* (going through the process of deification to attain salvation), there is no emphasis on paying for temporal punishments, as in Roman Catholicism. Nor are there any indulgences invoked to expiate sins for persons living or dead.

The Orthodox pray for those who have departed but not because they believe those souls are in purgatory. The Orthodox believe the departed are in a state of existence that is a place of rest quite different from the punishment connected with purgatory. Instead of having to be fully purified in order to enter heaven, the soul of the departed Orthodox believer is simply being strengthened by the prayers offered by the faithful still on earth, preparing him or her to be confident at the judgment seat of Christ on the Last Day.

WHY THE ORTHODOX PRAY TO SAINTS AND ICONS

The Orthodox pray to the saints, particularly to Mary, because these people have achieved deification. They stress that saints, including Mary, are not mediators but intercessors, and praying to them is not worshiping but venerating them.

Mary, of course, is the saint considered to have most completely achieved the goal of deification. She is venerated by the Orthodox as *Theotokos* (mother of God) according to the decision of the Third General Council at Ephesus in 431. The Orthodox also agree with the Roman Catholics concerning Mary's perpetual virginity, but they do not agree with the Roman Catholic doctrine of her immaculate conception. The Orthodox do find evidence for a strong and early tradition concerning Mary's assumption but do not feel it needs to be a dogma equal to such beliefs as the Trinity and the virgin birth.

Another important part of Orthodox tradition is their use of icons—colorful stylized paintings of Christ, the apostles, Mary and other saints, which adorn the walls of any Orthodox church, particularly the iconostasis, a screen that divides the sanctuary at the front of the church from the rest of the worship area. Orthodox believers sometimes prostrate themselves before the icons, kiss them and burn candles in front of them. All of these activities lead the typical Protestant to think of idolatry, believing that icons are being worshiped. But any Orthodox believer would disagree. The icon is not an idol but a symbol. The veneration being shown by the worshiper is not toward the picture but toward the person depicted in the picture.

One reason for the Orthodox insistence on icons, which continues to the present time, is that they are not just pictures but an important part of the Church's teaching of the faith. Those who lack learning or the time to study can enter the church and see on its walls all they need to know to understand their faith.[19] The icons are considered a source of revelation equal to the Bible.

ORTHODOXY STRESSES DEIFICATION ABOVE JUSTIFICATION

The Orthodox view of sin and salvation is much different from that of Protestants or Catholics. The Orthodox believe that, while the Fall was a disaster that plunged mankind into sin, they do not agree that man is bound by a totally corrupt, sinful nature. According to the Orthodox, through the Fall, mankind did not inherit guilt through Adam, but instead man inherited death, mortality and corruption.[20]

The Orthodox do not believe that man was created in communion and fellowship with God, but instead he was given the task of working toward it. When mankind fell in Adam, it was a "departure from a path," not a drastic plunge from a state of blessedness.[21]

The Orthodox agree that the Fall set up an impenetrable barrier between God and man, but while Protestants emphasize the Cross as Jesus' suffering God's wrath as a substitute for sinners, the Orthodox see Christ's sacrifice as a victory over sin and death. Protestants believe that putting faith in Christ's death—the atonement—fully restores man's fellowship with God. The Orthodox, however, view Christ's death on the cross and God's grace as the means to enable man to "become god, to obtain *theosis* ('deification' or 'divinization')."[22] The Orthodox get the term theosis from 2 Peter 1:4, which speaks of how God "granted to us His precious and magnificent promises, in order that by them you might become partakers of the divine nature" (*NASB*). The Orthodox also find the concept of theosis in other passages of Scripture (see Ps. 82:6; Eph. 4:24; 5:1; 1 John 3:2).

As early as the second century, the Church fathers from the eastern end of the Catholic (universal) Church were teaching theosis. Athanasius, defender of Christ's deity at the Council of Nicea in 325, said, "God became man so that men might become gods."

According to the Orthodox, theosis is not some kind of pantheism. Christians might become "gods," but they still have a human nature. To be deified is to become a partaker of the divine nature, but you are not changed into a divine being.[23]

Evangelical Protestant scholars believe that the Orthodox deification approach to salvation leaves them practically ignoring the doctrine of justification by faith. For example, Donald Fairbairn observes that "most elements of the Orthodox understanding of salvation actually pertain to sanctification."[24] Fairbairn also comments that the major Orthodox "proof text" for deification—2 Peter 1:4—"lies in the middle of a passage about sanctification."[25] Second Peter 1:3 has already spoken of God's divine power, which has given believers everything they need for life in godliness through their knowledge of Christ Himself. Because of the precious promises of full salvation that they have already received, believers can "participate in the divine nature" and escape the world's corruption.

In vv. 5-7, Peter lists specifically how believers can work at adding to their faith goodness, knowledge, self-control, perseverance, godliness, brotherly kindness and love—all qualities developed during sanctification, the growing process a Christian goes through after being justified by faith in Jesus Christ. The more believers possess these qualities, the more effective and productive they will be because they already have salvation in their Lord Jesus Christ.

Fairbairn believes that the Orthodox fail to stress the nature of salvation as a free gift. This results in a failure to "distinguish between justification as God's free acceptance of unworthy sinners and sanctification as the process of becoming righteous, a process which involves human activity and effort."[26]

JESUS CHRIST: THE "SOMEONE AT THE CENTER"

This all-too-brief look at Eastern Orthodoxy shows significant differences between their viewpoint and that of evangelical Protestants (for recommended reading to learn more about Orthodoxy, see appendix A). Nonetheless, evangelical Protestants have much in common with Eastern Orthodoxy. In particular, evangelical concern with defense of the fundamental truths of Christianity in the face of liberalism, secularism and modernism of all kinds is similar in many respects to the Orthodox devotion to a stalwart defense of the same truths. As Daniel Clendenin puts it, "Fidelity and an unwavering loyalty to the apostolic faith characterize eastern Christianity."[27]

There is still, however, the very real problem of the Protestant "sin of the Reformation"—putting Scripture over and above the Church and tradition. Does this mean that the Orthodox do not believe that Protestants are part of the Church or that they have salvation of any kind? Orthodox bishop and theologian Timothy Ware admits that some Orthodox would say yes and others would say no. The more moderate group in Orthodoxy contends that, while Orthodoxy is the Church, it is incorrect to assume that those who aren't Orthodox can't possibly belong to the Church. "Many people may be members of the church who are not visibly so," writes Ware. "Invisible bonds may exist despite an outward separation."[28]

Although Orthodoxy and Protestantism remain separated, certain of their leaders and scholars continue to dialogue,[29] because they believe they have much to learn from one another.[30] As C. S. Lewis pointed out, "At the center of differing Christian viewpoints . . . there is something or a Someone, who against all divergences of belief . . . speaks with the same voice."[31]

As all three of the main trunks of the Christian tree continue to hold firmly (and sometimes adamantly) to certain doctrines or traditions that appear to be nonnegotiable, it is good to remember that the "Someone at the center" is Jesus Christ, Lord of the universe, who died, was buried and rose again the third day, *according to the Scriptures*. His words of invitation are open to all who are willing to put their faith directly in Him alone: "All that the Father gives me will come to me, and whoever comes to me I will never drive away" (John 6:37).

SUMMING UP MAJOR DIFFERENCES BETWEEN ORTHODOX BELIEVERS AND EVANGELICAL PROTESTANTS

Regarding authority: Orthodoxy teaches that apostolic succession occurred through bishops and Church fathers who developed a "corpus of tradition"[32] equal to Scripture; the evangelical Protestant says the apostles were succeeded, not by bishops or Church fathers, but by the Scriptures only (see Titus 1:1-4; Jude vv. 3,17). Orthodoxy also says the Church is in authority over Scripture, which is only part of a larger tradition;[33] Protestants believe the Scripture is in supreme authority over the Church, the sole guide for faith and practice (see 2 Tim. 3:16,17; 1 John 5:13).

Regarding salvation: Orthodoxy teaches that man did not fall from perfect fellowship with God but departed from the path for attaining perfect fellowship and that man inherited mortality and corruption but not Adam's guilt;[34] Protestants teach that man fell from his perfect state with God and inherited Adam's guilt (see Rom. 5:12-21). The Orthodox believe salvation is attained through the process of *theosis*, becoming deified (like God). Protestants say justification comes through faith in Christ (see Rom. 3:24; Eph. 2:8,9), and then the Christian becomes sanctified by walking with Christ (see Eph. 2:10; 2 Pet. 1:3-11).

PART THREE

MAJOR RELIGIONS OF THE WORLD

JUDAISM

FOUNDATION FOR THE CHRISTIAN FAITH, BUT STILL LOOKING FOR THE MESSIAH

What makes a person Jewish? Is Jewishness a nationality, a religion or both? What can we say to our Jewish friends about Jesus Christ, born a Jew but rejected by many of His own people? (See John 1:11.) These are some of the questions often asked about the people who follow one of the world's oldest living religions.

To begin with, the Jewish people are descended from the ancient Hebrews. This name comes from Eber, their traditional ancestor (mentioned in Gen. 10:21). We can go back even farther to the name Shem, a son of Noah (mentioned in the same verse). From Shem comes the word "Semitic," which refers to a group of peoples that includes both Jews and Arabs.[1]

The history of the Jewish nation is contained in the Old Testament, the only Scriptures recognized by the Jewish people. Of particular importance is the Torah—the Law contained in the first five books of the Old Testament.

For Judaism, another critical part of the Old Testament are the writings of the prophets. These spokesmen for God stressed the importance of justice and love, placing that importance far above the empty ritualism of keeping the external regulations of the Law, while missing its intent (see Mic. 6:8). Striving for decent behavior (exhibiting justice and love) is still basic to Jewish thinking. It is no coincidence that many charitable organizations are led and supported by Jewish people.

Since the destruction of Jerusalem and the Temple by the Romans in A.D. 70, the Jews have had no place to offer sacrifices for their sins as required by the Law of Moses (see Deut. 12). After this dreadful loss, they scattered to almost every nation in the world where they established communities and built synagogues to keep their faith alive.

The Jewish people have been persecuted many times, worst of all by the Nazis who murdered 6 million Jews in the Holocaust. In 1948, the state of Israel was born and became a homeland to Jewish people immigrating from all over the world. In 1967, the Israelis captured all of Jerusalem, the first time they had held it as a free people since 586 B.C.

JEWISH CUSTOMS AND LAWS

Judaism, the religion, today exists in four different forms: Orthodox, Conservative, Reform and Messianic. We will look at the first three below and save Messianic Jews—those who believe that Jesus is the Messiah but still practice Jewish customs—for later in this chapter.

Orthodox Jews try to follow the letter of the Law. They carefully study the Torah (Law or teachings) written down by Moses. The Torah, meaning "teaching and direction," denotes the body of doctrine, written and oral, that has come down through the Jewish community.[2]

Orthodox Jews not only strive to obey the Hebrew Bible (what Christians call the Old Testament), but they also observe other teachings of famous rabbis that have been added through the centuries. Some of these teachings were written down around A.D. 200 in a book called the *Mishnah*. It is about 1,000 pages long and consists mainly of instructions for daily living known as *Halakah*, or "the way to walk."

Around A.D. 500 another book of Jewish learning was compiled called the Talmud. The Talmud runs to about 36 volumes. It is based on the Mishnah, but much more material has been added, especially certain famous stories called the *Haggadah*.

These three books—the Torah, the Mishnah and the Talmud—rule every facet of the Orthodox Jew's life.

Take dietary laws, for example. The Law of Moses forbids pork or shellfish (see Lev. 11:7,10). It also forbids the cooking of "a young goat in its mother's milk" (Ex. 23:19). As a result, Orthodox Jews will not eat meat and dairy products together, going so far as to use separate dishes for meat and dairy foods. In addition, because the Law forbids the consumption of fat or blood (see Lev. 3:17), animals must be slaughtered in a very specific way so that little blood stays in the flesh.

Another example is Sabbath law. The Law of Moses says to rest from work on the seventh day—the Sabbath, or day of worship (see Ex. 20:8-11). Orthodox Jews will not work, travel, use the phone, write, touch money or pose for pictures on the Sabbath.

Conservative Jews have a more lenient interpretation of the Torah, but they do believe the Law is vitally important. Conservatives also want to keep alive the Hebrew language and the traditions of Judaism.

Reformed Jews have moved some distance away from Orthodoxy. They teach that the principles of Judaism are more important than the practices. Most Reformed Jews do not observe the dietary laws or other laws, such as what a Jew should or should not do on the Sabbath.

But Orthodox, Conservative and Reformed Jews all agree on this: The Sabbath and the holy days must be observed. They have an old saying: "More than Israel kept the Sabbath, the Sabbath kept Israel."

For Jews, the Sabbath begins at sundown on Friday night and continues until sundown on Saturday. In devout Jewish homes, as the sun is setting on Friday, the woman of the house, with her family around her, lights the traditional candles and gives the age-old blessing:

"Blessed art Thou, O Lord our God, King of the Universe, Who has sanctified us by Thy laws and commanded us to kindle the Sabbath light." The father then blesses the wine, everyone has a sip, and then he slices the Sabbath loaf of challah bread.

After dinner on the Sabbath, Conservative and Reform families go to the synagogue. The main Orthodox service is on Saturday morning, and they and most Conservatives attend another service in the afternoon.

The High Holy Days of Judaism are Rosh Hashanah [Rosh hah-SHAH-nah], which is the Jewish New Year, celebrated in September or October; and Yom Kippur [YOME kee POOR], the Jewish Day of Atonement, which comes 10 days later. During this 10-day period, Jews take part in repentance and soul-searching.

Another important time is the Passover. This usually comes about the time when Christians celebrate Easter. Passover in the Jewish home begins with a question from the youngest child: "Why is this night different from all other nights?" An older member answers, "We were slaves to Pharaoh in Egypt. If God had not delivered our ancestors 'with a mighty hand and an outstretched arm,' we would still be slaves. That is why this night is different."[3] Thus begins an ancient ritual and celebration that includes everything from prayers and special foods to games for the children.

Christians share a great deal with Jewish people. To begin with, we share the Old Testament and its teachings. We share a belief in the same God—a God of holiness, justice, purity, righteousness and unity. Both faiths gladly proclaim, "The LORD our God, the LORD is one. Love the LORD your God with all your heart and with all your soul and with all your strength" (Deut. 6:4,5).

The moral and ethical teachings of the Bible are part of the Jewish and the Christian heritage. Both accept the Law given by the living God who created the world and is still the Lord of creation.

There are many more similarities between Judaism and Christianity: the need to worship God, the importance of the family, the obligation to love others. Many Jews accept Jesus as a great prophet and find good things in His teachings, but this is as far as they will go.

JESUS CHRIST: THE GREAT DIVIDE

It is on the question of Jesus Christ—who was this man?—that most Jews and Christians divide. This division began while Jesus walked the earth. The Jews of that time were looking for a messiah (literally "Anointed One"), spoken of by the Old Testament prophets as one who would redeem His people from their sins (see Heb. 2:16,17).

But by Jesus' time, Judaism was divided into many competing sects. Some, including many of the Pharisees, had become tradition-bound and focused on outward conformity to the Jewish laws, without the right heart attitude. Others, the Essenes, sought refuge in ascetic desert communities. Still others, the Sadducees, had emptied Judaism of the supernatural to the extent that it wasn't much different from Greek philosophy. And still others, the Zealots, hoped for a national deliverer, a warrior-king like David or Judas Maccabeus, who would drive out the hated Romans and restore the nation of Israel to its ancient glory. When we realize this, it's easy to see why many were disappointed by the humble Man of Galilee.

Yet Jesus claimed to be the Messiah, the Son of God. At a well in Samaria, He spoke to a woman and explained how she might satisfy her spiritual thirst. Even this sinful woman knew that the Messiah was to come. Jesus replied that He was the one who had been promised. She believed and was saved (see John 4:7-26; 39-42).

The New Testament contains many other references to Jesus as the Messiah, or Christ (see Matt. 16:16; 26:63-65; Luke 24:26; John 8:28). Christians see many messianic prophesies in the Old Testament fulfilled by Jesus' earthly life. Jesus explicitly claimed to be the Messiah (see John 4:25,26). For Christians, just a few of the prophecies that prove Christ's claim to be true include Micah 5:1-3 (the Messiah would be born in Bethlehem; see Matt. 2:3-6); Isaiah 7:14 (a virgin would bear a son and He would be called Immanuel; see Matt. 1:23); Zechariah 9:9 (the King would come riding on a donkey; see the Palm Sunday passage, Matt. 21:4,5).

THE "SUFFERING SERVANT" OF ISAIAH 53

Perhaps the greatest of these prophetic passages is in the book of Isaiah. Beginning with chapter 49, Isaiah describes God's "servant," the Messiah King, who will suffer to redeem His people from their sin and to turn Israel to the Lord (see vv. 5-26).

Isaiah opens chapter 53 by predicting that this servant will be despised, rejected, sorrowful and full of grief (see v. 3). These words are a perfect description of Jesus, who came to redeem the world but was rejected, especially by His own people (see John 1:10-12).

Isaiah also describes the redemptive ministry of the Messiah. The Messiah would bear punishment for mankind's transgressions (see Isa. 53:4-6). Peter reminds us that the Messiah died for all mankind and that His suffering brings us salvation (see 1 Pet. 2:24,25).

Finally, Isaiah describes just how the Messiah would die. In the gospels, we find Jesus fulfilling every detail of this prophecy (compare Isa. 53:7-9 with Matt. 27:57-60 and Luke 23:32,33).

The Old Testament also prophesied the Messiah's triumphant resurrection: "You will not abandon me to the grave, nor will you let your Holy One see decay" (Ps. 16:10). After Jesus' resurrection, Peter quoted this prophecy in the first sermon of the Early Church (see Acts 2:27-31). Many people had seen the risen Jesus. They knew that the prophecy had been fulfilled. They remembered what Jesus had said after His resurrection:

> This is what I told you while I was still with you: Everything must be fulfilled that is written about me in the Law of Moses, the Prophets and the Psalms. . . . This is what is written: The Christ will suffer and rise from the dead on the third day, and

repentance and forgiveness of sins will be preached in his name to all nations, beginning at Jerusalem (Luke 24:44,46,47).

So what's the difference between Christianity and Judaism? That question hinges on another question: Was Jesus the Messiah, as He claimed, or was He an impostor? Argument cannot settle this question. Each of us (Jew or Gentile) must look carefully at Jesus and answer the question for ourselves.

MESSIANIC JEWS BREAK THE MOLD

Messianic Judaism is a movement that gained increasing momentum during the last decades of the twentieth century. Messianic Jews, from every walk of life, believe that Yeshua (the Hebrew name for Jesus) is the promised Jewish Messiah and Savior for Israel and the world.

For more than 1,200 years it has been assumed on the part of Jewish and Christian communities that a Jewish person simply couldn't believe in Jesus and stay Jewish. If a Jewish person did come to believe in Jesus, the Christian community expected that person to leave the Jewish community and join a Gentile church. The Jewish community determined that anyone who believed in Jesus had betrayed the community by joining the Gentile religion of Christianity. It was not possible to imagine Jewish synagogues full of Jewish people who embraced Jesus as the Messiah.

In spite of these cultural barriers, throughout Church history there have always been some Jewish people who came to believe in Jesus as their Lord and Savior. But something really unanticipated and new began in 1967. At the end of the Six Day War, Jerusalem suddenly came back into Jewish hands after nearly 2,000 years under Gentile domination. Tens of thousands of Jewish people suddenly accepted Yeshua as their Messiah. Citing biblical prophecy (see Deut. 30:1-3; Hos. 3:4,5;

Joel 2:28,29; Luke 21:24), some Messianic leaders suggest that the movement of Jewish people embracing Jesus as Messiah and forming Messianic synagogues may be an important fulfillment and indicator of end-time restoration of Israel as a nation.[4]

Today it is estimated that there are over 350 Messianic Jewish congregations worldwide, with dozens in Israel. More Jewish people have put their trust in Jesus as their Messiah in the last 20 years than in the past 20 centuries.[5]

These Messianic congregations worship Yeshua and graciously welcome Gentiles, yet retain Jewish forms of worship, feasts, festivals, songs, customs and even humor. They are fond of reminding both Gentiles and Jews of the first-century Jewish origins of Christianity and that, after all, according to the New Testament, believing in Jesus is a very Jewish thing to do.

Gentile Christians should rejoice in the messianic Jewish movement as a possible indicator of the return of Jesus to the earth and (no less important) as an opportunity to put into practice what the apostles had in mind in Acts 15 and what the apostle Paul had in mind in Ephesians 2. Both of these passages speak of a Church in which the barriers of religious and cultural hostility between Gentile and Jew are broken down through the blood of the Messiah, a witness to all the earth that Yeshua is Lord. As the Messiah of prophecy, He stands ready to receive *all* who believe in Him. "For there is no difference between Jew and Gentile—the same Lord is Lord of all and richly blesses all who call on him" (Rom. 10:12).

SUMMING UP MAJOR DIFFERENCES BETWEEN JEWS (EXCLUDING MESSIANIC JEWS) AND CHRISTIANS

Regarding God: Jews believe that the Lord God is one (see Deut. 6:4); Christians believe there is one essence of the

Godhead in which reside three persons: Father, Son and Holy Spirit, coequally and coeternally God (see Matt. 3:13-17; 28:19; 2 Cor. 13:14).

Regarding Jesus Christ: Some Jews may accept Jesus as a good teacher or even a prophet, but they reject Him as Messiah, because He claimed to be divine and He failed to deliver Israel from oppression; Christians respond that Jesus is God as well as man, and He died to redeem all men from sin (see Mark 10:45; John 1:13,14; 1 Pet. 2:24).

Regarding sin: Jews believe that man is not born good or evil; he is born free to choose between the two. Christians teach that everyone is born in sin and falls short of God's standards (see Rom. 3:10,23; 5:12).

Regarding salvation: Jews believe that anyone, Jew or Gentile, may gain salvation through commitment to the one true God and through moral living; Christians counter that man is saved through faith in the atoning death of Christ on the cross (see Rom. 3:24; Eph. 2:8,9).

CHAPTER FIVE

ISLAM

ALLAH IS ONE, AND CHRIST WAS JUST A PROPHET

Here are some possible questions for *Jeopardy* or some other TV quiz show. What major religion

- has gained thousands of converts in North America, including many professional athletes?
- is the youngest among major world religions but still one of the largest?
- is so missionary minded that it is seeking to convert Western countries, not just African and Asian countries?

The answer to all of the above is Islam, a religion that claims nearly 1 billion followers in countries throughout the world. Islam originated in what is now Saudi Arabia, and from there it expanded along trade routes to Africa and Asia. The country with the most Muslims is Indonesia, with 120 million. In addition, there are millions more in parts of Eastern and Western Europe and in the Americas. One out of every six human beings on the face of the earth subscribes to the faith of Islam.[1]

Islam is the correct name for the religion often incorrectly called Mohammedanism. The word "Islam" means "submission" (to Allah, the God of Mohammed, the man who founded this religion). A believer in Mohammed's religion is a Muslim, meaning "one who lives his life according to God's will."[2]

HOW MOHAMMED BECAME A PROPHET

Born in Arabia in the city of Mecca in A.D. 570, Mohammed came from a prominent and highly respected family. His father died a few days before his birth, and his mother died when he was six years old. Mohammed's grandfather took him in but died when Mohammed was nine. Then he went to live in the home of Abu Talid, his uncle, where he herded flocks. As he grew older, Mohammed got into the caravan trade and accompanied his uncle on trips to Syria and Persia.

Scholars believe that, in his travels, Mohammed developed his concepts of monotheism from several sources, including the Monophysites, who believed that Christ had only a divine nature, and Nestorians, who divided the Incarnate Christ into two separate natures, divine and human, in one person (denying that the man Jesus of Nazareth was both fully God and fully man). In addition, it is believed he absorbed a great deal of teaching from Jews who exposed him to the Talmud.

As a result, it is unlikely that Mohammed's opportunities to learn about "the one true God" came in great part from anyone who really understood the Bible. Even a Muslim writer like Caesar Farah admits that Mohammed's narration of scriptural events shows he "could not have . . . had an educated knowledge of the sacred texts."[3] It is no wonder that Mohammed developed theologically flawed ideas, which he later expressed when developing the *Qur'an* (also called Koran).[4]

As a young man working in the caravan trade, Mohammed attracted the attention of his employer, a wealthy widow named Khadija. Although she was 40 years old and he was 25 when they were married, they lived happily together and she bore him several children. After his marriage, Mohammed spent much of his time during the next 15 years in solitary meditation. At the age of 40, he received his first revelation while contemplating in a cave on Mount Hira near Mecca. According to Mohammed, the archangel Gabriel came to him during a dream and brought the following command of God:

> Read in the name of thy Lord who created, who created man of blood coagulated. Read! Thy Lord is the most beneficent, who taught by the pen, taught that what they knew not unto men.[5]

From this command to "read" comes the name for the holy book of Islam, the Qur'an, meaning "the reciting" or "the reading." Because Mohammed could not read or write, the Qur'an is his reciting of revelations given to him.

After receiving his first revelation, Mohammed was deeply disturbed and told his wife he thought he might be possessed by jinns, supernatural beings that, according to Arabic folklore, could take human or animal form and influence human affairs. But Khadija assured him that his words were true, as did her cousin, Waraqua ibn Nawfal, who was somewhat familiar with the Jewish and Christian concepts of monotheism. It was through Waraqua's urging, as well as Khadija's, that Mohammed began to preach again in the streets and marketplaces in Mecca.[6] Mohammed never claimed to be divine but insisted that Allah had called him to be a prophet.

Mohammed hated the idolatry and the immorality of the Arabs who lived in Mecca or came there to trade their goods. The rich lorded it over the poor. Greed and selfishness were everywhere, and even infanticide was practiced among the Bedouin tribes.[7] He was met with bitter opposition, but for many years his influential uncle was able to protect him.

When both Khadija and Mohammed's uncle died in A.D. 620, plots were hatched to kill Mohammed and his followers. Finally, on July 16, 622, Mohammed was forced to flee to Yathrib, a friendlier city to the north. This flight, called the *hegira*, marks the beginning of the Islamic calendar. The years are counted from "A.H.," meaning "the year of the Hegira." Yathrib was later renamed Madinat an Nabi (City of the Prophet), in honor of Mohammed, but it is more commonly known as Medina. Mohammed became the religious and political leader of the city.

Soon the Meccans organized an army to destroy Mohammed and his followers. The fighting ended in 630 with Islamic forces triumphant. Mohammed entered Mecca and destroyed every idol in the *Kaaba*, the main temple, except the Black Stone, a sacred meteorite enshrined there. Mohammed then declared the Kaaba to be the most holy shrine in Islam. Since that time it has been the spot toward which all devout Muslims direct their prayers.

During the next two years, Mohammed strengthened his position as the leading prophet and ruler of Arabia. He united the tribes into a vast army to conquer the world for Allah. His death in 632 did not lessen the fervor of his followers. They carried their faith across Asia, Africa, even into Europe—and to this day the growth of Islam has steadily increased to its current worldwide status of nearly 1 billion.

THE TEACHINGS OF ISLAM

The Qur'an is the sacred scripture of Islam. About four-fifths the length of the New Testament, it includes 114 *surahs*, or chapters. While the ideas are all credited to God, Mohammed dictated parts of the

Qur'an, while the rest came from the writings of disciples who remembered his oral teachings after he died.[8] Much of the Qur'an jumps from one time and place to another, lacking a narrative unity. Muslims claim, nonetheless, that it is copied from an original in Arabic, which is in heaven.

In addition to the Qur'an, Mohammed developed important teachings and sayings called *Sunnah* (literally, "path"). The Sunnah became a base for traditions built on Mohammed's conduct as a prophet and how he handled things while being guide, judge and ruler of his Muslim followers.[9] The Sunnah were gathered into one body of work called the *Hadith*, which supplements the Qur'an in the same way the Talmud supplements the Hebrew Bible in Judaism.[10]

Still another important body of teachings in Islam is the *Shariah*, a combination of legal interpretations of the Qur'an and the Sunnah. Shariah means "law," and it lays down a strict and comprehensive guide of life and conduct for Muslims. It includes prohibitions against eating pork and drinking alcoholic beverages, as well as punishments for stealing, adultery, apostasy (denying Islam) and blasphemy (saying anything derogatory about Islam or Mohammed).[11]

THE SIX DOCTRINES OF ISLAM

Following are the doctrines that every Muslim is required to believe:

God. There is only one true God and His name is Allah. Allah is all-seeing, all-knowing and all-powerful.

Angels. The chief angel is Gabriel, who is said to have appeared to Mohammed. There is also a fallen angel named Shaitan (from the Hebrew "Satan"), as well as the followers of Shaitan, the jinns (demons).

Scripture. Muslims believe in four God-inspired books: the Torah of Moses (what Christians call the Pentateuch), the *Zabur* (Psalms of David), the *Injil* (Gospel) of Jesus, and the Qur'an. But, because

Muslims believe that Jews and Christians corrupted their Scriptures, the Qur'an is Allah's final word to mankind. It supersedes and overrules all previous writings.

Mohammed. The Qur'an lists 28 prophets of Allah. These include Adam, Noah, Abraham, Moses, David, Jonah and Jesus. To the Muslim, the last and greatest prophet is Mohammed.

The end times. On the "last day," the dead will be resurrected. Allah will be the judge, and each person will be sent to heaven or hell. Heaven is a place of sensual pleasure. Hell is for those who oppose Allah and his prophet Mohammed.

Predestination. God has determined what He pleases, and no one can change what He has decreed (also known as *kismet*, the doctrine of fate). From this doctrine comes the most common Islamic phrase, "If it is Allah's will."[12]

THE FIVE PILLARS OF THE FAITH

Besides the six doctrines to be believed, there are five duties to be performed.

Statement of belief. To become a Muslim, a person must publicly repeat the *Shahadah*: "There is no god but Allah and Mohammed is the prophet of Allah."

Prayer. Muslims pray five times a day—at daybreak, noon, midafternoon, after sunset, and early evening.[13] The Muslim must kneel and bow in the prescribed manner in the direction of the holy city, Mecca.

Alms. Muslim law today requires the believer to give one-fortieth of his profit (2.5 percent). This offering goes to widows, orphans, the sick and other unfortunates.

Ramadan. The ninth month of the Islamic lunar year is called Ramadan and is the highest of Muslim holy seasons. Muslims are required to fast for the entire month. Food and drink, as well as smoking and sexual pleasures, are forbidden, but only during daylight hours. During Ramadan, many Muslims eat two meals a day, the first just before sunrise and the other shortly after sunset. During Ramadan, the believer must not commit any unworthy act. If he does, his fasting is meaningless.

Pilgrimage to Mecca. This is called the *Hajj* and must be performed at least once in a Muslim's lifetime. However, if the pilgrimage is too difficult or dangerous for the believer, he can send someone in his place.[14]

HOW THE QUR'AN CONTRADICTS THE BIBLE

The Bible has had an important influence on the teachings of Islam. For instance, the Muslim proudly traces his ancestry to Ishmael, a son of Abraham. Muslim beliefs about the nature of God, the resurrection of the body and judgment are roughly similar to the teachings of the Bible. But there are some striking differences. Following are some of the Muslim ideas that contradict what is taught in the Bible.

For Muslims, God is one, period. The Qur'an explicitly attacks the Christian teaching on the Trinity, saying that anyone who ascribes "partners" to God is committing the sin of *shirk* (blasphemy). This prohibition is explicitly directed against the Christian doctrine of the Trinity and the teaching that Jesus is God. Many Muslims are also erroneously taught that Christians are really tri-theists who believe in God the Father, Mary the mother and Jesus the Son. This grotesque caricature of the Trinity is a complete misrepresentation of what biblical Christians believe and what the Bible teaches.

Muslims also teach that Allah is transcendent (all-powerful) and relatively impersonal. Of the 99 names ascribed to God in Islam, "Father" is omitted (to avoid the idea of the Father and the Son). This is in stark contrast to the Bible and to Jesus' own teaching, which says that God is our personal heavenly Father. (Compare passages on God's greatness, such as Ps. 77:10-15 and Isa. 43:13, with passages on God's love, such as Deut. 7:8; Jer. 31:3; Eph. 2:4; 1 John 3:1; 4:7.) While one of the 99 Muslim names for God is "the Merciful," He is not viewed primarily as a dispenser of love and grace but more as a righteous judge to whom the Muslim must give account.[15]

The Qur'an *denies that Jesus is the Son of God,* although it describes the virgin birth in a passage similar to Luke 1:26-38 (see Surah 3:45-47). The Qur'an calls Jesus a prophet, equal to Abraham, Jonah and others; but places Him in rank far below Mohammed. Surah 4:171 says that "Jesus . . . was only a messenger of Allah. . . . Far is it removed from His transcendent majesty that He should have a son."

Mohammed totally ignored what the New Testament says about Jesus' divinity (see, for example, Matt. 8:29; 17:5; John 1:1-5; 8:58; 10:30; 14:9; 20:28; Col. 1:15-17; 2:9). Instead of admitting that verses like these exist, Muslims claim Christians have changed the Bible.

The Qur'an *says that Christ never really died on the cross.*[16] "They slew him not nor crucified, but it appeared so unto them" (Surah 4:157). How could this be? According to Islam, Allah took Jesus to heaven just before the crucifixion, because it is unthinkable that an approved prophet of God should face such a humiliating defeat. Who, then, died on the Cross? Muslims say it was Judas (or possibly Simon of Cyrene), made up so cleverly to resemble Jesus that even Mary and the disciples were fooled! Another theory held by certain Muslim sects is that Jesus was taken down from the cross in a coma and that he later revived and traveled to another area where He finally died.[17]

Obviously, all this is in complete opposition to the teaching of the Bible. As we have seen, the Cross is the center of God's redemptive plan. The crucifixion of Christ was prophesied in the Old Testament. Eyewitness accounts of that crucifixion are contained in each of the four Gospels (see 1 Cor. 1:23; 2:2; 15:3,4: Gal. 2:20; 6:12,14; Eph. 2:16).

Jesus predicted His death many times (see Matt. 16:21). Why did He die? As a "ransom for many" (Mark 10:45); He promised that through His shed blood there would be "forgiveness of sins" (Matt. 26:28).

As for Judas, the Gospels tell us that he was the one who betrayed Jesus (see Mark 14:10,11,43-45); and in remorse for what he did, Judas hanged himself (see Matt. 27:5). Judas died at the end of a rope, not on the Cross of Calvary.

Surah 4:111 *declares that each person must take care of his or her own sins.* The Muslim must earn salvation from sin by following the Five Pillars of the Faith. If he doesn't make it, it's his own fault: "Whoever goes astray, he himself bears the whole responsibility of wandering" (Surah 10:109).

In contrast, the Bible teaches that we all have sinned and gone our own way (see Isa. 53:6). The only way mankind can find forgiveness is through faith in Jesus Christ (see John 3:16; Acts 4:12; Rom. 3:23-26; Eph. 2:4-9).

Mohammed sincerely tried to lead his followers out of idolatry by proclaiming himself a prophet and designing a religion of rules and regulations. Like Judaism, the religion of Islam places on each person a terrible burden of responsibility. But Jesus Christ has promised to lift such burdens from the human heart: "Come to me, all you who are weary and burdened, and I will give you rest. . . . For my yoke is easy and my burden is light" (Matt. 11:28,30).

LOVING IN THE WEST, OPPRESSIVE IN THE EAST

A distinction needs to be drawn between the friendly image Islam projects in the West as a religion of love, tolerance and justice with the uncompromising nature of Islam as it has consistently been practiced in history and continues to be practiced today, as a *political* religion in the East. Religious leaders of Islamic countries by and large believe that if Islam is to be practiced correctly, all of society must submit to Islamic law (Shariah). This means that everyone in Islamic societies, including non-Muslims, must either conform to Islamic laws, economics, politics and customs or suffer heavy consequences.

Historically, in countries where Islam has gained political power, people of all rival religions are either wiped out or, in the interest of "tolerance" and "open-mindedness," permitted to exist as second-class citizens.[18] As a cultural force, political Islam slowly squeezes non-Muslim people and crushes dissent, even though the Qur'an teaches there should be "no compulsion in religion" (Surah 2:256). The regular and continuing persecution of Christians in Muslim countries (which has included rape and murder) occasionally receives media attention. This persecution is part and parcel of political Islam's determination to force people to submit to Allah.[19]

Enslavement of thousands of Black Christians in Sudan by Muslim Arabs is also well documented. The Arab slave masters justify this horrific practice by claiming the Qur'an gives them the right to make slaves out of "infidels."[20]

This is not to say that conditions are the same in every Muslim dominated country. Islamic law is very strict in Saudi Arabia, Pakistan and Afghanistan; some Muslim countries are more lenient, like Qatar and the United Arab Emirates.

Islam in the West is completely different from Islam in Muslim-dominated countries. For one thing, Muslims who live in Western democratic countries enjoy all the benefits and privileges of freedom and democracy. They even have protected legal status as a minority religious group. Their civil liberties are secure; they may practice their religion freely and openly; they may build mosques, print literature, form organizations and associations, start schools, fund media outlets and preach their message from the street corners. Ironically, Muslims living in the United States reap the benefits available in a nation founded on biblical principles.

THE BLACK MUSLIMS ARE AMERICAN IN ORIGIN

A distinctly American adaptation of Islam is the Black Muslim movement. In 1913, Timothy Drew, who had changed his name to Noble

Drew Ali, taught that Blacks were originally from Morocco (not Ethiopia as many scholars say) and that they had been enslaved by the "Caucasian Devil." Ali called for the overthrow of the tyranny of the White culture. After Ali died in 1919, Wallace Fard Mohammed claimed to be "Ali reincarnated" and formed the Nation of Islam in Detroit in 1930.

Sometime after 1935, Fard disappeared and Elijah Mohammed assumed leadership of the movement. Elijah taught that a mad Black scientist had created Whites, who would rule the earth for 6,000 years. That period ended in 1914, and Blacks were now supposed to unite and bring sanity to the world. The Nation of Islam grew rapidly in the 1960s and 1970s, as Elijah focused on strict discipline and on bettering the education of Black people, while improving their economic and political prospects.

However, in the 1950s and 1960s, a very successful recruiter for the Nation of Islam, Malcolm X, began moving away from Elijah Mohammed's positions and teachings. Malcolm X made a pilgrimage to Mecca where he saw the multiracial character of orthodox (Sunni) Islam and came to believe this was the path to follow. He challenged the leadership of Elijah Mohammed and finally was assassinated by Black Muslims in 1965.

Malcolm X's beliefs, however, did not die with him. By the early 1970s, Black nationalism was disavowed by key Black Muslim leaders, links to orthodox Islam were established and non-Black members were admitted. When Elijah Mohammed died in 1975, his son, Wallace D. Mohammed, took over and relaxed the strict discipline and harsh rhetoric of the Black Muslim movement. He changed the group's name to the American Muslim Mission. This led in the latter 1970s and the 1980s to several breakaway groups, chief of which is led by Louis Farrakhan (born 1933). Believing that Wallace Mohammed's policies were lax, Farrakhan resurrected the Nation of Islam in 1978 and reclaimed the heritage and principles of Black separatism. He has emerged as the most influential leader among the Black Muslim community, but his racist tirades are considered "un-Islamic" by orthodox Muslims.[21]

In the West, whether members of the Nation of Islam or more orthodox Muslim communities, Muslims enjoy numerous freedoms that are unimaginable for Christians in almost all Muslim countries. Why the huge disparity? A large part of the answer is that the West's Judeo-Christian heritage provides a theological foundation for the dignity of each individual's freedom of conscience. In 1,500 years of Islamic history, it has yet to be proven that democratic values and Islam can comfortably coexist.

The key point, however, is that, whether in the East or the West, Islam is a religion of self-reliance and self-effort. Muslims, who are trying to follow a religion that puts the responsibility for their salvation squarely on their own shoulders (or on kismet), can only do their best and hope that Allah might have mercy on them. As people whose confidence is not in themselves but in the God who sent His Son to reconcile them to Him, Christians have incredibly good news to share with Muslims who are willing to listen.

SUMMING UP MAJOR DIFFERENCES BETWEEN MUSLIMS AND CHRISTIANS

Regarding God: Muslims believe there is no God but Allah; Christians believe that God is revealed in Scripture as Father, Son and Holy Spirit, three persons who are coeternally God (see Matt. 3:13-17; 28:19; 2 Cor. 13:14).

Regarding Jesus Christ: Muslims believe that Jesus was only a man, a prophet below Mohammed in importance, who did not die for man's sins; Christians say Christ is the Son of God, the sinless Redeemer who died and rose again for sinful man (see John 1:13,14; 1 Pet. 3:18).

Regarding sin: Muslims claim that humans are born with hearts that are clean slates. If they commit sins, these can be overcome by acts of the will; Christians counter that we are born corrupted by sin, spiritually dead apart from God's grace, and that no one does good apart from faith (see Rom. 3:12; Eph. 5:8-10).

Regarding salvation: Muslims say that Allah does not love those who do wrong, and each person must earn his or her own salvation; Christians contend that a loving God sent His Son to die for our sins, according to the inspired Word (see Rom. 5:8; 1 Cor. 15:3,4).

CHAPTER SIX

HINDUISM

WE ARE ALL DIVINE

To the typical Western way of thinking, Hinduism and other Asian views of life appear strange. That's because we who live in the Western world[1] have a religious and cultural heritage much different from that of people of the East.

Western thought began in ancient Greece where men like Socrates, Plato and Aristotle saw that the universe had a plan and purpose. To these early Greek ideas, Judaism and Christianity added the teachings of the Bible, which explained that this plan and purpose reflected the nature of a rational and energetic God who had created the universe. The Bible taught that the infinite God is personal, that He loves people and, because He is their creator, He has the power to make moral demands upon them. In addition, the Bible taught the dignity and worth of each person, created "in the image of God," with the power of reason, the ability to make choices and the capacity to relate to God (see Gen. 1:26,27). The Bible also taught that time and history are progressing to a definitive judgment day.

Things developed much differently in the East. Typically, Eastern religions emphasize that *everything* in the world is temporary, changing, ephemeral and unreal and that our perceptions of the world are most often misleading and illusory. The physical universe is not seen as a rational, ordered universe revealing God's glory (see Ps. 19:1-4), but as a *hindrance* to experiencing "Ultimate Reality."

In the East, Ultimate Reality is thought of as attainable *within* each individual by realizing intuitively that the "self" is Divine, or at least part of the Divine. God is, for the most part, seen as an impersonal, unifying force who takes no personal interest in individuals. The idea of a creator having authority over the universe and making universal moral demands is, by and large, rejected.

ORIGINS AND BACKGROUND OF HINDUISM

The word "Hinduism" comes from the Indus River, which flows through what is now Pakistan. In the third millennium B.C., the great civilization of Mohendo-jaro flourished there, populated by the dark-skinned Dravidians. From what archaeologists have been able to discover, the Dravidians had a polytheistic fertility religion that centered upon worship of the forces of nature and use of rituals, merging human sexuality with the hope for abundant crops.[2]

About 2000 B.C., the light-skinned and warlike Aryans came over the Caucasus Mountains and conquered the people of the Indus Valley. The Aryans also had a polytheistic religion, and some of the most popular Dravidian gods received new Aryan names but retained their old functions. The Aryans wrote down their hymns, prayers, mythic stories and chants into the *Vedas, Brahamanas, Aranyakas* and *Upanishads,* composed between 2000 and 700 B.C., and known as the *Vedic* literature.[3]

These writings are considered by Hindus to be supernaturally inspired and are as sacred to them as the Bible is to Christians.[4]

Dravidian polytheistic fertility religion and the early Aryan Vedic polytheistic religion laid the foundations of what later became Hinduism. While the earliest Vedas were blatantly polytheistic and devoted to rituals and sacrifice, the later Vedas showed a movement toward pantheism (from the word "pan," meaning "everything," and "theos," meaning "God"). According to pantheism, God did not create the world; God *is* the world, along with everything in it.

Although the earlier Hindu scriptures had mentioned many gods, the highest goal, according to the later Vedic literature, was union with Brahma, the impersonal absolute. The priests of Brahma became known as the Brahmins, who performed the ritual duties for the community, which were demanded in the early Vedic writings to appease the many gods. The Brahmins also maintained a monopoly on the higher truths of pantheistic Brahmanism. Brahmins grew more and more powerful until they became the highest social class.

Around 500 B.C., still more writings were added to the Hindu scriptures. Their purpose was to establish *Varna*, a rigid caste system, or social hierarchy. One hymn tells how four castes of people came from the head, arms, thighs and feet of the creator god, Brahma. The four castes were the *Brahmins* (priests); the *Kshatriyas* (warriors and nobles); *Vaisyas* (merchants and artisans); and *Shudras* (slaves). Each caste was then subdivided into hundreds of subcastes, arranged in order of rank. Only Brahmins, Kshatriyas and Vaisyas were allowed to take full advantage of all that the Hindu religion has to offer, but the Shudras were not allowed to hear the Vedas or to use them to try to find salvation.

Even lower on the social totem pole were the Untouchables who, until the twentieth century, were considered so low they were outside the caste system and, most of the time, were treated as subhuman. In the past, Untouchables always had the dirtiest and filthiest jobs, drank polluted water, ate carrion meat, wore clothing of disgrace and watched their children die of malnutrition. They were denied property, education and dignity.

When India became a nation in 1947, the government officially outlawed discrimination against Untouchables. The greatest force for changing these laws and customs, which kept Untouchables in virtual slavery, has been the influence of Christian missionaries, who have played a major role in challenging the social-economic-religious power blocs in India.[5] Still, the social reality in many Indian villages is that change comes slowly and grudgingly.

TWO CORE BELIEFS OF HINDUISM

Hinduism is not really one religion, but many religions that interact and blend with one another. There is no known founder of Hinduism, no creedal statements of faith to sign and no agreed-upon authority. In fact, one can be a good Hindu and believe in one god, many gods or no god at all! This is because, for Hindus, contradictory ideas are not a problem. All reality, contradictory or not, is seen as "one." There are, however, two foundational assumptions that almost all Hindus believe without question: reincarnation and karma.

Reincarnation is the belief that the *atman*, a person's uncreated and eternal soul, must repeatedly be recycled into the world in different bodies. In some forms of Hinduism, souls may be reincarnated as animals, plants or even inanimate objects. Reincarnation is the process that takes the Hindu through the great wheel of *samsara*, the thousands or millions of lives (all full of suffering) that each atman must endure before reaching *moksha*—liberation from suffering and union with the infinite.

Karma ("action") has to do with the law of cause and effect. For the Hindu, karma means merit or demerit, which attaches to one's atman (soul) according to how one lives one's life. Karma from past lives affects a person's present life, and karma from this life will determine a person's station in the next life.

The Bible flatly contradicts Hindu ideas of reincarnation and karma. Hinduism teaches that the atman (soul) is uncreated and eternal. The Bible teaches that each person is created by God, will die once and then be resurrected once at the judgment (see John 5:17-30; 1 Cor. 15:1-58; Heb. 9:27). Hinduism teaches that the atman is perfect, free and unlimited, and no matter how many lives it takes, eventually each and every atman will realize its divine nature. The Bible teaches that each person has one life to live, and after this comes the judgment (see Heb. 9:27).

PATHS TO MOKSHA

For Hindus, the great spiritual challenge is that the soul, or atman, is separated from Brahma (Ultimate Reality) and trapped in samsara, the seemingly endless process of being reincarnated over and over. Moksha, which is liberation from samsara and reunion with Brahma, is the goal. In Hinduism, there are basically three paths to moksha: the path of works (*dharma*), the path of knowledge (*inana*) and the path of passionate devotion (*bhakti*).

When following dharma, the path of works, a person has a set of specific social and religious obligations that must be fulfilled. He must follow his caste occupation, marry within his caste, eat or not eat certain foods and, above all, produce and raise a son who can make a sacrifice to his ancestors as well as perform other sacrificial and ritual acts. By fulfilling these obligations, the person using the path of works may hope to attain a better reincarnation and *perhaps*, after thousands or tens of thousands of reincarnations, achieve moksha.

A more difficult way to achieve moksha is the path of knowledge (inana), which includes self-renunciation and meditation on the supreme pantheistic reality of Hinduism. This very aesthetic path is open to men only in the highest castes, and it is described in the *Upanishads*, a series of philosophical treatises composed beginning around 600 B.C.[6] The Upaninshad texts teach that the world as we experience it is mere *maya* (illusion) and that Brahma is the only thing that really exists and has meaning.

The path of knowledge most often includes the practice of yoga (yoking, or union). Yoga is the attempt to control one's consciousness through bodily posture, breath control and concentration, to the extent that one comes to understand experientially that one's true self, one's undying soul (atman), is identical with Brahma. This leads to the famous Hindu saying, "Aham asmi Brahma" ("I am Brahma").[7]

The path of passionate devotion to a god (bhakti) is the most popular way to achieve moksha. This path is described in earliest form in the epic poems of the *Ramayana* and the *Mahabharata*, composed somewhere between 300 B.C. and A.D. 300.[8] Bhakti is also found in the *Puranas*, folktales and erotic stories composed between the fourth and sixteenth centuries A.D.[9]

According to the way of bhakti, a devotee may choose any of the 330 million gods, goddesses or demigods in the Hindu pantheon and passionately worship that particular god. In actual practice, almost all Hindus following the way of bhakti worship Vishnu or Shiva.

Most popular is the god Vishnu, who has many names and has appeared as *avatars* (saviors—the incarnation of deity) in the form of a giant turtle, as *Gautama* Buddha (see chapter 7) and as *Rama* and *Krishna*, the two important heroes of *Ramayana* and *Mahabharata*. Vishnu also has many sexual consorts (wives), as does Shiva, who is worshiped by other millions of Hindus. Shiva can be linked to the ancient pre-Aryan fertility god of the Dravidians. Rituals performed by Shiva worshipers are not unlike the worship of the Canaanites, whom God commanded the Israelites to destroy (see the book of Joshua).[10]

The way of bhakti appeals to the lower classes (the vast majority of the inhabitants of India) and offers a much easier path for their souls to progress to higher forms of birth through reincarnation—and eventually to reach moksha. Through bhakti the worshiper bypasses going through as many rebirths and lives as the other paths demand. There are no torturous yoga exercises to perform, nor is there a need to be part of the intelligentsia or a special caste.

HINDU "EVANGELIZATION" OF THE WEST

Hindu ideas began to influence Western thought in the mid-nineteenth century when Ralph Waldo Emerson, a leading American exponent of transcendentalism, steeped himself in Hindu writings. His doctrine of the "Oversoul" was an expression of pantheism, and his concept of self-reliance is remarkably similar to the Hindu understanding of atman as Brahma. Henry David Thoreau, a contemporary of Emerson and fellow transcendentalist, was inspired by the *Upanishads* and *Bhagavad Gita* when he wrote *Waldon* and some of his other books.[11]

The first significant breakthrough, however, came in 1893 at the World Parliament of Religions in Chicago, Illinois. At that meeting, Swami Vivekananda made a sizable impression on the cream of American intellectual society. In the 1930s the Ramakrishna Order of India sent another young monk, Swami Prabhavananda, to establish the *Vedanta* Society of Southern California.

The followers of the modern Vedanta movement believe that the most recent incarnation of Vishnu is that of Sri Ramakrishna (after whom the Ramakrishna Order was named). Ramakrishna lived in Bengal toward the end of the nineteenth century. His followers say that he practiced all the spiritual disciplines of Hinduism, Christianity and Islam and that he attained a vision of God in each one. Ramakrishna would often say, "Many faiths are but different paths leading to the one reality, God."

Vedanta, which played a major role in the New Age movement (see chapter 11), purports to be friendly toward all religions. Aldous Huxley, author of *Brave New World* and one of Vedanta's ardent followers, said, "It is perfectly possible for people to remain good Christians, Hindus, Buddhists or Muslims and yet to be united in full agreement on the basic doctrines of the Perennial Philosophy."[12]

In the 1960s, the Beatles went to India and were taught transcendental meditation (TM) by Maharishi MaheshYogi. They brought TM back to the United States and other nations, where it became extremely popular. Since then Hinduism in various forms has entered the mainstream culture of the United States to such an extent that certain ancient Vedantic ideas are unquestioned by millions of Americans. One basic example is the Vedantic motto: All approaches to God are true and valid.

Teachers of Vedanta, such as Swami Prabhavananda, say that a Hindu "would find it easy to accept Christ as a divine incarnation and to worship Him unreservedly, exactly as he worships Krishna or another avatar ('savior') of his choice. But he cannot accept Christ as the *only* son of God."[13]

The great Indian leader Mohandas K. Gandhi made a similar statement: "It was more than I could believe that Jesus was the only incarnate son of God. And that only he who believed in him would have everlasting life." Gandhi also said that he could not believe there was any "mysterious or miraculous virtue" in Christ's death on the cross.[14]

Gandhi, like other Hindus, could not accept the Christian answer to the problem of sin, yet he felt a deep hunger for real salvation from sin. He wrote, "For it is an unbroken torture to me that I am still so far from Him, who, as I fully know, governs every breath of my life, and whose offspring I am."[15]

HINDUISM VERSUS JESUS CHRIST

Along with their rejection of God as sovereign creator of the world, Hindus also part company with Christianity on the critical issue of Jesus Christ as God's incarnate Son. Hindu worshipers of Vishnu, for example, believe that God has become incarnate many times in the past.[16] The Bible teaches that God became incarnate only once in human history (see John 1:14). Jesus came not to teach humanity various "ways" to salvation, but to be "the way and the truth and the life"

(John 14:6) and "to take away the sins of many" (Heb. 9:28).

The resurrection of Christ demonstrates His absolute uniqueness as God the Son, His victory over death and His divine approval from God the Father. It also refutes the Hindu teaching of continuous reincarnation and their belief that Christ is just another teacher-avatar (super-savior).

WHY THE HINDU'S GOD IS TOO SMALL

Actually, Hinduism is more a philosophy than a theology (a study of God). The Hindus try to make a tremendous case for the bigness of their impersonal god—Brahma—the "that" behind and beyond reality. But where does the Hindu seek Brahma? Within himself. For the Hindu, each person is "god" (or at least part of "god"). The Hindu's god is too small. The biblical record (see 1 John 5:11,12) states that God has given us eternal life, and this life is in His Son. If we have the Son, we have eternal life (not a series of mythological, absolutely unproven reincarnations). As an Indian folksong puts it: "How many births are passed, I cannot tell. How many yet to come, no man can say: But this alone I know, and know full well, that pain and grief embitter all the way."[17]

Christians, however, can rest in "the blessed hope—the glorious appearing of our great God and Savior, Jesus Christ" (Titus 2:13).

SUMMING UP MAJOR DIFFERENCES BETWEEN HINDUS AND CHRISTIANS

Regarding God and Jesus Christ: Hindus do not believe in a personal, loving God, but in Brahma, a formless, abstract, eternal being without attributes, who was the beginning of all things.[18] They believe that Jesus is not God but just one of many incarnations, or avatars, of Vishnu.[19] Christians believe that God is an eternal, personal, spiritual Being in three persons—Father, Son and Holy Spirit (see Matt. 3:13-17; 28:19; 2 Cor. 13:14). Jesus Christ is God as well as sinless man and He died for our redemption (see John 1:13,14; 1 Pet. 2:24).

Regarding sin and salvation: Hindus call sin "utter illusion" because they believe all material reality is illusory. They seek deliverance from samsara, the endless cycle of death and rebirth, through union with Brahma, which is achieved through devotion, meditation, good works and self-control.[20] Christians believe that sin is prideful rebellion that leads to eternal separation from God after living only one life, not many (see Rom. 3:23; Heb. 9:27) and that salvation is gained only through believing in the sacrificial death and resurrection of Jesus Christ (see Rom. 3:24; 1 Cor. 15:3).

CHAPTER SEVEN

BUDDHISM

YOU YOURSELF MUST MAKE THE EFFORT

Unlike the Hindu religion, Buddhism can point to an individual founder and can look back to a date for its beginnings. The man who formulated Buddhism was Siddhartha Gautama, who was born a Hindu about 560 B.C., at Lumbini near the border of India in what is now Nepal.

Tradition says that when Gautama was born, a seer prophesied that he would become the greatest ruler in human history. The seer added that if Gautama ever saw four things—sickness, old age, death and a monk who had renounced the world—the boy would give up his earthly rule and discover a way of salvation for all mankind.

To refute the prophecy, Gautama's father built a palace for his son, giving orders that neither the sick, the old, a dead body nor a monk be allowed near the palace. Gautama grew up in this way, protected from the world. He later married a beautiful girl named Yasodhara, who bore him a son.

But the "gods" had other plans for Gautama. One day, as he rode though the park that surrounded his palace, he saw a man who was covered with terrible sores, a man who tottered with age, a corpse being carried to its grave and a begging monk who appeared to be peaceful and happy.

That night, as Gautama reported later, he began to think about the look of peace on the face of the monk. He began to wonder if there was more to life than the luxuries of his palace. Late that night he took a last look at his sleeping wife and child, then left the palace forever.

Gautama, 29 years old, was determined to solve the riddle of life. He shaved his head, put on a yellow robe and wandered the countryside as a beggar monk. First he studied the Upanishads with the finest teachers, but he could find no satisfaction in these writings. Then he tried to find salvation through self-denial. He starved himself until he was a walking skeleton, but this brought him no happiness either.

GAUTAMA BECOMES THE "ENLIGHTENED ONE"

Finally, he sat under a tree for 40 days and nights. He swore that he would not move until he found what he was searching for. During this time, Mara, the evil one, tried to make him give up his quest. At the end of the 40 days, he experienced the highest degree of God-consciousness—*nirvana*—literally, the "blowing out" of the flame of desire and the negation of suffering. Through this experience, Gautama felt he had found "salvation." From then on, he was known as Buddha or the "enlightened one."

After his life-changing experience, Gautama Buddha went back to the world of man. He began to preach and teach about the meaning of life and his way to nirvana. Soon he founded the *Sangha*, an order of monks. By the time Gautama Buddha died, 45 years later, many thousands had adopted his teachings.[1]

In some ways, Buddhism is similar to the Hinduism from which it evolved. In other ways, it is quite different, and many of Buddha's teachings were rejected as heresies by the dominant teachers of Hinduism, the Brahmin priests. For example, Buddha denied that the Vedas and the Upanishads were divine writings, saying they were of no help in finding the way to nirvana. He also denied that man has an atman (soul), which is part of the Brahman (world soul), and that the present world is maya (unreal).

Other Hindu concepts Buddha rejected included the Brahmin priesthood and the entire Hindu sacrificial system; instead, he emphasized ethics over ritual. He rejected the caste system and taught that enlightenment was open to anyone—including women—not just Brahmin males. Finally, Buddha radically challenged all the indifferent Hindu gods and goddesses, saying they were essentially unimportant in the quest for enlightenment.

Buddha did accept the Hindu teachings on reincarnation, along with karma (the soul gains merits or demerits according to how one lives his life) and dharma (the duty one has to perform according to his station in life). Buddha taught that one could be reborn as a human, an animal, a hungry ghost, a demon or even as a Hindu god. He also incorporated yoga and meditation, which were highly developed skills in Hinduism, into his teachings.

THE MIDDLE WAY AND THE EIGHTFOLD PATH

One of Buddha's most important teachings was his theory of the Middle Way. For Buddha, the Middle Way was a spiritual path of salvation, winding between the extreme asceticism and the unrestrained sensuality he had known while a Hindu. To describe his Middle Way, Buddha offered four main principles, which have come to be called the Four Noble Truths:

1. *Suffering is universal.* Buddha taught that the very act of living involves suffering from birth until death. Even death brings no relief, however, because of the cycle of rebirth, suffering and death. Salvation (nirvana) is to be released from this unending cycle of suffering.

2. *The cause of suffering is craving (selfish desire).* People remain in this endless cycle, because they are too attached to their health, wealth, status and physical comfort. This is because they are ignorant of the nature of reality and they fall victim to what Buddha called *tanha* (attachment, desire).

3. *The cure for suffering is to overcome ignorance and eliminate craving.* Since to live is to suffer and suffering is caused by craving, if a person could remove craving from his or her life, suffering would end.

4. *Suppress craving by following the Middle Way—the Noble Eightfold Path.* First, Buddha isolated the cause, tanha—humanity's inability to escape from the squirrel cage of death and rebirth. Next he worked out a system called the Eightfold Path by which a Buddhist could rid himself of tanha. The Eightfold Path consists of eight ways of right living: (1) right viewpoint, (2) right aspiration, (3) right speech, (4) right behavior, (5) right occupation, (6) right effort, (7) right mindfulness and (8) right meditation.

Buddha claimed that whoever could follow this Eightfold Path would eventually reach nirvana, a release from the endless cycle of death and rebirth. When Buddha was asked to define the state of nirvana, he replied that he had never tried to solve this question. His mission was to show man the way to escape the suffering of life, not to describe what he would find once he had been liberated.

The Hinduism that Buddha rejected said that life in this world is maya (illusion); thus, suffering, which is part of this world, is also illusion. Buddha, however, proclaimed that life in this world is quite real. It involves real suffering; because of this suffering, the world must be escaped by following Buddha's Eightfold Path.

Buddhism has always had great appeal for the peoples of the East. Unlike the elitist ideas of Hinduism, Buddhism offers a precise definition of man's problem, along with an exact "plan of salvation" for everyone.

MAJOR BRANCHES OF BUDDHISM

Buddhism was popular in India for several centuries until it was absorbed by Hinduism. The Brahmin priests even promoted the Buddha to an incarnation of Vishnu. During the first thousand years of Christianity, while the gospel was being carried all over Europe, Buddhist monks spread their religion throughout the Orient. Today, from Ceylon to Japan, over 350 million people follow the teachings of Buddha.[2]

Buddhism takes a wide variety of forms, but the three main kinds are *Hinayana*, *Mahayana* and *Tantrism*. Hinayana means "the doctrine of the lesser way," referring to the belief that, for all intents and purposes, only a fortunate few lifelong monks can find nirvana by absolutely following the way to Buddha. Since the term "lesser way" was a derogatory name given by critics, proponents of this path later changed the name to *Theravada* Buddhism ("way of the elders"). The best that laypeople can hope for in Theravada Buddhism is to rise to a higher level when reborn in their next life so they may become monks. The Theravada branch of Buddhism has become very wealthy through gifts of land and money for monasteries and is dominant today in Sri Lanka, Thailand, Laos and Kampuchea.[3]

Mahayana Buddhism, the doctrine of the "greater way," teaches that Buddha believed that nirvana is available to all people. Buddha originally taught that the only person who can save you is you, but Mahayana developed the idea of savior gods or *Bodhisattvas*. Followers of Mahayana reasoned that Buddha had remained on the earth for 45 years when he could have gone straight to nirvana. He decided, however, to stay to save mankind and became the first and supreme Bodhisattva, a savior to mankind who can be called on by the faithful. Other Buddhist monks who achieve nirvana and become enlightened as Buddha did are also Bodhisattvas.

From all this, you can gather that Theravada and Mahayana Buddhism differ radically in their opinion of Buddha. To Theravada, Buddha was only a teacher (as Buddha himself claimed), but Mahayana has raised him to the position of a savior-god for all people. Because of this, Mahayana Buddhism is by far the more popular. It is influential in Nepal, China, Tibet, Japan, Vietnam and Korea.[4]

A popular form of Mahayana Buddhism in the West is *Zen*, a discipline with the primary goal of experiencing enlightenment through meditation (reaching *satori*).[5] Zen teachers emphasize the saying of the Buddha: "Look within, you are the Buddha."[6]

After World War II, Zen made significant inroads in the West through the influence of the Japanese scholar D. T. Suzuki (1870-1966), as well as through influential artists, philosophers and psychologists. Hundreds of thousands of Americans converted to Buddhism, including notable entertainers and film stars such as Joan Baez, Tina Turner, Richard Gere, Larry Hagman and Harrison Ford.[7]

The third major division of Buddhism is called *Tantrism*, a blending of Mahayana Buddhism with the ancient occult practices of Tibet. Tantric Buddhism uses incantations and occult signs. It contains strong elements of animism (attributing conscious life to inanimate objects or objects in nature) and is one of many false religions that can leave its followers open to demonic activity. Tantrism is considered the official religion of Tibet and is practiced extensively in Nepal.

COMPARING BUDDHA'S TEACHINGS WITH THE BIBLE

Five hundred and twenty years after the death of Buddha, Jesus came to bring full and abundant life, not only in the world to come but also in this world. Buddha claimed to have found a way, but Jesus claimed that He is *the* way. How do these two claims compare?

Buddha said that "to live is to suffer," and he said that the reasons for suffering were ignorance and craving. The Bible agrees that suffering is everywhere and that a good deal of suffering is due to misplaced desire, but at the core, the Bible provides a very different explanation for suffering. The Bible explains that the entire world "groans" and that all men suffer because of sin (see Rom. 8:18-23). All of us have put our own personal desires ahead of God's. All of us are sinners by choice. We decide to live our lives independently of God and His laws (see Isa. 53:6).

Buddha observed that suffering comes from craving—desire or attachment of any kind. For Buddha, all desire was bad and had to be eradicated. The Bible, however, teaches that, while there are bad desires, there are also good ones. For example, we are encouraged to have great desire for God, His glory in our lives and for His kingdom (see Ps. 27:4; Matt. 6:33).

As for bad desires, James 1:13-15 points out that a man is enticed from *within* by "lusts"—passions or appetites that tend to get out of control. When a person yields to these temptations, he sins. The result of sin is spiritual suffering and death (see Rom. 6:23). Christians agree that the cause of much suffering is selfish desire, but they disagree with Buddhism's way of removing this desire.

Buddha taught that the only way to rid oneself of selfish desire was through self-effort. For centuries his followers have tried to stay on the Eightfold Path, but many have found that "the heart is deceitful above all things" and will sabotage the best of human intentions (Jer. 17:9).

For a person to master himself, he must have a higher source of strength. But Buddha was agnostic. He ignored the possibility of help from God. The apostle Paul (see Titus 3:3-8) reminds us that every Christian was once a slave to desire and selfish hungers but that Christ came into the world as God and as man to supply the strength to overcome these desires. Without the help of God, the only way to end desire is to die. But with God, we can become "new creatures" who die (figuratively) to selfish desires (see John 3:5; 2 Cor. 5:17; Gal. 2:20).

CHRISTIANITY GOES BEYOND BUDDHISM

Buddha said that to end desire one must follow the Eightfold Path—a noble goal that must be pursued solely through one's own determination and resources. Jesus gave a similar set of standards in the Sermon on the Mount (see Matt. 5), but He also promised to give us His personal strength through the Holy Spirit so that we might live this kind of God-pleasing life (see John 16:7-15; Rom. 8; Gal. 5).

Christ shares in the life of the true believer and gives His followers two vital ingredients for effective living: power and authority. The Christian increases or limits that power in direct proportion to how much of his life he really shares with and submits to his Lord (see John 15:1-8).

THE CHOICE EVERYONE MUST MAKE

The Theravada Buddhist has eight guidelines for the right way to live, but Buddha promised him no power to live that way. Also, the Buddha had no authority for saying these eight steps are right, as noble as they may sound. Mahayana Buddhists find the Eightfold Path a lonely one and look to the Bodhisattvas for help.

Buddha taught that you yourself must make the effort. Christ teaches us to turn ourselves over to Him and He will give us power to live successfully. Christ does not simply give the Christian a list of commandments and orders to obey. He promises to help the Christian grow, change and develop.

Every person, Christian or otherwise, faces a choice: self-effort or yielding everything to Christ as Savior *and* Lord. When Christians accept Christ as Savior but fail to obey Him as Lord, they shortchange themselves and, in some respects, are no better off than the Buddhist who has to grapple with craving (selfish desire) using only his own strength.[8]

Perhaps Christians can learn from Buddhism to recognize that, even though they are saved through faith in Christ, they still have selfish desires. The way to deal with those desires is to turn them over to the One who has plainly said, "Apart from me [without living all of your life in Christ] you can do nothing" (John 15:5).

SUMMING UP MAJOR DIFFERENCES BETWEEN BUDDHISTS AND CHRISTIANS

Regarding God and Jesus Christ: Buddhists deny the existence of a personal God or say that God's existence is irrelevant;[9] Christians say that God is personal, omniscient and omnipotent (see Job 42:1-6; Ps. 115:3; Matt. 19:26); Buddhists identify Christ as a good teacher but less important than Buddha; Christians believe that Jesus Christ is the unique Son of God who died for mankind's sin (see Matt. 14:33; John 1:34; Rom. 5:6-8).

Regarding Sin and Salvation: Buddhists believe that sin is the lust that arises in one's life, and they seek to rid themselves of lustful desires by self-effort or by calling on Bodhisattvas for help;[10] Christians believe that sin is any thought, deed or desire contrary to God's will, and that salvation comes only through faith in what Christ has done for us (see Acts 4:12;

Rom. 3:10, 23; Eph. 2:8-10). Through faith and the gracious
working of the Holy Spirit, God transforms our desires to be
more and more in conformity with God's desires (see Rom.
12:1,2).

PART FOUR

CULTS, NEW RELIGIONS AND THE OCCULT

CHAPTER EIGHT

WHERE DID THE CULTS COME FROM?

Before discussing some of the cultic movements that are directly at odds with biblical Christianity, we need to define what we mean by the word "cult." In this postmodern age that puts such a high value on tolerance, use of such a label is often seen as insensitivity at best and arrogant name-calling at worst. To mention a cult evokes images of brainwashed weirdos conducting strange rituals that sometimes end in death.

But what is a cult? What do its members believe? The word "cult" (from the Latin for "worship") is defined by Webster as "a religion regarded as unorthodox or spurious." In Webster's eyes, a cult is an organization opposing orthodoxy. When Christians speak of cults, they mean groups which they believe do not hold "orthodox [biblical]

Christian views." Therefore, the label "cult" as used here is not intended to be derogatory but only a semantic way of recognizing the *difference* between biblical Christianity and the beliefs that certain groups might hold.

In fact, some cults (the Mormons, for example) might call biblical Christians "cultists" because of their belief in creeds that are, in the opinion of the Mormons, based more on Greek philosophy than on the teachings of the New Testament. Early Christianity was seen as a cult by much of the Jewish establishment from which it sprang, as well as by the Roman government, which found Christians to be a pesky bunch that wouldn't conform to the first-century religious norm and posed a serious threat to peace and tranquility.

The late Walter Martin, who spent over 30 years researching cults and working with cultists, defines cults as groups which hold doctrines "contradictory to orthodox Christianity," yet claim to trace their origin to orthodox sources and may even be in harmony with some of those sources.[1] Another typical characteristic of a cult, says Martin, is that it is "a group of people gathered around a specific person or person's misinterpretation of the Bible."[2] Obvious examples are Jehovah's Witnesses, who began with Charles Taze Russell; the Mormons, who look back to Joseph Smith as their founder and first prophet; and Christian Scientists, who follow the teachings of Mary Baker Eddy.

FIVE MAJOR CHARACTERISTICS OF CULTISTS

On the following pages, we will look at a number of groups that fall under our definition of cults, with particular emphasis on Jehovah's Witnesses and the Mormons, by far the most successful cults in history.

There are several characteristics of all major cults. The first is that they reject the Trinity; that is, they *disbelieve* in Jesus Christ as God. Cults may say good things about Jesus and assign Him a certain position of importance, but they almost always attack or undermine the true biblical deity of Jesus Christ, either lowering Him to the level of man or raising man to His level.

Second, cultists usually believe that all Christian churches are wrong and that their group has the only real truth about God.

Third, they claim to believe the Bible but they distort its teachings to suit their own peculiar view of mankind, God, the Holy Spirit, heaven and hell, salvation and many other doctrines. They usually find the source of these peculiar beliefs in their leaders, who claim to have new interpretations of the Bible or even valuable additions to it.

A fourth point is that all cults deny that people can be saved by faith in Christ alone. They teach their members that they can make themselves right with God through good works and through obedience to the doctrines and requirements the cult has set down as "God's will" for their lives.

Fifth, cults are skillful at using Christian terminology, but they are not talking the same language as biblical Christians. Beware of the semantics barrier. Commonly understood words like "God," "Christ," "faith," "sin," "salvation," etc., mean entirely different things to a cultist and a Christian. The first task, then, when sharing your faith with someone who seems to have different ideas, is to define terms.

WHY CULTS GROW SO FAST

If cults teach error and heresy, why do many of them grow so fast? A major reason is that cults offer answers to human needs that aren't being met by Christian churches. People, many of whom grew up as Baptists, Presbyterians, Methodists, etc., wind up in a cult because that cult seems to offer practical solutions to problems like loneliness, spiritual emptiness and the desire to find a way to please God by serving Him faithfully.

What cults offer is counterfeit salvation, no matter how real it may seem for a while. The fellowship in many cults is conditional—that is, you must stay in line. Express even the smallest deviation in doctrine and you usually will be rejected, shunned or expelled. Also, being in a cult is hard work. Keeping pace with all the effort you are expected to expend can easily wear you out, if not physically, then mentally, emotionally and spiritually. Deep down inside, despite all the assurances by the cult that God needs to "see some effort" to be sure you have *real* faith, there is the gnawing doubt that works aren't cutting it, that you can't possibly do (or be) what the cult says God demands.

The following discussions are intended only as introductions to the thinking of various cults operating throughout the world today. Their different approaches range from all-out frontal assaults that leave no doubt about their disagreement with Christianity, to the subtlest of semantical game-playing designed to make them sound and look genuinely Christian. Some cults are odd, even bizarre; others are deadly to the spirit, mind and even the body.

As you learn about these various groups, be aware that your first line of defense against their lure and attractiveness is to know God's Word and be able to "test all things" with biblical truth (see 1 Thess. 5:21,22; 2 Tim. 2:4-16). Only by knowing the real *difference* between what you believe and what certain cultists believe can you reach out to them with the all-fulfilling truth and power of the gospel.

But don't stop with knowing the *written* Word. You need to know the *living* Word. Trusting Christ alone for salvation is a good start; knowing Him as a friend and helper will spur you to do good works—not to earn or secure your salvation but simply to live out what comes from within—a love for God and man because of what Christ has done for you.

As King Solomon said, "It has all been done before. Nothing under the sun is truly new" (Eccles. 1:9, *NLT*). In the case of today's cults, there is no heresy which they have not invented (or reinvented). For a key example, there is no better place to begin than with Jehovah's Witnesses, who openly and fervently teach that Christ is a created being, undeserving of the title of "God."

CHAPTER NINE

JEHOVAH'S WITNESSES

THERE IS NO HELL . . . HARD WORK EARNS "PARADISE"

Knock on any door in the United States, as well as in many countries around the world, and the odds are excellent that Jehovah's Witnesses have been there ahead of you. Above all else, Jehovah's Witnesses (hereafter referred to as JWs) are known for their aggressive door-to-door witnessing program. They are a serious challenge to Christians for several reasons.

JWs continue to grow at a rapid pace. In the early 1980s, the JWs claimed a half million members in the United States and more than 2.25 million throughout the world. According to their 1998 report, the JWs claimed just over 1 million members in the United States and a grand total of just under 5,900,000 in 233 countries worldwide.[1]

The amount of time JWs spend "preaching" (going door-to-door or standing in front of restaurants and other public places sharing literature) is enormous. In 1998, JWs spent almost 183,000,000 hours preaching in the United States alone. Total hours worldwide were almost 1.2 billion. In addition, the JWs also conducted 4.3 million Bible studies for those who showed interest in their doctrines.[2]

Officially called The Watchtower Bible and Tract Society (WTBTS), JWs arm their members with the printed page in astounding amounts. In 1997, circulation of their semimonthly magazine *Awake!*, designed to attract and intrigue nonmembers, hit over 18 million copies in 80 languages; *The Watchtower*, a semimonthly magazine designed to instruct the society's members in doctrine and practice, reached almost 21 million copies in 126 languages.

All JW witnessing efforts and tools are designed to oppose and contradict biblical doctrines and teachings and to twist Scripture to make the Bible fit a preconceived theology it simply does not teach. One of the major JW tools is The Watchtower Society's own version of the Bible, *The New World Translation of the Holy Scriptures* (NWT), which is filled with mistranslations designed to prove JW doctrines.

The JWs are totally convinced by Watchtower headquarters that all those who disagree with them—particularly biblical Christians—are not only wrong but are mortal enemies who will finally be destroyed by Jehovah at the great battle of Armageddon, which is yet to come.

JWs are tightly controlled by Watchtower headquarters and are constantly told they cannot interpret the Bible for themselves in any way; they must avoid independent thinking; they are never to question the counsel provided by the Watchtower.[3]

CHARLES TAZE RUSSELL: HOW IT ALL BEGAN

The roots of the JWs go back to Charles Taze Russell (1852-1916) who, as a teenager, rejected many of the views taught in his Congregational church, particularly the doctrines of hell and the Trinity, which struck him as unreasonable. For a while, the teenage Russell was a skeptic, but soon he was influenced by Adventist teaching that assured him there was no eternal punishment, because the wicked were annihilated. His faith in Scripture was restored, but he remained totally distrustful of all churches and denominations.

By the time he was 18, Russell formed his own Bible study and began developing his own system of theology, emphasizing the second coming of Christ, which many Adventists had predicted would happen in 1874. When it didn't happen, Russell was further influenced by some Adventists who decided that Christ's coming had happened in a "spiritual and invisible way" in 1874.[4]

In 1879, Russell parted company with the Adventists and launched his own magazine, eventually known as *The Watchtower*. Financing the magazine and the spread of his movement with personal income from his profitable men's clothing business, Russell set 1914 as the year of the battle of Armageddon when God would destroy all present governments of the earth, end "Gentile times" and establish His kingdom.

By 1896, Russell had founded the Watchtower Bible and Tract Society. In 1908, he moved his headquarters from Pennsylvania to New York City, and the WTBTS soon owned entire blocks in Brooklyn. Watchtower headquarters are still in Brooklyn today, where it owns a huge up-to-date printing plant, a modern apartment building, offices, a Bible school and other enterprises.[5]

Russell never had any formal theological training, and his tempestuous career included his exposure in court in 1912 as a perjurer. He claimed to know the Greek alphabet, but under examination he could not read Greek letters.[6] Nonetheless, he wrote a six-book series called *Studies in the Scriptures*, which he described as "practically the Bible itself."[7]

When World War I started in 1914, Russell claimed that it was the "beginning of Armageddon." But Armageddon never happened that year, or even the next. Russell died in 1916, a failed Watchtower prophet, but he would not be the last. Following is a condensed version of JW history from 1916 on, as the WTBTS and its leaders tried vainly to predict the end of the world.

RUTHERFORD SETS NEW DATE FOR ARMAGEDDON

In 1917, Joseph F. Rutherford, a lawyer who had served as legal advisor to the WTBTS, became its new president. A charismatic and dominating figure, Rutherford instituted many changes that alienated some of the other leaders of the Society. He set 1925 as the new date for Armageddon, which was widely advertised across the nation, particularly in *The Watchtower*, as being not of man but of God and "absolutely and unqualifiedly correct."[8]

When 1925 came and went without Armageddon, the WTBTS and Rutherford backed away from his prediction, claiming that he had been "misunderstood" by JW faithful who had "erroneously" anticipated the end, which wasn't what the Lord had stated at all.

Undeterred by the 1925 debacle, Rutherford pressed on. In 1931 he pushed through the adoption of a new name for the Society—Jehovah's Witnesses—taken from Isaiah 43:10 *(KJV):* "Ye are my witnesses, saith [Jehovah]."[9] One of Rutherford's main motives for adopting the name of Jehovah's Witnesses was to avoid confusion between the WTBTS and certain splinter groups, such as the Dawn Bible Students Association, which had been formed by disenchanted former members who had left because of Rutherford's domineering policies.

Another Rutherford innovation was the door-to-door visitation program for which JWs are famous. As president of WTBTS, one of Rutherford's main goals was to increase membership, which he attempted to do by spreading the word that only 144,000 people were going to make it to heaven.[10] Throughout the 1920s, JWs preached this message from door-to-door, but as the 1930s arrived, Rutherford and the Watchtower had a real problem. The ranks were filling fast, Armageddon still had not happened, and soon there would be more than 144,000 members in the Watchtower organization.

Rutherford then announced that everyone who had become a JW before 1935 would go to heaven (the "little flock"), while everyone who became a JW after 1935 would be among the "great crowd" who would not go to heaven but could look forward to living on Earth in a new paradise after Armageddon and the Millennium.[11]

In the late 1930s, Rutherford continued to be known for his scathing denouncements of traditional Christianity, and the JWs kept growing in influence and numbers. While no more dates were set, Rutherford and The Watchtower magazine kept saying that Armageddon was "coming soon." The WTBTS predicted 1940 as the "most important year yet." In 1941, the WTBTS mentioned "there were just a few remaining months before Armageddon."[12]

When Rutherford died in 1942, there still had been no Armageddon. The next Watchtower president, Nathan Knorr (1905-1977), was cut from different cloth than Rutherford or Russell. An almost reticent man who stayed in the background, Knorr changed Watchtower policy and made all its books and other publications from that point on anonymous.

In 1943, the WTBTS released a book entitled The Truth Shall Make You Free, which was the first step in coming up with a new dating system teaching that Jesus had not returned invisibly in 1874, as Russell had taught. The new Watchtower revelation taught that Christ had returned invisibly in 1914; and, in accordance with Matthew 24:34, the generation that had been alive in 1914 would not "pass away" before Armageddon would occur.

As the years went by with no Armageddon, Knorr and the Watchtower did some shuffling of the 6,000 years of history concept that originally had been taught by Charles Russell. According to Russell, the 6,000 years were supposed to have ended in the 1870s with Christ's return, followed by Armageddon. When this didn't happen, Russell revised his thinking to say that Christ had returned invisibly and the 6,000 years of human history would end in 1914. The new system installed during Knorr's presidency taught that the latest—and certainly the "absolutely final"—date for Armageddon would be 1975.[13] This left plenty of room for JWs who had been alive in 1914 to be around when Armageddon came, thus fulfilling the Watchtower interpretation of Matthew 24:34: "This generation will certainly not pass away until all these things have happened."

And so, in the late 1960s and early 1970s, Watchtower leaders used the same strategy employed in the 1940s when they strongly urged JWs not to marry or have children. They even asked JWs to give up college or professional careers so they could spend their time working for the WTBTS in the few years and months left before "the end."[14]

The year 1975 arrived, but Armageddon did not. Although he joined Rutherford and Russell as a failed prophet, Knorr's presidency was, nonetheless, marked by a strong emphasis on training and education, as well as increases in world mission work and individual evangelism. Many new JW textbooks and doctrinal teachings were written and published during this span, as well as the JW "translation" of the Bible, *The New World Translation of the Christian Greek Scriptures*. Despite the reversals of 1975 and huge defections from the ranks, when Knorr died in 1977 there were still over 2 million active JWs around the world.

In 1977, Frederick Franz (1893-1992), Watchtower's vice president, succeeded Knorr as president. Touted as the Watchtower's most "knowledgeable" Hebrew scholar, Franz suffered the same fate during a court trial as did Charles Russell. In Franz's case, he had to confess he could not cast a simple Bible verse (Gen. 2:4) back into Hebrew, even though he claimed he was knowledgeable in Greek and Hebrew, as well as many other languages.[15]

Franz's embarrassment in court over his lack of Hebrew training happened over 20 years before he became president, and the incident was forgotten (or perhaps unknown) by most JWs. Franz was able to guide the Watchtower through stormy waters caused by the failed

1975 prophecy. Once again, JWs were told they had "missed the point" of all the statements made in Watchtower publications and had erroneously thought the Bible chronology being used taught a "specific date."[16]

During his term as president, Franz refrained from setting any more specific dates, but he steadfastly taught that persons alive during 1914 would definitely experience Armageddon. Franz died in 1992 at the age of 99, and JWs were running out of time and people who had been alive in 1914. They solved their problem, however, through Franz's successor, 72-year-old Milton G. Henschel. In November 1995, Henschel discarded the entire 1914 generation prophecy by producing more "new light" (a favorite JW term to explain its many changes in doctrine and teachings). An article in *The Watchtower* explained that the word "generation" had nothing to do with individuals who had been alive in 1914; now it simply applied to *all* people of the earth in *any* generation who would see the signs of Christ's coming but "fail to mend their ways."[17]

And so the position held by the WTBTS for 80 years was totally abolished, replaced by a more flexible point of view claiming that anybody who lived in "today's wicked system," or in such a system hundreds of years in the future, could be in the generation who would see Armageddon. At the same time, Watchtower scholars assured the world that numerous biblical condemnations of false prophets did not apply to them.[18] Despite the repeated failures of their prophecies to come true, the JWs insist vehemently that they have never made any false prophecies.

In 1943, an issue of *The Watchtower* claimed it is God who interprets the prophecies, and Jesus Christ then proclaims them to Watchtower leaders, who merely publish what they have been told. Out of the other side of their mouths, Watchtower leaders have said they are "deeply grateful that God has been pleased to use them" *as His prophets*. All of this backpedaling and doublethink is fully recorded in *The Watchtower* magazine.[19]

RUSSELL'S THEOLOGY STILL IN USE

Although JWs admit that Russell was the founder of the Watchtower Society, they try to distance themselves from his theology and teachings, even claiming in an issue of *Awake!* that they do not quote him as an authority or publish his writings.[20] The truth is that today the WTBTS still operates on the same foundation laid by Russell's preconceived theology that denied the Trinity, Christ's deity and bodily resurrection, the Holy Spirit's deity and personality, and hell as a place of eternal punishment, as well as teaching that all other religions, especially Christendom in general, are doomed to extinction; and that only JWs have the truth.[21]

Russell was a great believer in reason—making the Bible logical. But instead of going to the Bible to reason out what Scripture said, he brought his own preconceived notions to the Bible and then proceeded to twist and rearrange the Word to fit his own theology. On the following pages, we will examine three of Russell's most heretical teachings, all of which are taught by JWs today.

JEHOVAH'S WITNESSES DENY THE TRINITY

JWs deny the doctrine of the Trinity, calling it an insult to "God-given intelligence and reason." And, because God is not a God of confusion (see 1 Cor. 14:33), they reason that He would never author such a confusing doctrine; Satan is the author instead.[22]

JWs love to point out that the word "Trinity" is not in the Bible, and this adds to the "unbiblical" nature of the term. An obvious response is that the word "Bible" is not in the Scriptures either. Nor is the word "theocracy" (a favorite JW term for God's rulership). The point, however, is that the *concept* of the Trinity is definitely in the Bible. The doctrine does not teach there are three Gods in one or that

"God has three heads," typical misunderstandings of the Trinity voiced by JWs.

A favorite question JWs are trained to ask when going door-to-door is, "Who ran the universe for the three days Jesus was dead and in the grave?" Because the JW concept of death is annihilation, they reason that if Jesus was God when He died, God had to be dead, too; therefore, no one was in heaven minding the store. The biblical response to this rather childish question is, "God did. Though Jesus' body died, He continued to exist, and the triune God continued to rule the universe."[23]

Biblical Christianity has always taught that the eternal God exists in three coequal and coeternal persons—Father, Son and Holy Spirit. All three have the same divine nature (essence) and, therefore, exist as one divine being.[24] In the Old Testament, references to the Trinity include Genesis 1:26, where Jehovah speaks in the plural, saying, "Let *us* make man in *our* image" (emphasis added; see also Gen. 11:7; Isa. 6:8). While the Old Testament suggests plurality in the Godhead, the New Testament states it clearly. Three distinct, divine persons of the Trinity are specifically mentioned in John 14:26; 15:26; 2 Corinthians 13:14; and 1 Peter 1:2.

JEHOVAH'S WITNESSES DENY CHRIST'S DEITY

A natural outgrowth of the denial of the Trinity by JWs is their denial of Christ's deity. It is not that they do not give Christ "honor." That they do, but they damn Him with faint praise. In fact, JWs teach a kind of polytheism with their doctrine of "two gods." They say Jehovah is the *Almighty God* who created Jesus. Then Jesus, the *mighty god*, created everything else. This was essentially the same view held by one of the first great heretics of the Church—Arius—who caused the Council of Nicea in A.D. 325. Arius, a pastor's assistant from the church at

Alexandria, also claimed that Christ was a created creature. His views became very popular because he used easy-to-understand and even colorful methods to teach heresy, just as JWs do today.

Following the teachings of Charles Russell, JWs say Jesus Christ had been the archangel Michael in heaven before He came to Earth. Michael supposedly gave up his "godlike" characteristics, leaving only his "life force." Jehovah then placed the "life force" of Michael in the womb of the virgin Mary so Jesus could be born a human being.[25] While on Earth, say JWs, Jesus was a perfect man but nothing more than that. After dying on the Cross, His humanity was annihilated; then He was raised as an immortal spirit who returned to heaven to become once again the archangel Michael.[26]

JWs twist the scriptural phrase "the only begotten Son of God" (see John 1:14,18; 3:16,18), claiming that Jesus was the "first and only being created directly by Jehovah." They also twist the reference to Jesus being "the Word" or "Logos" (see John 1:1,14) to mean one who simply "speaks for Jehovah"—as a sort of chief executive officer. With this kind of Scripture distortion, JWs try to "prove" that Jesus might be called a "mighty god," but He was not Almighty God—Jehovah Himself.[27]

Two outstanding examples of passages JWs have tampered with to "prove" Jesus was a created being are John 1:1-5 and Colossians 1:15-19.

In any reputable translation of the Greek, John 1:1 clearly states, "In the beginning was the Word and the Word was with God." In the *NWT*, however, the JWs translate the verse, "In the beginning was the Word and the Word was *a god*" (emphasis added).[28] Numerous Greek scholars, particularly the eminent Dr. Julius R. Mantey, have refuted the *NWT* version of John 1:1. In an interview with Dr. Walter Martin, Dr. Mantey testified that the JW translators had misquoted him in their attempts to twist the meaning of what the Bible says in the Greek.[29]

While the rules of Greek grammar would allow the insertion of an indefinite article before the word "god" (something JWs argue), the context of the passage clearly teaches that Jesus is equal to God and not "a god." John 1:3 states, "Through him all things were made; without him nothing was made that has been made." This clearly says that the Word (Jesus) is Creator of *everything*. How can He be Creator of everything if He was created Himself?[30]

The *NWT* also misconstrues Colossians 1:15-20 by describing Jesus not as "firstborn over all creation," a term showing His preeminence, but as "first created" by God. Colossians 1:16 goes on to say that Jesus is the preeminent One, because through Him "all things were created." The JW translation inserts the word "other" into the passage in several places to make it look as if Jesus were created first by God, and then He created "all other things." The problem, of course, is that the word "other" is simply not there in the Greek text.[31]

JEHOVAH'S WITNESSES DENY JESUS' BODILY RESURRECTION

As for Jesus' resurrection, the JWs insist that Christ did not rise bodily from the dead, but only as a spirit who looked as if He were a body.[32] Their theology does not leave any room for the existence of the spirit apart from the body after death. JWs teach that Jehovah does not resurrect bodies, He "re-creates" them. The form the disciples saw after the Resurrection was Jesus' "re-created body." According to JW reasoning, because the body and soul of the individual (which are one) have been annihilated at death, God must re-create the "life pattern" of a person, and He can easily do this by retrieving that life pattern from His memory.[33]

A standard reply to the JW insistence that Jesus did not rise bodily from the dead is to cite Luke 24:36-43. Following His resurrection, Jesus appeared to His disciples, and they were frightened, thinking they were seeing a ghost. Jesus asked them to touch Him and see that He had flesh and bones. Then, for good measure, He ate a piece of broiled fish.

The JW response to these Scriptures is that the body the disciples saw and touched was not the same body that had been crucified and buried. Instead, He had "materialized" the look of a body, much as angels had done in the past when appearing to humans. His supposed reason for doing this was to "strengthen His disciples' faith." The obvious question is why Jesus would seek to strengthen His disciples' faith with a masquerade and a lie.[34]

JEHOVAH'S WITNESSES DENY THE HOLY SPIRIT IS GOD

In keeping with their highly questionable logic, JWs claim the Holy Spirit is not God. The WTBTS teaches that the Holy Spirit is an "invisible act or force" that God uses to inspire His servants (JWs) to do His will. According to the Watchtower, the "holy spirit" is like electricity.[35]

For just a few references that clearly attribute personal traits to the Holy Spirit, see Acts 13:2, Romans 8:14,26,27; 1 Corinthians 12:11; Hebrews 3:7 and Revelation 2:7.[36]

JEHOVAH'S WITNESSES DENY CHRIST'S FULL ATONEMENT

Many Christians may be aware that JWs are "working their way to heaven," but what they might not understand is that JWs readily give Christ credit for giving them the opportunity to do so. You can even find Watchtower writings that say salvation is "of grace," which was granted by Jehovah. But nowhere will you find anything saying salvation is by faith in Christ alone, a cardinal doctrine taught throughout the New Testament (see John 5:24; 11:25; 20:31; Rom. 3:24,25; 10:9,10).[37]

JWs also talk about Christ's being a "ransom to God for Adam's sin," but by this they mean that Christ (Michael the Archangel in human form and not equal to God) was a sort of fair trade to pay for Adam's sin. Jesus—the perfect human—was redemption for Adam's sin, and being such He made it possible for all mankind to be saved. How then is mankind saved? Through works and perfect obedience to Jehovah—by being and doing exactly what the WTBTS teaches.[38]

To be a JW means constantly trying to affirm your salvation, even though that "salvation" will not include going to heaven. Only 144,000 JWs will do that, and those ranks were closed decades ago. What JWs are working for now is a place in an earthly paradise where they will have everlasting life, but not in the presence of a loving Jehovah God. Instead, they will be ruled by Christ and the 144,000 anointed ones who remain in heaven throughout eternity to enjoy immortality, as they serve as joint heirs and co-rulers of Jehovah's glorious theocracy.

THE LAST DAYS ACCORDING TO THE WATCHTOWER

The JWs have an elaborate doctrine regarding the last days, the Millennium and the Final Judgment, which includes the destruction of 99.9 percent of mankind during Armageddon.[39] According to the Watchtower, during the Millennium the earth will be repopulated by faithful JWs who survive Armageddon, plus billions of people who are "resurrected" (re-created from Jehovah's memory bank).[40]

During the Millennium, those on Earth will be taught the truth (as JWs see it) and constantly evaluated on how faithful they are to Jehovah. At the end of the 1,000 years, there will be a final test when Satan and his demons are let loose from the abyss where they have been imprisoned. They will be allowed to challenge Jehovah and tempt His people. All those who remain faithful will enjoy everlasting life on a paradise Earth. Some, however, may be led astray and will suffer a final, horrible fate when Jehovah casts them into the lake of fire to be annihilated (wiped forever from existence).[41]

HOW TO ANSWER JEHOVAH'S WITNESSES WITH LOVE

That the scenario the JWs teach about the end times is not in the Bible does not deter them in the least. They believe it is there because the Watchtower has convinced them. They continue to misinterpret Scripture as they go from door-to-door, warning of the perils of Armageddon and attacking all biblical doctrines. And they continue to be successful at luring unsuspecting and unschooled people into their ranks, placing particular emphasis on recruiting the millions of professing Christians who may not be biblically well grounded.

When one looks at the JW weekly schedule, it is easy to understand why they are so effective in sharing and defending their faith. Every Kingdom Hall (the JW term for their church buildings) has five meetings a week, and all members of the congregation are expected to attend. On Sundays there is the Public Talk, followed by Watchtower Study. Theocratic Ministry School is offered on a weekday night, followed by a Service Meeting. In addition, every JW is required to attend a weekly book study and, after that, do "field work"—door-to-door or street-corner witnessing.[42]

The late Walter Martin, who wrote and spoke extensively to combat the false teachings of the Watchtower, observed that the average JW "can cause the average Christian untold trouble" by sprinkling the conversation with Greek or Hebrew terms, while repeating Scripture out of context.[43]

Martin went on to say that every Christian needs to be absolutely sure of what the Bible teaches regarding the Trinity, Jesus' deity and resurrection, the Holy Spirit and salvation through grace, not works. If you hope to answer, (much less witness to) the JWs who come to your door, *you need these Bible basics to give a reason for the hope that is within you* (see 1 Pet. 3:15). Above all, you need to know in your heart—not just according to "reason"—that Christ is, indeed, God, and He died for our sins and was raised on the third day according to the Scriptures.

SUMMING UP MAJOR DIFFERENCES BETWEEN JEHOVAH'S WITNESSES AND CHRISTIANS

Regarding authority: JWs may do no independent thinking[44] and must absolutely adhere to the decisions and scriptural understanding of the Watchtower Society.[45] Christians depend on the guidance of the Holy Spirit as they read the Scriptures and learn to obey God, not man (see Acts 5:29; 17:11; 1 John 2:26,27).

Regarding the Trinity, Christ's deity and the Resurrection: JWs find it difficult to worship "a three-headed God."[46] They call Jesus a "mighty god," but not the Almighty God—Jehovah;[47] they say Jesus was raised from the grave, "not a human creature but a spirit."[48] Christians believe that God is three coequal, coeternal Persons who exist as one divine Being (see Matt. 3:13-17; 2 Cor. 13:14).[49] Christ is divine, the second person of the Trinity, and equal to the Father and the Holy Spirit (see John 1:1; Col. 1:15-19; Phil. 2:5-11). Christ rose bodily from the grave, was touched by His disciples and ate before them (see John 20:24-29; Luke 24:36-43).

Regarding salvation: JWs say Christ's death provides the opportunity for men and women to work for their salvation;[50] Christians believe that Christ's death completely paid for all mankind's sins and that believers are justified freely by God's grace through redemption in Christ (see Rom. 3:24,25; 5:12-19; 1 Pet. 2:24).

Regarding Christ's return and man's immortality: JWs believe that Christ returned to Earth invisibly in 1914 and now rules from heaven, "no longer visible to human sight."[51] They claim that man does not have an immortal soul;[52] and at death man's spirit (life force) goes out and "no longer exists."[53] Christians believe that Christ will return to Earth physically, visibly and audibly (see 1 Thess. 4:1-17) and that man has an eternal, immortal soul (i.e., spirit) that, at death, either goes to be with Christ (see Luke 23:46; 2 Cor. 5:8; Phil. 1:22,23) or awaits judgment (see John 5:24-30).

CHAPTER TEN

MORMONISM

AS GOD IS, MAN CAN BECOME

The fastest growing and most successful cult in the history of the United States, and perhaps the world, is the Mormons, officially known as The Church of Jesus Christ of Latter Day Saints (LDS). Increasing at an average rate of 300,000 converts a year (as many as 75 percent of whom may be former Protestants), membership in the Mormon Church reached 10.6 million worldwide in 1999.[1]

In their multimillion dollar promotion program, as well as their practice, the Mormons create a highly attractive and admirable facade that communicates caring, a strong emphasis on building the family, clean living and a commitment to Christ that would appear to outdo many Christians in evangelical churches.[2]

Why, then, refer to them as a cult? Mormons strongly insist they do not fit the definition of a cult (see chapter 8) and claim they are bona fide Christians who believe in the Father, Son and Holy Ghost and in the saving power of the Lord Jesus Christ.

The first difference to grasp between the Mormon Church and biblical Christianity is one of semantics. The Mormons use but have redefined many key terms employed by evangelical Christians—a definitive sign of a cult. Analysis of Mormon views, past and present, reveals that they dismiss, twist, change or add to all biblical doctrines, particularly revelation, the Trinity and salvation by grace alone through faith alone.

In recent years, some Mormon scholars and leaders have taken positions that seem to refute what Mormon prophets, apostles and other leaders clearly taught during the nineteenth century and most of the twentieth. This "later viewpoint" insists that Mormons and evangelicals are far closer in doctrine than they might think and that anti-Mormon views expressed over the years are all wrong about what LDS believe.

The rest of this chapter will cover what LDS prophets and other main leaders have historically taught, followed by a brief look at the new view, which is ably represented by Stephen Robinson, a Brigham Young University professor. Mormonism disagrees with biblical Christianity at many points, but two of the major issues are: (1) What is authoritative revelation (Scripture)? (2) Who (or what) is God?

JOSEPH SMITH, JR.: HOW IT ALL BEGAN

Examining the issue of trustworthy revelation means going back to the origins of Mormonism. (Although we will only cover key events in brief form, sources of more complete discussions by Mormon and non-Mormon writers are listed in the endnotes for this chapter and in the Resources in appendix A.)

The story of Mormonism started when a 14-year-old boy named Joseph Smith, Jr., had a vision in which two personages—whom he believed to be the Father and the Son—appeared before him. He asked them which Christian denomination he should join and they told him to join none of them because they were all "wrong and corrupt."[3]

In 1823, Smith, then 17, saw the angel Moroni appear at his bedside and tell him of a book written on golden plates by former inhabitants of the continent that would contain "the fullness of the everlasting gospel." Four years later, Smith dug up the plates and began translating their "Reformed Egyptian" writing with the help of two special stones called "Urim" and "Thummim."[4]

As Smith translated the plates, he sat behind a curtain, gazing into a hat, supposedly reading lines of the *Book of Mormom* (BOM) as they appeared on "seer stones" and dictating each line to a scribe outside the curtain. It should be noted that as a youth and young man, Joseph was a well-known hunter for buried treasure with the aid of a seer (or peep) stone.[5] Using a seer stone to get information otherwise unavailable is called "scrying" (from *descry*, "to read"), an occult practice still popular in contemporary witchcraft.

Despite Mormon denials of Smith's occult practices, incontrovertible evidence shows that in 1826 he was convicted of "glass looking" (using a seer stone), a misdemeanor, because those who did scrying were often con men.[6]

Martin Harris, a wealthy farmer assisting Smith, decided to check and see if the plates and translation were genuine. He showed a sample to Professor Charles Anthon of Columbia College and reported back to Smith that Anthon recognized the characters he had been shown as "Egyptian, Chaldaic, Assyriac, and Arabic," and that the translation was "correct."[7] Anthon later learned of Harris's report and wrote a lengthy letter to Mr. E. D. Howe, a prolific researcher of Joseph Smith and the origins of Mormonism. The gist of Anthon's letter to Howe was, "The whole story about my having pronounced the Mormonite inscription to be 'Reformed Egyptian hieroglyphics' is perfectly false." Anthon well remembered "that the paper contained anything else but 'Egyptian hieroglyphics.'"[8]

By 1830, Smith had published the *BOM*, financed by Martin Harris's mortgaging of his farm, and had founded the Mormon Church, which grew quite rapidly. From 1831 to 1844, Smith established Mormon strongholds in Ohio, Missouri and Illinois. Wherever they went, the Mormons drew hostility and persecution, either because non-Mormons did not trust Smith or they were suspicious of Mormon teachings and practices.[9] At times, Mormons were treated horrifically. At one point, the Missouri militia slaughtered, raped and pillaged Mormon believers, obeying an "extermination" order issued by the governor.

From the early 1830s to the early 1840s, Smith continued to receive revelations that guided him in where to go and what to do next, as well as how to establish new and different doctrines. The first edition of the compilation of these revelations—65 chapters—was published in 1833 under the title *Book of Commandments*. By 1835, a second edition was released under the new title *Doctrine and Covenants*, which would become "inspired Scripture" alongside the *BOM*.

By 1838, the Mormons had been driven completely from Missouri into Illinois, where Smith led in the development of the thriving city of Nauvoo. It was here that he came up with revelations concerning the Godhead, origin and destiny of the human race, eternal progression, baptism for the dead, plural marriage (polygamy) and sacred temple ordinances. Smith's revelation regarding polygamy was released on August 12, 1843, and included a threat that Smith's first wife, Emma, would be "destroyed" if she resisted the idea.[10]

Tension between Mormons and non-Mormons increased when the *Nauvoo Expositor* published stories exposing the Mormon practice of polygamy. As mayor of Nauvoo and "lieutenant general" of the 4,000-man Nauvoo legion, Smith felt he had unlimited power. He ordered the destruction of the newspaper, and for non-Mormons in Illinois, this was the last straw. Smith wound up in jail in nearby Carthage, Illinois, awaiting trial.

A crowd of around 200 attacked the building, and a gunfight ensued. Mormons claim their founder died as a "Christian martyr," but the truth is he died fighting, using a six-shooter that had been smuggled to him, and he succeeded in killing at least two of his assailants.[11]

Following Joseph Smith's death, Brigham Young won a power struggle for leadership and led a large number of LDS west, where they settled in the Valley of the Great Salt Lake in 1847. Under Young, polygamy became a formal practice of the church, and he himself had 20 wives and fathered 57 children.[12]

But not all Mormons followed Young west. A significant minority, headed by Smith's wife Emma and his son Joseph III, remained in Missouri and Illinois and formed the Reorganized Church of Jesus Christ of Latter Day Saints, headquartered today in Independence, Missouri. Many other Mormon splinter groups also survived, and some still exist.

The Mormons officially practiced polygamy until 1890. Due to increasing enforcement of a federal law against polygamy, which included fines and imprisonment, Wilford Woodruff, fourth president/prophet, rescinded polygamy as a practice (but not as a doctrine) out of practical necessity. Government pressure threatened the very existence of all Mormon temples, and polygamy had been a chief reason Utah had been denied statehood at least six times.[13]

Despite all their troubles with the United States government over polygamy, the Latter Day Saints built a prosperous church and society under the ironfisted rule of Brigham Young, who advocated the death penalty for any White mixing blood with a "Negro" and taught that Jesus had been conceived through literal sexual relations between God the Father and the Virgin Mary.[14]

As the Mormon Church headed into the twentieth century, with polygamy rescinded and statehood gained, a more positive public image was sought in order to gain more converts. A new strategy, designed to blend the Mormon Church with mainstream Christianity, claimed, "Mormonism is Christianity; Christianity is Mormonism; they are one and the same."[15]

Millions of converts to Mormonism base their definition of "Christian" on four "standard works" of Scripture. Besides the Bible,

Mormons trust the *BOM*, *Doctrine and Covenants* (*D&C*) and the *Pearl of Great Price* (*PGP*) as containing the word of God. The LDS Church claims the biblical canon never closed and revelation continued with Joseph Smith, as well as other presidents/prophets of the church, right up to the present day.

IS THE BOOK OF MORMON CORRECT?

The *BOM* covers the history of two great civilizations, the most important of which is supposed to have arrived in America from the Middle East around 600 B.C. These Jewish people are reported to have become two great nations, the Nephites and the Lamanites, who fought intermittently over many centuries.

Most of the *BOM* was allegedly put down on gold plates by Mormon, commander in chief of the Nephites. After completing his part of the account, Mormon gave the plates to his son, Moroni, who hid them in the Hill Cumorah after adding a few words of his own. The Nephites then fought the Lamanites to the death and all were killed. The Lamanites went on to become the "principal ancestors of the American Indians."[16]

The Mormon Church has gone to incredible lengths to justify the *BOM*, coming up with its own archaeological theories and justifications for its authenticity. But non-Mormon archaeologists and biblical Christians look askance upon the *BOM* for many reasons. For example, the *BOM* speaks of at least 38 "mighty cities" built by the Nephites and Jeredites (people in the first migration around 2200 B.C.). No trace of these cities or any other archaeological evidence reported in the *BOM* has ever been found.[17]

In summary, there is no institution of higher learning in America except Brigham Young University (pride of the Mormon educational system) that tries to substantiate or support the *BOM*. Even some Mormon professors have admitted the weakness and, in some cases, fallaciousness of Mormon attempts to find archaeological support for the *BOM*.[18]

Despite its numerous problems, Smith claimed the *BOM* to be the "most correct of any book on the earth."[19] The LDS firmly maintain the *Book of Mormon* is the inspired Word of God and they make this same claim for *Doctrine and Covenants* and *Pearl of Great Price*, two other books produced for the most part by Joseph Smith. While Mormons claim absolute accuracy and full inspiration for their three "standard works," they see the Bible as inspired only so far as it is "translated correctly."[20] LDS apostle Orson Pratt said he doubted even one verse of the New Testament had escaped pollution or conveyed the same sense now as it did in the original manuscripts.[21] This comment is interesting in that the *BOM* contains some 27,000 words copied, often verbatim, from the *King James Version* of the Bible (compare, for example, 2 Nephi 12–24 to Isaiah 2–14).

Mormons ignore modern textual studies[22] that consistently confirm the validity of the Bible and dwell instead on establishing reliability for the *BOM*, yet they have no manuscripts for the *BOM* whatsoever. According to Joseph Smith, the gold plates were taken back by the angel Moroni, and Mormons simply rely on his "word as a prophet."

MORMON THEOLOGY GOES BEYOND THE BOM

Although Joseph Smith claimed that the *BOM* was the most complete book on Earth and that it contains "the fullness of the gospel," he added 13 key Mormon doctrines in *D&C* that aren't found anywhere in the *BOM*. Among these new revelations were: plurality of gods (polytheism), God as an exalted man, a human being's ability to become God, three degrees of heaven, polygamy, eternal progression and baptism for the dead.[23] In addition, *D&C* contains a number of prophesies by Smith that did not come true, which makes him a false prophet, according to the Bible (see Deut. 18:20-22).[24]

Like the *BOM*, *D&C* underwent many changes and additions from one edition to another. Examination will show that very few of the "revelations" in the current edition of *D&C* read as they did in the first compilation of Smith's *D&C* revelations in 1833.[25]

What appears obvious is that Joseph Smith continued to get ideas about what to put in his "scriptures," and that's why so many of these changes in the very "revealed words of God" continue to appear. And Mormon Church officials have made many changes themselves, including deletion of "Lectures of Faith," in which Smith clearly taught that God has no beginning or end and is unchangeable—direct contradictions of what Mormon theology teaches today.[26]

THE "PEARL" WITH A HUGE BLEMISH

Unlike the *BOM* and *D&C*, the *PGP* was translated (in part) from papyri fragments, which Smith bought, along with some Egyptian mummies, from a traveling lecturer in 1835. According to Smith, the Egyptian hieroglyphics on the parchment were a record of writings by Abraham while he was in Egypt. The "Book of Abraham" became part of *PGP*, which was first compiled and published in 1851 and incorporated into the canon by the LDS Church in 1880.

Assumed lost or destroyed for many years, the papyri fragments turned up in 1967 and were returned to the Mormon Church. Investigation of the fragments by Mormon and non-Mormon Egyptologists showed that the papyri contained nothing more than an Egyptian funeral text with instructions to embalmers. Smith had taken Egyptian characters that actually translate into one or two words, such as "water," and created long passages teaching Mormon doctrines such as preexistence, the priesthood and the nature of the Godhead.[27] Undismayed by this scientific evidence, *The Encyclopedia of Mormonism* unblushingly states that when Smith looked at the

Egyptian hieroglyphics on the piece of papyrus, he "sought revelation from the Lord" and "received the Book of Abraham."[28]

A key to understanding Mormons is that they have absolutely unshakable faith in Joseph Smith, their first prophet. Facts do not matter. Whatever happened, Smith is still their source of divine revelation, the foundation of their entire viewpoint.

The above only touches on the first huge difference between orthodox Christianity and Mormonism—the LDS claim to "further revelation," which, if granted, opens the door to unlimited speculation, as we will see in the next section.

ETERNAL PROGRESSION: HEART OF MORMONISM

The biblical Christian's doctrine of God says He is eternal, the only God in the universe, the supreme creator of everything out of nothing. He has always been and always will be. The Mormon doctrine of God says He is "progressive," having attained His exalted state by advancing along a path that His children (Mormons) are permitted to follow. As LDS apostle James Talmadge wrote, "The Church proclaims the eternal truth, 'as man is, God once was: as God is, man may be.'"[29]

Briefly stated, the historic Mormon view of God includes the following: God—the heavenly Father—is really an exalted man. He is one of a "species" that Mormons call "gods." These gods existed before the heavenly Father who rules Earth today. In Mormon thinking, God is not the eternal creator, the first cause of everything. He was created or begotten Himself by another god who had been created and begotten by someone else, ad infinitum.[30]

When the LDS's Father-God of our present universe was created, he became a spirit-being who grew to full maturity and was then sent to a planet other than Earth where he lived as a man, learning all he could as he grew up, finally dying and then being resurrected. Having attained Godhood, he returned to a heavenly abode with a body of flesh and bones, where he joined with his goddess wife (Mother-God) to copulate and have millions of spirit children who would eventually populate planet Earth. The spirit world domain where all this takes place is called by Mormons "the preexistence."[31]

According to Mormon thinking, the Father-God of our present universe was not created *ex nihilo* (out of nothing). The "god" who created the Father-God did so out of eternal matter, which is full of "intelligences." Everyone who ever lived is actually an intelligence who resided at one time in eternal matter. For Mormons, God is not eternal, but matter is.[32]

When God had all those spirit children, His firstborn "creation" was Jesus Christ, followed by Jesus' brother Lucifer; and then all the other innumerable spirit children were created to populate the earth. After God finished creating all the spirit children, he held a meeting called the Council in Heaven. He told everyone about a plan He had for His spirit children to live on Earth to be tested and then returned to Him after death. There were two likely candidates to be the savior of all those who would be born on Earth—the premortal Jesus and His younger brother Lucifer.

When Jesus was chosen to be Savior, Satan rebelled, fought a great war against the armies of heaven, led by Michael the Archangel, and lost. He was cast down to Earth, where he was condemned to live as a spirit who would never have a human body.[33] Meanwhile, under His Father's instructions, Jesus, with the help of other spirit children, used eternal matter to create the earth with all its animals and the first human inhabitants, Adam and Eve.

Among those descended from Adam and Eve were certain spirit children who fought halfheartedly against Satan during the Great War in heaven. They were sentenced to be born mortals with black skin as part of the lineage of Cain. Using this doctrine, which Joseph Smith teaches in *PGP* (see Moses 7:7,22), LDS prophets and apostles of the church, including Smith, Brigham Young and Bruce McConkie, have

articulated racist attitudes and teachings that still have not been officially repudiated by the church despite its declaration in 1978 that
allows Blacks into the priesthood.[34]

Mormon theology teaches that when Jesus came to Earth from the
spirit world to become Savior of mankind, He was born of Mary but
not conceived by the Holy Spirit as the Bible teaches. A common
Mormon teaching over the years has been that God the Father came
down to Earth in human form to have sexual intercourse with Mary,
and she conceived the baby Jesus. Many Mormon leaders have believed
this, from Brigham Young (1801-1877) to Ezra Taft Benson (1899-
1994), thirteenth prophet/president of the LDS.[35]

While the Mormon Church today has no "official position" as to
whether or not Jesus married, the logic of the Mormon system
demands it because celestial marriage is one requirement for godhood
or exaltation. That's why Mormon apostles like Orson Pratt strongly
imply that Jesus did marry and commit polygamy as well, being wed to
Mary, Martha and the other Mary during the wedding at Cana. Also,
following Mormon celestial logic to its conclusion, apostle Orson
Hyde taught that Jesus had children by the women he married before
He died on the cross.[36]

After His death on the cross, Jesus "gained fullness," which he
attained through a resurrected body. He returned to heaven, fully exalted, and from there He reigns with the Father-God in power and glory.
According to Smith, Jesus will eventually take the Father-God's place
as Father-God moves on to even higher realms of glory, exaltation and
progression.[37]

Just like Jesus, all those who are born to Earth come from the spirit world where they have been waiting in the preexistence for their turn
at earthly experience. They are on exactly the same track as that of
Father-God and Jesus Christ. If they become Mormons, they, too, can
rise higher and higher, progressing further and further toward godhood. In fact, if they take part in celestial marriage (being married in a
Mormon temple), a man and his wife can eventually have their own

planet. There they can continue to procreate spirit children for all eternity, and so the cycle will continually repeat itself, resulting in millions of gods on millions of planets, finding eternal exaltation through obedience and progression.[38]

It is important to note that around 1830, when Joseph Smith started out with his new religion and translated the *BOM*, he was monotheistic and even used terms that sounded Trinitarian. In the early 1830s, however, Smith started studying Hebrew and learned that the word for God is *Elohim*, which can be translated as either plural or singular, depending on how it is used. From this he deducted that, instead of one God, there are many gods (polytheism). He went on from there to lay the foundation for the Mormon view of the godhead.[39]

Smith taught, "You have got to learn to become Gods yourselves . . . the same as all Gods have done before you—namely, by going from one small degree to another."[40] The Bible, however, clearly teaches, "Before me no god was formed, nor will there be one after me" (Isa. 43:10); "I am God, and not man" (Hos. 11:9); "I the LORD do not change" (Mal. 3:6).[41]

OTHER MAJOR MORMON ERRORS

From their two basic errors—additional revelation and eternal progression—flow other Mormon teachings that are clearly heresy.

To Mormons, the Trinity is not one God whose essence is found in three persons, but three Gods—three distinct bodies (the Holy Ghost has only a spirit body; He has never been able to become a man, according to the Mormon system). Despite the teaching of Father, Son and Holy Ghost as one God in the *BOM* and in early revelations in *D&C*, Smith later taught that the Father, Jesus Christ and the Holy Ghost were distinct personages—three distinct Gods (see *D&C* 20:28). In his *Documentary History of the Church*, Smith made light of the Trinity, saying, "It would make a strange God anyhow . . . he would be a giant or a monster."[42]

The Mormons take standard Scripture passages that Christians use to teach the Trinity and turn them around to teach their own doctrines. For example, when God said, "Let us make man in our image" in Genesis 1:26, or when Jesus used the names Father, Son and Holy Spirit in Matthew 28:19, these verses only show Mormons there is "more than one God."

John 1:1, which teaches that Jesus Christ—the Word—was with God the Father in the very beginning and, in fact, made the worlds, is said by the Mormons to teach "two Gods."[43] Because of their worldview, which says that God is an exalted man and that all men can attain godhood, the Trinity—one God existing as three persons—is simply incredible, illogical and nonsensical to Mormons. Their polytheism (in the case of the Trinity, their tritheism) makes more sense to them.[44]

Salvation, according to Mormonism, comes in two parts: general and individual. General salvation is what Mormons mean when they say, "We believe that through the atonement of Christ, all mankind may be saved."[45] All mankind will be saved in a general sense when they are resurrected, and later they will be judged according to their works. General salvation is given regardless of a person's actions or beliefs (except for "the sons of perdition," who will be assigned to the fires of hell). But because Christ's atonement paid for Adam's sins only, people are still responsible for their personal sins. Christ's atonement provides the opportunity, then, to earn individual salvation by obeying the laws and ordinances of the gospel (i.e., the teachings of the LDS church).[46]

Mormons list eight requirements that must be met if a person is to merit forgiveness from personal sins and thereby attain godhood. Some of these include: faith in Christ, being baptized, becoming a member of the LDS church, keeping the commandments, doing temple work and accepting Joseph Smith and his successors as "God's mouthpiece."[47]

HOW WIDE IS THE DIVIDE?

As the Body of Christ moves into the third millennium, the gap between Mormons and biblical Christianity seems hopelessly wide; yet at least one effort has been made to close it. The book *How Wide the Divide?* contains a dialogue between Stephen E. Robinson, professor of Ancient Scripture at Brigham Young University, and Craig L. Blomberg, professor of New Testament at Denver Seminary.[48]

As he dialogues with Blomberg, Robinson corrects, "interprets" or dismisses as speculative almost all of earlier Mormon teachings used as examples of what Mormons have believed since 1830. According to Robinson, anti-Mormon extremists have used these historic teachings to falsely criticize the LDS Church.

In his part of the introduction to *How Wide the Divide?* Robinson says he believes the real problem is the different "view of the nature of the universe into which Mormons fit the gospel. . . . [W]e believe that God and humans are the same species of beings and that all men and women were his spiritual offspring in a premortal existence."[49]

Robinson strongly insists that "there is not a single verse of the Bible the Latter Day Saints do not accept";[50] but in many places he makes it clear that LDS reject the Greek philosophy they believe is in the Creeds hammered out by Early Church councils.[51] As Robinson mounts his arguments, he continually assures the reader he believes in "Jesus Christ as the Way, the Truth, and the Life: the only name given under heaven whereby we may be saved."[52]

Reaction to *How Wide the Divide?* has been mixed. Several books have been written in response, as well as any number of critical reviews appearing in periodicals and on the Internet, some of which are described in the endnotes for this chapter.[53] Much of the criticism of *How Wide the Divide?* focuses on Robinson's "minimalism," meaning his way of not telling the whole Mormon story.

While Robinson admits he is not representing the LDS Church but only giving his own opinions, he adamantly insists that what he says is standard LDS theology believed today by the Mormon Church. Yet he does not really do much, if any, quoting of current LDS General Authorities who supposedly agree with him.

In fact, Robinson limits LDS orthodoxy to the four standard works (*KJV, BOM, D&C* and *PGP*) "as interpreted by the General Authorities of the Church, the current apostles, and prophets."[54] In this way he conveniently gets rid of a great deal of other material by Joseph Smith, Brigham Young, et al., that he does not wish to explain, defend or contradict.

Reviewers from the Mormonism Research Ministry (MRM) have observed that "Robinson is a clever writer who is able to make Mormonism sound like Christianity";[55] and while he may sincerely believe the views he has put in *How Wide the Divide?* "he absolutely does not represent the normal LDS position on many points."[56] MRM reviewers believe the public would have been better served if an LDS General Authority had represented the Mormon position; but in their opinion, LDS General Authorities choose not to discuss issues in this kind of format.

If any more dialogue between Mormonism and biblical Christianity is to take place, it would make sense for current LDS General Authorities to step forward and participate. Then, perhaps, some progress could be made toward spelling out and clarifying the real differences between biblical Christianity and Mormonism, where the divide remains wide indeed.

SUMMING UP MAJOR DIFFERENCES BETWEEN MORMONISM AND BIBLICAL CHRISTIANITY

Regarding Scripture: The Mormons believe that the canon of Scripture is not closed and that "modern revelation is necessary . . . (God) continues to speak, because He is unchangeable."[57] The LDS Church accepts as Scripture the *Book of Mormon, Doctrine and Covenants, Pearl of Great Price,* and the Bible (*KJV*), with the reservation that the Bible is "the Word of God as far as it is translated correctly."[58] Biblical Christians hold that the canon is closed and accept only the Bible as Scripture, believing it is "God-breathed" (see 2 Tim. 3:16) and complete, containing "the faith that was once for all entrusted to the saints" (Jude 3; see also Gal. 1:8: 2 Pet. 1:3).

Regarding God and the Trinity: Joseph Smith taught that "The Father has a body of flesh and bones as tangible as man's."[57] Apostle James Talmadge said, "We believe in a God who is . . . a Being who has attained His exalted state by a path which now His children are permitted to follow . . . the church proclaims the eternal truth: 'as man is, God once was; as God is, man may be.'"[58] Talmadge also said the doctrine of the Trinity was a jumble of "inconsistencies and contradictions."[59] Joseph Smith taught that Jesus Christ, God the Father and the Holy Ghost were "three distinct personages and three Gods."[60] Biblical Christians believe God is a Spirit (see John 4:24) and creator of the universe (see Gen. 1:1). The biblical God says, "I am God, and there is no other" (Isa. 46:9), and "Before me no God was formed, nor will there be one after me" (43:10). The word "trinity" means "three-in-oneness" and summarizes Scripture's teaching that "God is three Persons, yet one God" (see Deut. 6:4; Matt. 28:19).[61]

Regarding sin and salvation: Joseph Smith taught that "men will be punished for their own sins, but not for Adam's transgression."[62] The *BOM* says Adam and Eve were foreordained to sin in order to provide parentage for the spirit children of God, who were waiting for the experience of earthly life (see

2 Nephi 2:25). According to Apostle Bruce McConkie, "general salvation" means "all men are saved by grace alone."[63] Full (individual) salvation comes only through the LDS Church, and without the Mormon priesthood and continuous revelation, "there would be no salvation."[64] Biblical Christians believe salvation is a free gift, provided by God's grace for all who believe in Christ and His atoning work on the cross (see Eph. 2:8,9). Christians do good works not to *earn* salvation but because they *have* salvation (see Rom. 3:24-26; Eph. 2:10).

Regarding heaven: Joseph Smith taught that most of mankind will enter one of three levels of heaven: telestial, terrestrial or celestial (see *D&C* 76:30-119). Apostle Bruce McConkie taught that eternal life in celestial heaven is for Mormons only.[65] Biblical Christians believe heaven is the dwelling place of God (see Ps. 73:25), which will become home for *all* believers in Christ's full atonement for personal sins (see 1 John 4:10). To be in heaven is to be in Christ's presence (see Luke 23:43; John 14:3; 2 Cor. 5:8; 1 John 3:2).

For where to find more information on Mormon doctrines and practices, see appendix A.

CHAPTER ELEVEN

NEW AGE

THE SERPENT'S OLD LIE IN AN UPDATED PACKAGE

Among the myriad new religions and cults on today's scene, nothing is more far-reaching or hard to define than the New Age Movement (NAM). Russell Chandler, former religion writer for the *Los Angeles Times*, observed that "New Age is not a sect or cult, per se."[1] Instead, the NAM is a worldview that claims to offer a new way of thinking. Despite a lack of formal structure and organization, millions of New Age activists hope to transform society by bringing about a reawakening that will emphasize self-discovery, spiritual growth and enlightenment.[2]

THE NEW AGE IS NOT NEW AT ALL

If you have read the chapters on Hinduism and Buddhism, many of the ideas in this chapter will sound familiar because New Age thinking really isn't new. In fact, New Age ideas go all the way back to the garden, where the serpent asked Eve if God really said she couldn't eat from that tree (see Gen. 3:1-5).

New Age concepts find their roots in many ancient sources, including the Babylonian mystery rituals, which are supposed to elevate humans to godlike status; nature worship; occult practices and reincarnation.

The New Age draws heavily from Hinduism, which, besides reincarnation, teaches concepts like monism (all is one) and pantheism (all is god). Another contributing stream of the New Age movement is Buddhism, which teaches mind control, meditation and spiritual enlightenment, as well as reincarnation.

New Age thought also borrows from Taoism (pronounced "dowism"), a Chinese philosophy that teaches that all things are constantly changing (the process called Yin and Yang); and, therefore, nothing is absolute; all is relative, including morals and ethics.

From Gnosticism, the New Age adapts the concept of esoteric knowledge, which is supposed to ignite a divine spark and power within and, therefore, negates the need for Christ's atoning death.[3]

New Age thinking is a hybrid or blend of all of the above, plus several other ideas and phenomena of modern origin, such as unidentified flying objects (UFOs), extraterrestrial intelligence and psychokinesis (bending objects like silverware into pretzel shapes by applying the mind).[4]

So eclectic is the NAM that it is difficult to describe a "complete" New Ager; some buy into one portion of New Age thinking, while others accept and practice other pieces and parts. In addition to those who consider themselves New Agers, there are millions more who have adopted New Age understandings of reality and are using these ideas to develop what they consider a practical and useful philosophy of life. The NAM has even caught many Christians (and pseudo-Christians) in its web.

Because the NAM is so diverse, it is difficult to estimate the number of people who are New Agers. Various polls taken in recent years provide considerable evidence that a large number of people are interested in New Age activities. For example, 66 percent of American adults claim to have had a psychic experience. Thirty million Americans (one in four) say they believe in reincarnation. Ten million Americans say they are involved in some sort of Eastern mysticism. Forty-two percent of American adults believe they have been in contact with someone who has died (spiritism). Fourteen percent of Americans endorse the work of spirit mediums or channelers. Another survey found that 67 percent of American adults read astrology columns.[5]

ALICE BAILEY MADE "NEW AGE" POPULAR

The New Age label has been around for over 50 years, first popularized by Alice Bailey, a British-born Episcopalian who, for a time, followed the teachings of Madame Blavatsky, founder of the Theosophical Society.

While Bailey's writings laid groundwork for the NAM of today, it was the events of the 1960s that really set the stage for attracting increasing numbers of people—particularly those in the younger generation—to New Age ideas. During the '60s, the nation was ripped, splintered and demoralized by the Vietnam War and the assassinations of political figures.

The counterculture was fed up and disillusioned, looking for new truth and reality wherever they could find it. The '60s became a springboard for the generation gap, anti-establishment thinking and psychedelic expression through LSD and other drugs. The '60s also saw the Beatles help to introduce transcendental meditation (TM) to America after a trip to India where they were "enlightened" by practicing TM with the Maharishi Mahesh Yogi, a Hindu guru. After that, Eastern ideas flooded the United States in all forms, including the hit musical *Hair*, which opened on Broadway in 1968.

Hair included the stirring hit "The Age of Aquarius," which became, in many respects, the theme song of the NAM. With direct references to astrology, the song mentions the moon being in the seventh house, Jupiter aligning with Mars, peace guiding the planets and love steering the stars. According to astrology, the Aquarian Age will begin when the vernal equinox passes from Pisces (the fish) to Aquarius (the water bearer). For New Agers, this will mean the end of the Christian era and the beginning of a new age symbolized by Aquarius, the water bearer, pouring water over the earth to heal the planet and cause mankind's problems to disappear, "submerged into a great cosmic consciousness."[6]

HOW NEW AGERS DEFINE "GOD"

There is no central New Age organization or headquarters, nor is there a basic authoritative set of writings that present New Age doctrines in 1-2-3 order. Instead, New Agers tend to adhere to certain principles or beliefs. For example, monism—the idea that everything flows together, that human beings, natural phenomena and even "God," are not separate but actually one—is foundational to New Age thinking. For New Agers, the reality is that everything is interrelated, interdependent and interpenetrating.[7] The concept of monism leads logically to another basic New Age principle—pantheism, which simply means "all is god." You, everything around you, the entire creation, is god. In fact, there is nothing you would not call god.

The New Age god is more of an "it" than a "he." New Agers have no concept of a personal creator who exists outside of and exercises control and authority over his creation. The creation is not held together for the New Ager by Christ (see Col. 1:17). In fact, for New Agers, the creation account in Genesis is a quaint myth, because there is no creator. All that is here was always here. How it got here is not the New Ager's concern. Instead, the New Ager is more interested in how he can develop his "godlikeness" because, if all is god, then he, too, is god.

For some New Agers, there is no supreme being to whom worship is due because all of us are supreme. Shirley MacLaine, movie star turned evangelist for the New Age movement, said it as well as anyone in her best-selling book *Dancing in the Light*: "I *know* that I exist, therefore, I AM. I know the god-source exists. Therefore, IT IS. Since I am part of that force, then I AM that I AM."[8]

NEW AGERS FIND "SALVATION" IN THEMSELVES

For the New Ager, salvation is not a matter of the saving of one's soul from being fallen and sinful, but instead achieving a new "awareness" of his or her divinity and oneness with all things. This new state of awareness is called by many different names—cosmic consciousness, God-consciousness, God-realization, self-realization, enlightenment or illumination. Instead of repenting from sin, the New Ager reawakens to himself or herself. Prayer to a personal God is replaced with meditation—a journey within. Being born again from above is therefore unnecessary.[9]

Atonement from sins is not found in Christ, say New Agers. In fact, Christ is demoted from second Person of the Trinity to one of many "cosmic Christs," including Buddha, Moses, Elijah and Mohammed. In a play on the Christian term "atonement," the New Age awareness is sometimes called "at-one-ment." Whatever you want to call it, the "self" is lifted up to the highest levels and "seen as the cosmic treasury of wisdom, power, and delight."[10] Shirley MacLaine sums it up in *Dancing in the Light* when she tells a friend, "You are unlimited. You just don't realize it."[11]

As New Agers seek to unlock and unleash the divine self within, they follow the well-known New Age admonition to "create your own reality." Whatever New Agers do or practice, they almost all agree on one central dogma: *All truth is relative, there are no absolutes, and you find "God" within yourself.*[12]

CHANNELING—NEW AGE VERSION OF CONTACTING SPIRITS

Practices of the occult, like spiritism, constitute a major strand of today's NAM. Madame Blavatsky and Alice Bailey were both heavily involved in spiritism, which Russell Chandler calls a fad that "swept the nation like an uncontrolled brush fire in the 1850s."[13]

Alice Bailey was a voluminous writer who put out two dozen books on occult philosophy between 1919 and her death in 1949. She claimed that she was in contact with a Tibetan teacher named Djwhal Khul and that most of what she wrote was really his teachings.[14]

The spiritism movement that swept the United States a century ago had two goals: (1) to obtain information about the life beyond (would it be happy, sad, etc.); (2) to get in touch with departed loved ones.[15] The channeling that goes on in the NAM today centers on messages from a "higher source," such as the ideas that death isn't real; all is one; all of us are divine but we exist in physical bodies; we can control reality through the powers of Universal Mind.[16]

According to New Agers, spirit entities speak through mediums, or channelers. One is known as Ramtha, supposedly a 35,000-year-old warrior who channels through a rural Washington housewife named J. Z. Knight. Ramtha has spoken to millions via TV on such programs as the "Merv Griffin Show." To receive messages from Ramtha, Ms. Knight goes into a seeming trance. In an authoritative masculine voice Ramtha speaks through her, emphasizing that all of us are God, all of us have infinite potential and that we create our own reality. Moreover, there are no moral absolutes that can bind and restrict us, and none of us will be judged by God.[17] Ramtha advises New Agers never to go against any feeling. If you feel like doing something, then do it because the experience will make life so much the sweeter.[18]

One of the most anti-biblical messages received through channels is the three-volume A Course in Miracles, written by the late Helen Schucman, a psychology professor at Columbia University. Schucman, who claimed to be an atheist and "reluctant scribe" of the Course, kept hearing an inner voice that dictated a message to her for seven years. The course has been studied by hundreds of groups in various settings across America (including churches), and sales have been estimated as high as half a million copies.[19]

While *A Course in Miracles* contains Christian terms, it is filled with anti-Christian ideas, such as the idea that God did not create the world, Jesus was not the only Son of God and He did not suffer and die for our sins. In fact, the Course clearly communicates that sin is an illusion. None of us has ever had our relationship with God broken or marred: this only happened in our thinking. Sin as the Bible explains it never really happened, according to *A Course in Miracles*.[20]

Ever since Satan told Eve, "Eat the fruit; become like God Himself," men and women have been trying to "do it on their own," or at least with the help of spirits and demons—what Paul calls "the powers of this dark world and . . . the spiritual forces of evil" (Eph. 6:12). It is no coincidence that the Bible firmly forbids contacting spirits or getting in touch with the dead (see Lev. 19:31; Deut. 18:10-13). Other New Age concepts or practices condemned or countered in the Scriptures include:

- many gods, goddesses, spirits and demons: see Gen. 1:1; Exod. 15:11; 20:2-6; Deut. 6:4; Isa. 45:5,6,21,22.
- manipulating or bartering with the spirit world: see Deut. 13:1-5; 18:9-14; 1 Kings 11:33.
- continuing blood sacrifice rituals: see Heb. 7:27; 10:10-13; 1 Pet. 3:18.
- mythological, unhistorical legends: see 1 Cor. 15:1-8,12-19; 1 Tim. 1:4; 2 Peter 1:16.
- secret knowledge only for elite "knowers": see John 1:12; 3:16; Col. 2:8-10; 1 Tim. 2:4.
- magic arts, spells, taboos, astrology: see 2 Kings 17:16-18; Isa. 47:12-15; Acts 8:9-24.

- confusion of identity between the creator and the created: see 1 Kings 8:27; Ps. 8:1-9; 24:1-10; 89:5-14; Isa. 40:12-17; 1 Pet. 1:24,25.
- ethics and morals derived from humans or the self; no absolutes, everything is relative: see 1 Kings 8:46; Ps. 51:1-4; 143:2; Eccles. 7:20; Rom. 2:14-16; 1 John 1:5-10.
- reincarnation: see Rom. 6:23; Heb. 9:27.
- salvation by human effort: see Rom. 4:3; Gal. 2:15,16.
- picking and choosing among religions: see Exod. 20:2-5; 23:13; John 1:7-9.
- worshiping other gods, especially fertility religions: see 2 Kings 17:9-12; Jer. 2:20; Ezek. 6:13.
- the idea that Christ is optional, only one of many spiritual masters: see John 14:6-8; Acts 4:12; 1 Tim. 2:5,6.

REINCARNATION—A KEY PART OF THE NEW AGE

Permeating New Age thinking is the concept of reincarnation—the idea that death is not the end of earthly life but only a passage to a cycle of unending deaths and rebirths. As we have seen, reincarnation is a key part of Hindu and Buddhist religions. And in many cases, the law of karma (cause and effect as one's good and bad actions are totaled up) determines what an individual may "come back as" in the next life. In some forms of Hinduism, bad karma (caused by bad actions) can result in coming back as an animal, a worm or even a rock or a tree.

In New Age thinking, however, reincarnation has been turned into a hybrid that almost always emphasizes progressing upward toward final self-redemption. According to Russell Chandler, "Most, though not all, New Age reincarnationists reject the idea that the human soul can transmigrate backward to lower life forms."[21]

For example, film star Shirley MacLaine, one of the most high-powered promoters of New Age thinking through her books and lectures, plays down negative karma in favor of working on realizing personal divinity. MacLaine, whose errors and twisting of the Bible are believed by millions due to her great media exposure, says in her bestseller *Out on a Limb*, "I read that Christ's teachings about reincarnation were struck from the Bible during the Fifth Ecumenical Council meeting in Constantinople in the year A.D. 553."[22]

The actual ruling of the Fifth Council included 15 condemnations of the Church father Origen, none of which actually referred to reincarnation. Origen rejected reincarnation in several of his writings, but in one place he had taught the preexistence of souls. One of the condemnations did say, "If anyone asserts the fabulous preexistence of souls . . . let him be anathema." The Council did not strike anything from the Bible.[23]

Contrary to New Age thinking, the Bible overwhelmingly teaches resurrection, not reincarnation (see Ps. 49:15; John 5:25; 6:40; 11:25; 1 Cor. 15; 2 Cor. 4:14; 1 Thess. 4:16). New Agers like to think they have all kinds of time to "get it right" as they progress toward some kind of self-induced salvation. The Bible clearly says you get one chance and after that comes the judgment (see Heb. 9:27).

SYNCRETISM: ALL RELIGIONS LEAD TO THE SAME PLACE

One of the key concepts of New Age thought is *syncretism*, the idea that all religions are one and they all lead to the same place. In other words, there are many ways to God and heaven—or whatever you perceive either one of these to be. Syncretism is a natural step beyond monism and pantheism. If all is one and all is God and we are God, then it is not surprising that New Agers believe all religions have the same ultimate goal.

But the New Age concept of syncretism does not square at all with biblical Christianity. Jesus' words alone are enough to counter the concept of syncretism. Jesus told His disciples, "I am the way and the truth and the life. No one comes to the Father except through me" (John 14:6).

New Age writers like James Redfield, author of *The Celestine Prophecy*, sell the concept of *synchronicity* (the underlying interconnectedness, in the face of seeming coincidence, of everything in the universe) as the way to eventually solve problems like poverty, world hunger, crime, war and terrorism by bringing forth peace, light, energy, cooperation, human growth and happiness—all made possible through human development and progress.[24] But all of this is a false lure, a lie that is based on fallen human resources and abilities. The Fall did happen. Sin is a pervading, all-encompassing disease of the human soul that cannot be cured by trying harder or "finding new paradigms of thinking and acting." All religions are not one, despite New Age claims that the Age of Aquarius will usher in new world order with three ideals: one world government, one world leader and one world religion.

IS THE NAM A WORLDWIDE CONSPIRACY?

A number of Christian writers have warned against a "New Age conspiracy" to take over the world. Some conspiracy theorists point back to Alice Bailey's writings, which New Agers are now following "like a recipe" for world domination.[25] Included in one of Bailey's books is "The Great Invocation," part of which New Agers refer to as "The Plan":

> From the centre which we call the race of men
> Let the Plan of Love and Light work out.
> And may it seal the door where evil dwells.
> Let Light and Love and Power restore the Plan on Earth.[26]

That everyone connected with the NAM is in on the "conspiracy" and is following the Plan like a recipe is hard to prove. A number of hard-core New Agers are, however, definitely in favor of the Plan and of having one world government led by one great leader. New Age writers like Marilyn Ferguson believe that networking is a key to spreading the New Age "gospel."[27] This networking has been going on since at least the mid-1980s, when organizations and groups with common New Age goals began to link up to share ideas for how to become a collective force to transform the world. One estimate says that at least 10,000 different New Age organizations and groups network with each other in one way or another.

The bottom line is that, while the New Age movement appears to lack form, direction or organization, its multitiered system of networks gives it a means to share goals, spiritual experiences and aspirations. Many people following or using New Age concepts are not even aware of the network or the overall "Plan," but it is still being pursued by thousands of dedicated New Agers who are seeking to bring the world into the Age of Aquarius.

What can be said with certainty about a NAM "conspiracy" is that New Age spirituality is totally at odds with the Christian faith. Ever since Lucifer's expulsion from heaven, Satan has had a plan to rebel against His creator and even become "like the Most High" (Isa. 14:14). Because its principles and doctrines are the very antithesis of Scripture, the NAM is a "viable contemporary component of Satan's plan . . . to defeat the Kingdom of Jesus Christ."[28]

THE "OSTRICH MENTALITY" IS NO ANSWER

In responding to the New Age, Christians might be tempted to use the turtle shell or ostrich mentality, which views New Age as something so far out that no one in his right mind would consider it. The truth is, a lot of people, including some Christians, are unconsciously or unintentionally accepting and practicing New Age concepts in many areas of everyday life, including the following:

- Some forms of holistic care that feature "the power to heal yourself."
- The corporate arena, where major firms, such as Ford Motor Company, pay huge sums to offer motivational seminars designed to help employees tap the "divine energy source within."
- Some public schools where youngsters as young as those in first grade are exposed to "transpersonal education," featuring "confluent curriculum" designed to help them tap into a "universal mind" where they can receive information through meditation and contact with "spirit guides."[29]
- Music and films. Many New Age albums can be used to trigger meditation and mystical experiences.[30] Slick, engaging films with New Age messages appear regularly and have included *ET* and *Close Encounters of the Third Kind* (extraterrestrials are good, helpful and even lovable); *The Sixth Sense* (psychologist tries to help boy seeing ghosts); the *Star Wars* episodes ("May the force be with you.").
- TV and video games, including the likeable, even lovable, Ninja Turtles who actually send a thinly veiled Zen Buddhism message.[31]
- Even more popular has been Pokemon (short for POCKEt MONster, pronounced poh-keh-mon), cute little toy figures, which actually can entice children and youth to become fascinated with occult powers as they "summon" the forces displayed on their Pokemon cards.[32] (To learn more about Pokemon and other occult toys, see appendix A, Resources for Further Study.)

Because the New Age seems to be everywhere and in practically everything, it would seem logical to see all of the NAM as taboo and dangerous. But there are some things New Agers talk about that Christians can agree with, to a point. Saving the environment is one. Trying to end war, terrorism, bigotry and racial and gender discrimination are others. The New Age solution to these problems, however, is found only in fallen mankind, and that is doomed to a dead end.

To respond to New Age thinking, Christians must have a thorough understanding of their own faith. To know what God's Word teaches is imperative. Even more important is to know the living Word—His Son—in a personal, vibrant way. A favorite response of the New Ager to the Christian who tries to point out the absolute truth of the Bible is, "That's your reality, but it's not mine." Christians can only respond confidently but humbly that, in the end, only one reality will turn out to be real: Jesus Christ—the only way, the only absolute truth and the only source of life.

SUMMING UP MAJOR DIFFERENCES BETWEEN NEW AGERS AND CHRISTIANS

Regarding God and Jesus Christ: New Agers say, "God is us and we are God";[33] and Jesus Christ was just one of a "line of spiritual teachers" that continues today.[34] Christians believe God is separate from His creation, and that only He can be called God (see Isa. 45:12; Rom. 1:25); that Jesus Christ is God, the only mediator between God and man (see John 14:6; 1 Tim. 2:5).

Regarding revelation (the Bible): New Agers claim that revelation came through leaders of other world religions, not just through Jesus. One NAM writer says God is seen from different points of view and He does not seem the same to everyone. "You Brahmans call him Parabrahm; in Egypt he is Thoth; and Zeus is his name in Greece; Jehovah is his Hebrew name".[35] Christians believe that revelation is contained only in the Bible, God's inspired, infallible and final Word (see 2 Tim. 3:16,17; Jude 3.

Regarding sin, salvation and reincarnation: New Agers say human nature is neither good nor bad but open to continuous transformation;[36] salvation is enlightenment, "the realization of our at-one-ment with God."[37] Most New Agers believe in reincarnation that keeps the soul progressing "until you get it right."[38] Christians believe all mankind is born in sin and stands condemned before a righteous, holy God (see Rom. 3:9-11,23); salvation comes by putting faith in Jesus Christ's atonement for sin on the cross (see Rom. 3:24,25; Eph. 2:8,9). The Bible does not teach reincarnation. Man has one life and then is judged (see Matt. 7:13; Heb. 9:27).

CHAPTER TWELVE

NOTHING NEW UNDER THE SUN

ELEVEN MORE VIEWPOINTS THAT UNDERMINE, CHALLENGE OR ATTACK BIBLICAL CHRISTIANITY

As we have seen throughout this study of differences, the exclusive claims of Christianity as the only holder of absolute truth in Jesus Christ, second Person of the Trinity, have been undermined, criticized or attacked ever since the first century. As we have also seen, many of these attacks come from within as well as from without. Indeed, biblical Christian churches are a favorite hunting ground for cultists or other groups who are looking for Christians who really don't understand their own theology but may "feel" that it just isn't meeting all their needs. There are dozens of such cults or groups, and more seem to pop up every day.

The following 11 viewpoints present something of a cross section of what is currently competing for the hearts and minds of men and women, as well as children and young people. Space limitations force a shorter treatment of these groups, but their origins, history, practices and beliefs are succinctly presented and compared with biblical teachings to answer the question, So what's the difference?

BAHA'I

Origin/Background

Baha'i is a movement started by an Iranian wool merchant and Shi'ite Muslim to reform Islam. Many Muslims had been waiting for another prophet to succeed Mohammed; and in 1844 Mirza Ali Mohammed (1819-1850) claimed to be the one who would herald the coming of that prophet. Mohammed became known as "The Bab" (pronounced "bob," meaning a gate leading to a new era for man), and his followers were called Babists (or *Bobis*). He was executed in 1850 by Muslim zealots who wanted no part of reform.[1]

Thirteen years later, one of The Bab's followers, Mirza Husayn Ali (1817-1892), took the name Baha'u'llah and announced that he was the long-awaited prophet. Baha'u'llah began organizing and writing many of the teachings of the new movement, which became known as Baha'i. Baha'u'llah's writings (estimated between 100 and 200 books and papers) were eventually considered inspired by his followers. One of the most important is *The Most Holy Book*, containing the laws governing Baha'i.[2]

After Baha'u'llah died in 1892, his son Abdu'l Baha' (1844-1921) assumed leadership and was instrumental in bringing Baha'i to the United States in 1893. An outstanding teacher and interpreter of his father's works, Abdu'l Baha' led in the building of a $2.5 million Baha'i temple in Wilmette, Illinois, just north of Chicago. Abdu'l Baha' died in 1921 and his Oxford-educated grandson, Shoghi Effendi, was appointed to lead Baha'i as Guardian of the Faith. Effendi died in 1957 with no appointed successor. In 1963, the first Baha'i Universal House of Justice was elected—a nine-person board, held to be infallible as it governs the affairs of 6,500,000 members of the Baha'i faith from world headquarters in Haifa, Israel.[3]

Teachings/Practices

Baha'i is syncretistic, claiming that the world's major religions are not contradictory or competitive but equally true. According to Baha'is, Judaism, Islam, Buddhism, Christianity and Hinduism all agree in their basic principles; the only differences are "inconsequential details."[4] Baha'i also teaches that Adam, Abraham, Moses, Krishna, Buddha, Jesus and Mohammed were all equal manifestations of God, each a genuine prophet and each divine, sinless and infallible.[5] Each lived and taught in his own time or cycle, instructing his contemporaries in a way they could understand.

Without question, the very heart of Baha'i teachings is found in the writings and claims of Baha'u'llah, who is considered God's appointed prophet, superseding all other prophets. Although he stopped short of claiming to be God, Baha'u'llah did claim to be more important than all previous manifestations, including Jesus. As he developed the law for Baha'i followers, he laid down strict rules about daily worship, including the duty that three times a day followers wash faces and hands, turn toward his (Baha'u'llah's) tomb and recite the Obligatory Prayer. In addition, they must repeat daily the words "Allah-u-Abha" (God of highest glory). Every March, Baha'is must fast from sunup to sundown for 19 days.

A major goal of Baha'i is unity of mankind. By this they mean an international political empire where Baha'ism would be the state religion. According to Baha'i thinking, all nations would give up national sovereignty and allow the Baha'i world super-state to rule. Every human being on planet Earth would be under the Baha'i World Parliament.[6]

So What's the Difference?

1. The Baha'i view of God is the same strict monotheism of
   Judaism or Islam—God is one, period. Compare Genesis
   1:26; 3:22; 11:7; Isaiah 6:8 for Old Testament references
   where God refers to a plurality of persons in Himself.[7]
   Also compare Matthew 28:19; John 14:6; 15:26;
   2 Corinthians 13:14; 1 Peter 1:2 for New Testament references to the Trinity—Father, Son and Holy Spirit.

2. Baha'is see Jesus as just another man whose career as Lord
   ended when Mohammed founded Islam in the seventh
   century.[8] Teachers of Baha'i categorically reject the Trinity,
   Jesus' incarnation, His bodily resurrection from death and
   the need for Jesus' sacrificial atonement for sin.[9] Compare
   Matthew 1:23; 3:16,17; 28:19; Mark 16:1-6; John 1:1-5;
   Romans 3:24-26; 1 Corinthians 15:12-15; 1 John 2:2; 4:10.

3. Baha'is claim that Baha'u'llah is the fulfillment of Christ's
   promise of the Holy Spirit. Baha'u'llah's teachings belittle
   Jesus, reducing Him from God to a "manifestation" whose
   time has passed and who has been replaced by a more
   recent and greater manifestation—Baha'u'llah himself.[10]
   Compare John 14:1-9, where Christ clearly claims deity,
   and John 14:16-18 and 16:12-15, where Jesus clearly says
   that the Spirit of truth will come to glorify Him and help
   the Christian.

4. Baha'i theologians deny that Christ is the only way to
   God. According to Baha'is, religious truth is relative, not
   absolute, and revelation is continuous and never final.[11]
   Compare John 1:14; 14:6; 18:37, all of which clearly teach
   that Christ is the source of life and truth.[12]

Summary

The differences between Baha'i and Christianity are numerous, but perhaps the key difference is Baha'i syncretism—a type of monism—that says all religions are one and all agree with one another (as long as they give final loyalty to Baha'u'llah, the last great manifestation). Baha'is teach some good principles for developing personal integrity, but their absolute dependence on works to avoid judgment leaves them relying on obeying the law (and Baha'u'llah's laws at that) to achieve what they call salvation.

CHRISTIAN SCIENCE

Origin/Background

Christian Science is the mother of the mind sciences family of religions (Religious Science, the Unity School of Christianity and many New Age groups).[13] Christian Science arose out of the religious and intellectual ferment of the nineteenth century, which included everything from adaptation of Hindu pantheistic beliefs into New England Transcendentalism by Ralph Waldo Emerson and Henry David Thoreau to experimentation with mesmerism (hypnotism), occult metaphysics, mental healing and attempts to contact the dead and other spirits through séances.[14]

Mary Baker, born in 1821 to humble but strict Congregationalists, was frequently ill as a child. She married at 22, but her husband, George Glover, died only seven months later. Pregnant, she was reduced to a highly emotional and unstable state, depending from time to time throughout her life on morphine as a medication. After a second (failed) marriage to Dr. Daniel Patterson, she was married a third time at age 56 to Asa Eddy.[15] Five years later, Asa died. Mary broke a cardinal Christian Science rule and demanded an autopsy. In a newspaper article, she accused her former students of mentally poisoning her husband with malicious mesmerism in the form of arsenic.[16]

Eddy is heralded as the discoverer and founder of Christian Science, but her claims to originality and truthfulness do not hold up. For one thing, her teachings are dependent upon her association with Phineas Parkhurst Quimby, a metaphysical healer from Maine, who treated Eddy for "spinal inflammation." Her book *Science and Health with Key to the Scriptures* (the authoritative text of Christian Science, which she claims to have had no help in writing), steals passages almost verbatim from Quimby's own book.[17] In addition, modern historians have proven that Eddy also plagiarized other authors' works without giving them credit.[18] Furthermore, Eddy's claim that, after being severely injured in a fall and near death, she read the Bible and rose the third day completely healed, were exposed as falsehoods by her own physician, Dr. Alvin M. Cushing.[19]

Nevertheless, Eddy was an energetic leader and great promoter. She founded her Church of Christ, Scientist, in Boston in 1879. By the time of her death in 1910, there were approximately 1 million members worldwide. Today Christian Science has an estimated 200,000 members in 66 countries.[20] In the '90s, several child-neglect court cases involved Christian Science parents; the children died after the parents decided to rely on Christian Science prayer alone, even though their children's deaths had been easily preventable.[21]

Teachings/Practices

Christian Science and the other mind sciences interpret the Bible from the perspective of a belief system that rejects the idea of a Creator God who is infinite, personal, good and qualitatively distinct from His creation. Christian Science teaches that God "is not a person. God is a principle," the principle of Impersonal Mind.[22]

Science and Health teaches that "there is no life, truth, intelligence, or substance in matter. All is Infinite Mind and its infinite manifestation, for God is all in all." Furthermore, "man is not material; he is spiritual."[23] According to the Christian Science worldview, there is no reality to the physical world; therefore, it is only a small step to the conclusion that evil, sin, disease, sickness and death are mere "illusions of the Mortal mind."[24]

The Christian Science denial of the reality of the physical is similar to Hindu pantheism, reducing God to an impersonal force or idea. Furthermore, the material world is mere illusion. The practical outworking of Christian Science is that sin, sickness, suffering and evil have no objective existence ("it's all in your mind"); therefore, *materia medica* (material medicine) is unnecessary.[25] However, the biblical worldview clearly teaches that the infinite and personal God created the physical universe outside of Himself and that what He created was real and originally good (see Gen.1:4,10,12,18,21,25,31). According to the Bible, evil, sin, sickness and death are the results of the Fall (see Gen. 3 regarding Adam's disobedience and Rom. 3:10-23; 5:12-21; 6:23 for the results of that disobedience). While Christian Science denies the validity of the science of medicine, a biblical Christian worldview welcomes the advances of medical science, which explains and helps us counteract the physical causes of many human ailments.

So What's the Difference?

1. Christian Science says the Bible must be interpreted through the higher and final revelation of Mary Baker Eddy's *Science and Health with Key to the Scriptures*.[26] Compare Deuteronomy 4:2; 2 Timothy 3:16; Hebrews 1:1,2; Jude 3, which teach the divine inspiration of Scripture.

2. Christian Scientists claim that healings using Christian Science methods "prove" that Christian Science is authentic. Compare Exodus 7:11,12,22 and Matthew 7:22,23, which clearly show that false prophets could perform miracles and lead people away from God.

3. Christian Science teaches that "the theory of three persons
   in one God (that is, a personal Trinity or Triunity) suggests
   polytheism, rather than the one ever-present I AM. . . . Jesus
   Christ is not God, as Jesus himself declared, but is the Son
   of God."[27] In contrast, the Bible clearly says Jesus was God.
   There is no contradiction between saying Jesus is God and
   Jesus is the Son of God, because of the doctrine of the
   Trinity (see John 1:1,2; 5:19; 8:58; 14:6-9; 2 Pet. 2:1).

4. Christian Science claims that "God is the principle of man;
   and the principle of man remaining perfect, its idea or
   reflection—man—remains perfect."[28] In contrast, the Bible
   clearly teaches that men and women are created by God,
   they are qualitatively different from God and they are far
   from perfect (see Gen. 1:26,27; 2:7; Rom. 3:9-23; 5:12-21).

5. Christian Science says "the material blood of Jesus was no
   more efficacious to cleanse from sin when it was shed
   upon 'the accursed tree' than when it was flowing in His
   veins. Jesus' students . . . learned that he had not died."[29]
   On the contrary, the central truth of the gospel is the
   atoning death and resurrection of Jesus Christ (see Matt.
   27:50-60; Rom. 10:9; 1 Cor. 15:1-4).

6. Christian Science teaches that "the sinner makes his own
   hell by doing evil, and the saint his own heaven by doing
   right. . . ."[30] Man as God's idea is already saved with an
   everlasting salvation."[31] In contrast, the Bible strongly
   warns that sin leads to death and separation from God
   and that we are not "already saved" but in desperate need
   of salvation through Christ's death and resurrection for
   us. Jesus also clearly warned against a real hell (see Rom.
   3:23; 6:23; also Matt. 8:12).

7. Christian Science denies that the Holy Spirit is the third "person" of the Trinity, because God is impersonal.[32] This is clearly refuted by John 14:15-18,26,27; 15:26; 16:7-14, which state that the Holy Spirit is sent by the Father and Christ to be with believers as God.

8. Christian Science denies prayer: "The mere habit of pleading with the divine Mind, as one pleads with a human being, perpetuates the belief in God as humanly circumscribed—an error which impedes spiritual growth."[33] Compare 1 Chronicles 16:11; Matthew 7:7, 26:41; Luke 18:1; John 16:24; Philippians 4:6; 1 Thessalonians 5:17, all of which tell us to pray always about everything. God wants us to communicate with Him.

Summary

Due to Mary Baker Eddy's worldview and totally different interpretation of reality, Christian Science and Christianity are 180 degrees apart. Eddy said, "The sick are not healed merely by declaring there is no sickness, but by knowing that there is none."[34] But the Bible teaches that sickness—physical and spiritual—is very real, and Christ is the great Physician (see Matt. 4:23,24; Luke 4:40).

EVOLUTIONISM

Origin/Background

Evolutionism, which also falls under the labels of Darwinism and Scientism, is a "religion" based on Charles Darwin's theory that *all* life forms have evolved from a common ancestor. The idea of evolution has been around since the ancient Greek philosophers. Darwin (1809-

1882) was the first to popularize the concept in his book *The Origin of Species by Means of Natural Selection*, published in 1859.

In *The Origin of Species*, Darwin left room for belief in the creator, but not as a relevant part of the process. While his theory of evolution by natural selection was heralded as an "astounding scientific breakthrough," what he was really doing was using science to "prove" the worldview of naturalism (nature is all there is). In this sense, evolutionism or Darwinism can be seen as a "religion," particularly among those in the scientific community who refuse to allow the possibility that God—a supernatural cause—created life. As Charles Colson puts it, "Naturalism may parade as science, martialing facts and figures, but it is a religion."[35]

According to Darwin's theory of natural selection, plants and animals prey on each other to survive; as they cope with their environment, some, through mutation, develop new characteristics, capacities or features that give them a better chance at survival. These characteristics and capacities allow only the species most well adapted to their environments to survive. As these capacities become permanent, a new species evolves.

Darwin believed that from one or a few simple original forms natural selection ("survival of the fittest") had produced every species of animal that ever existed. Darwin had no objective proof of evolution from "amoeba to man." Nevertheless, his theory hit society like a bombshell. Those who didn't want to believe in God or His "interference" with natural order embraced it as a scientific "reason" to dismiss God and the "creation myth" of the Bible. Many Christian leaders vehemently rejected evolution—Charles Spurgeon called the idea a "monstrous error which would be ridiculed before another twenty years."[36]

Far from being ridiculed by the general public, Darwin's theory gained credibility and popularity. In the latter part of the nineteenth century and into the twentieth, Christians fought a losing battle trying to defend Genesis in the face of what seemed like all-powerful science, which suddenly looked as if it could explain everything. Some Christians, both in theological schools and in universities found a way to accommodate their faith with evolution, becoming "theistic evolutionists."

As the controversy ebbed and flowed, academic circles became increasingly intolerant of anything that smacked of authority coming from outside of the realm of science.[37] Completely naturalistic evolution became the reigning scientific "orthodoxy" in American education, and disbelief in evolution became academic "heresy."

Teachings/Practices

Today evolution is taught as a fact, when it is actually a theory that supports the philosophy of naturalism, a worldview that says nature is all there is, God is not in the picture. Typical of what appears in college textbooks is the following: "By coupling undirected, purposeless variation to the blind uncaring process of natural selection, Darwin made theological or spiritual explanations of the life processes superfluous."[38]

In 1995, the National Association of Biology Teachers summed up its approach to teaching high school students about the origin of life by saying life results from "an unsupervised, impersonal, unpredictable, and natural process."[39]

What statements like these say is that the educational establishment is in the hands of people who believe that life is the outcome of purely material processes that have acted blindly by chance. God is absent; and if God—the creator—did not make life, then we don't need God or His morals. As biologist William Provine says, "No life after death; no ultimate foundation for ethics; no ultimate meaning for life; no free will."[40]

Although Darwin himself was not sure how the first crude lifeform started, he hesitated to say it came from nowhere. As he ended *The Origin of Species*, he spoke of how life could have "been originally breathed by the Creator into a few forms or into one."[41] But once scientists and secular humanists decided that evolution "had to be the way it happened," they filled in any blanks that Darwin may have left.

Evolutionists generally believe that 3 or 4 billion years ago the universe began with a "Big Bang," and somehow the planet Earth formed with conditions that were "just right" for life. The first speck of life came into existence (it was not created) through a series of "accidents" that combined chemicals and energy (possibly lightning). Another possibility is that life formed in the oceans in what some evolutionists call "prebiotic soup." At any rate, this first little speck of life somehow survived and reproduced itself. This process went on until finally a cell emerged. Certain evolutionists believe that it took as long for that first little speck of life to become the first cell as it did for the first cell to progress to man.

That first living cell, then, reproduced and evolved through the eons by natural process alone (natural selection, mutation, etc.), and eventually developed into simple plants and animals, then fish, then into amphibians, then reptiles, then mammals. From among the mammals came the primates—monkeys, apes and, finally, man.[42]

According to Darwin's theory, all this happened not with any great leaps or sudden changes, but only by incremental steps. Small changes in species are recognized by everyone—creationists and evolutionists alike—as microevolution. Darwinism claims that, given enough time, microevolution in species resulted in macroevolution—evolution from species to species, causing the major transitions necessary to prove Darwin's theory to be a "fact."

From the beginning, Christians have contested Darwin's theories, not just because of the worldview assumptions of macroevolution, but on the basis of the evidence itself. Darwinian evolution is not a fact because *macroevolution has not happened.* The major evidence against macroevolution is in the fossil record and the complexity of the cell. There is simply no conclusive fossil evidence of how single-cell organisms changed step-by-step into complex plants and animals.

As for a single cell somehow developing out of "pre-biotic soup" and then evolving up to man, this too has proven to be a dead end for Darwinians. In his book *Darwin's Black Box,* molecular biologist Michael Behe spells out the "irreducible complexity of molecular mechanisms."

As Behe explains, the cell was a "black box" as far as Darwin was concerned. In other words, how it worked was a total mystery to him. But now Behe has opened up the black box, and his work—which has been recognized throughout the scientific community—has proved that the complex systems in a cell depend on far too many interconnected parts to have been built up gradually, step by tiny step, over a long period of time.[43] Behe says there is not enough time for macroevolution to have happened, no matter how much time might pass.

Because of the time problem, new evolutionary theories have been proposed, such as Stephen Jay Gould's "punctuated equilibrium," the theory that evolution could have happened in extremely short time periods. Without hard evidence, these theories are still very much in flux and very much unproven.[44]

Beyond the problems for evolutionists in the fossil record and in the irreducible complexity of the cell is the primary question of them all: If, indeed, everything started with "The Big Bang," then where did the elements of The Big Bang come from, and what was there before The Big Bang?

So What's the Difference?

1. Believers in naturalistic evolution claim the process of evolution is unsupervised by any deity and is, therefore, caused purely by chance. In contrast, the Bible teaches the mighty and personal God, who lovingly and caringly created the universe, the earth and all the living creatures in it (see Gen. 1:1-31; Ps. 24:1; Rom. 1:18-20).

2. Naturalistic evolution teaches there is no purpose or meaning to life, which arose spontaneously out of a blind combination of time, chance and matter. The Bible, however, tells us that God created (see Ps. 33:6-9 and Isa.

45:18); that creation clearly shows the glory of God (see Ps. 19:1-4 and Rom. 1:18-20); that Jesus Christ was there in the beginning (see John 1:1-5 and Col. 1:16-18); and that instead of nothingness God offers eternal life and the opportunity to belong to Him (see John 1:10-12; 3:15,16; 1 Cor. 8:6).

3. Evolutionism claims there is nothing special or sacred about humanity. Evolution reduces man to a highly developed animal who is really no more valuable than a cow or chicken.[45] Compare Genesis 1:26,27; 5:1; James 3:9, all of which teach that man is created in God's image and likeness. Also see Genesis 1:28; Psalm 8:4-8; Matthew 6:26; 12:11,12, which teach man's value in God's sight and his preeminence over animals and the rest of creation.

4. Evolutionism theorizes that humans are not "free" but are determined by their genes and environment. Compare Genesis 2:17; Deuteronomy 30:19; Joshua 24:15; 1 Kings 18:21, all of which outline the choice ever before us; see also Mark 8:36; Luke 15; Romans 6:23, for consequences of our freedom to choose.

5. An inescapable conclusion to be drawn from evolution is that natural selection (survival of the fittest) does away with universal moral values based on divine law. Scripture teaches that morality is not for sinful man to decide (see Exod. 21:1-17; Matt. 22:37-40). See also Deuteronomy 6:25; John 19:11; Romans 13:1; 1 John 3:4, which teach law and authority as coming from God alone.

6. Naturalistic evolution and Christian faith are incompatible. "Human beings did not fall from perfection into sin as

the Church had taught for centuries; we were evolving, and indeed are still evolving, into higher levels of consciousness."[46] Compare Matthew 9:13; John 3:16,17; Romans 10:13; 1 Timothy 2:4; Titus 2:11; 1 John 3:18, which all say that sinful man's only hope is the salvation provided by God, not evolution.

Summary

Even though many highly qualified scientists who are not creationists say macroevolution is a bankrupt theory and some other solution must be found, believers in evolutionism continue to preach their gospel, which one eminent zoologist has said "is a fairy tale for grownups . . . it is useless."[47] Nonetheless, Isaac Asimov, avowed secular humanist and atheist, repeats the evolutionist's creed with conviction: "Simple forms of life came into being more than 3 billion years ago, and have formed spontaneously from nonliving matter."[48]

Asimov's statement of faith (not fact) is reminiscent of a story that has made the rounds on the Internet. It seems that one scientist was picked by his peers to tell God that, because cloning people was practically a reality and with many other scientific miracles an everyday occurrence, He wasn't needed. Perhaps He could retire or just "get lost."

After listening patiently, God said, "Very well, how about this? Let's have a man-making contest."

"Okay, great!" the scientist replied.

"But," God added, "we're going to do this the same way I did it back in the old days with Adam."

"Sure, no problem," said the scientist, as he bent down and grabbed a handful of dirt.

God smiled and said, "No, no, no. You go get your own dirt."[49]

While this tale is obviously facetious, it does make a good point: Brilliant as scientists are, they don't know how to go get (make) their own dirt out of nothing. There is, however, one explanation that increasing numbers of scientists are giving strong consideration: *In the beginning, God created the heavens and the earth.*

FREEMASONRY

Origin/Background

Freemasonry is the largest international fraternal order in the world. It is a secret society that seeks to perpetuate its traditions through symbolism, rituals and oaths taken on pain of death if broken.[50] Freemasonry is a diverse movement with many distinct branches (the main ones being the York Rite and the Scottish Rite). There is no single central authority, book or even definition of Freemasonry that all Masons accept.[51]

To gain credibility and stature, Masons claim to have ties to ancient biblical accounts. Masonic legends include unproven assertions that the first Masonic aprons (used in initiation rites) were Adam and Eve's fig leaves; that Freemasonry dates back to the time of Solomon, who employed stonemasons to construct the temple; that Freemasonry is connected to biblical accounts of the Tower of Babel, of Noah and of Seth.[52]

More traceable origins of Freemasonry go back to James Anderson, George Payne and Theopholis Desaguliers who founded the first Masonic Lodge in London, England, in 1717. Other lodges soon sprang up in England and Europe. The first Masonic Lodge in the United States began in Boston in 1733. During the 1800s, Freemasonry became a powerful institution with several thousand lodges organized throughout the United States. But during the 1800s, there was a strong backlash against Freemasonry, partly because of the disappearance and apparent death of William Morgan, a former Mason who had exposed Masonic secrets. Masons were suspected of foul play but no proof was found.[53]

Many famous Americans have been Freemasons, including George Washington, John Wayne, Henry Ford and Gen. Douglas

MacArthur.[54] In 1991, there were nearly 2.5 million Masons in the United States, down from a high of 4 million in 1959.[55]

Teachings/Practices

Freemasonry teaches the civic values of brotherliness, charity and mutual aid[56] and that all religions acknowledge the same God.[57] The Lodge blends its own myths and rituals with elements from other religions, including Christian, Islamic, Jewish and Egyptian.[58] Joseph Smith, founder of the Mormon Church, was a Mason, and Mormon and Masonic rituals are similar if not identical.[59]

The attraction in Freemasonry is that it calls itself a men's fellowship to "make good men better" and professes to contain "no contradictions with Christianity." In truth, Freemasonry's bedrock ideas come from ancient Gnostic, esoteric and pagan sources.

At beginning levels, the religious worldview behind Freemasonry is Deism or Unitarianism, both of which teach that God is the creator and worthy of worship, that virtue and piety are good, that humans should repent from sin and that in the afterlife there will be rewards and punishments.[60] But Freemasonry emphatically rejects the idea that God reveals Himself clearly and specifically through the history of Israel, the Bible and Jesus the Messiah. Almost all church denominations that are committed to biblical truth and have studied the matter have concluded that Freemasonry is incompatible with Christian faith.[61]

At the higher levels of Masonry, the religious worldview is occultic and very similar to New Age teachings. The higher someone progresses in Freemasonry, the deeper one gets involved in the occult, spiritism, deception and blasphemies against God.[62] The eclectic mixing and matching of religions found in Freemasonry dovetails with the New Age and postmodern desire people have to construct their own truth and spirituality.

Amazing as it may seem, many Christians see Freemasonry as relatively harmless fun and games, a networking arrangement for businessmen with the added benefit of service to humanity through the Shriner's hospitals and other excellent forms of good works. They do not see it as a religion and philosophy that, at its core, is in conflict with foundational Christian truths.

So What's the Difference?

1. The Bible is not the unique Word of God. "The Bible is used among Freemasons as a symbol of the will of God, however it may be expressed. Therefore, whatever . . . expresses that will may be used as a substitute for the Bible in a Masonic Lodge" (i.e., the Qur'an or the Vedas).[63] Compare Psalm 119:105; Isaiah 48; 2 Timothy 3:15,16; Hebrews 4:12; 2 Peter 1:16-21 for examples of how the Bible is the Christian's final, eternal and trustworthy authority for faith and practice.

2. The God of the Bible is identified with other gods, and God's true name is "Jabulon," which explains why "Jah, Bel and On appear in the American ritual of the Royal Arch degree on the supposition that Jah was the Syriac name of God; Bel (Baal), the Chaldean; and On, the Egyptian."[64] Contrast Judges 3:7; 2 Kings 17:9-18; Jeremiah 19:4,5,15, for why Masonic identification of the God of the Bible with pagan deities is blasphemy and under His condemnation.

3. Jesus is not God the Son, nor is He the Savior of the world. "Jesus was just a man . . . one of the great men of the past, but not divine and certainly not the only means of redemption of lost mankind."[65] In direct contradiction, the Bible says Jesus was uniquely God the Son and Savior of mankind (see John 1:1,14; Phil. 2:9-11; Col. 1:15-17; 2:9).

4. Humans are basically good, even divine, and human nature is perfectible. "The perfection is already within. All that is required is to remove the roughness . . . divesting our hearts and consciences of all vices . . . to show forth the perfect man and Mason within."[66] Compare Titus 2:11-14; 1 John 1:5-10; 3:1-3, for why perfection is not possible in this life. Also compare Mark 7:20-23; Galatians 2:15,16; Ephesians 2:1-13 for what Scripture says about humans and why they need salvation from spiritual death.

5. Freemasonry uses the Bible but deletes Jesus' name from Scripture references. Speaking Jesus' name is forbidden in Masonic rituals and prayers.[67] See John 14:13,14; Acts 4:12; 2 Thessalonians 1:12, for the importance of Jesus' name to the Christian.

6. Freemasonry is the one true faith to lift spiritual darkness from the world. "Masonry is the universal, eternal, immutable religion, such as God planted in the heart of universal humanity . . . all [religions] that ever existed have had a basis of truth; and all have overlaid that truth with errors."[68] Compare John 1:14; 14:6; 18:37; Galatians 1:6-9; 1 John 2:22, for the source of real truth and Scripture's condemnation of those who claim otherwise.

HARE KRISHNA

Origin/Background
Known officially as the International Society for Krishna Consciousness (ISKCON), Hare Krishna was started in the United States by Abhay Charan (1896-1977), a Hindu from Calcutta. Charan arrived in New

York City in 1965 and immediately gained a following among young members of the counterculture who gave him the title of Swami Prabhupada (meaning "at whose feet masters sit").[69]

Soon Swami Prabhupada had established ISKCON centers in many major cities. Before his death at 82, he had published 70 volumes of translation and commentary on the Hindu scriptures, including the *Bhagavad Gita (As It Is)*. In addition, he had organized ISKCON into a worldwide network of *ashrams* (religious communities), schools, temples and farms.[70]

Swami Prabhupada was the latest and greatest in a long line of Krishna gurus. In the sixteenth century, Caitanya Mahaprabhu, who came from a priestly Brahman family in Bengal, India, founded the Krishna sect by teaching and practicing the ancient tradition of adoring Krishna that had begun between the second century B.C. and A.D. second century. Hindu scriptures written during that period spoke of Krishna, who was the eighth *avatar* (incarnation) of Vishnu, one of the three major deities of Hinduism.[71]

According to Hindu theology, any time that dharma (order) would be threatened and the need to set things straight was evident, an incarnation of Vishnu would appear, foremost among whom was Krishna. In the Bhagavad-Gita epic, Krishna is a charioteer who serves the great warrior Arjuna and teaches him to do what is right. In other popular writings called the *Puranas*, which became the text of the common Hindu people, Krishna was depicted as a great lover who seduced 100 maidens at one time, finally choosing one as his wife. The relationship between Krishna and his wife, Radha, symbolizes the "divine human relationship which is the heart of the Krishnaite religion."[72]

When Caitanya founded Krishnaism in the early 1500s, he had already become a *sannyasi* (one who has renounced the world). As a dynamic advocate of *Vishnuism* and especially the worship of Krishna, he attracted followers by dancing and chanting the name of Krishna in the streets. Caitanya taught that direct love of Krishna was the surest way to get rid of ignorance and karma (consequences of past actions) and attain *nirvana* (bliss).[73]

Caitanya attracted many followers in Bengal and northeast India, and Krishnaism continued to flourish down through the centuries. In the 1930s, Abhay Charan (who would become Swami Prabhupada) was initiated into the Caitanya sect. A Sanskrit scholar educated in Eastern and Western schools, Charan became a sannyasi and, at age 58, renounced his promising pharmaceutical business, as well as his wife and five children, to become a Hindu monk and later to take the title of swami (Hindu religious leader).

When Charan came to the United States to start ISKCON, he was 70 years old. He died 12 years later and, instead of picking a certain disciple to carry on his teaching, he left the movement to 11 senior disciples. Today ISKCON membership includes approximately 2,500 monks, 250,000 lay priests and 1 million worshiping members.[74] A well-known Westerner who became a follower of Krishna was George Harrison, one of the Beatles, who dedicated his hit song "My Sweet Lord" to Krishna.[75]

Teachings/Practices

In ISKCON, chanting the name of Krishna (*sankirtana*) is the best way to attain freedom from *samsara* (endless reincarnation). In the first three decades of the movement, devotees would often be seen chanting in public places such as airports, sporting long robes and shaved heads, selling literature, playing drums and finger cymbals and singing the 16-word chant "Hare Krishna, Hare Krishna, Krishna, Krishna, Hare, Hare, Hare Rama, Hare Rama, Rama, Rama, Hare, Hare." (Krishna means "The All-Attractive," Hare addresses "the energy of God," and Rama means "The Greatest Pleasure.")

In the 1960s and 1970s, Hare Krishna drew attention and criticism for its aggressive (and sometimes misleading) means of soliciting donations and recruiting followers with techniques that used brainwashing and severe discipline, such as keeping Krishna devotees existing on minimum amounts of food and rest.[76]

Today the Krishna movement looks much different. Full-time members no longer have long robes and shaved heads (although some shave their heads but wear wigs in public). Since a 1992 Supreme Court decision, they are no longer allowed to seek donations at airport terminals. Members are no longer required to live in temples, providing they worship before altars in their homes. Nonetheless, discipline is still strong, and the Krishna follower must give total devotion of mind, body, soul and senses to the cause of Krishna consciousness.[77] Full-time members of ISKCON take vows of abstinence from eating meat, drinking alcohol in any form and sex. They rise at 3:00 A.M. and chant 16 "rounds" of the chant, each round consisting of singing the Krishna mantra once on each of 108 prayer beads.

So What's the Difference?

1. No person or religion can claim absolute truth, since absolute is beyond man's reasoning powers (Swami Prabhupada).[78] Compare this teaching with John 1:14; 14:6; 18:37; Romans 3:4.

2. ISKCON says salvation comes through a personal relationship with the god Krishna, and complete surrender in devotion to him. Compare this with Romans 3:24; Ephesians 2:1-9; Titus 2:11; 3:7).

3. ISKCON claims to "revere" Jesus Christ, but Jesus is considered to be the son of Krishna and inferior to Krishna, who is "the original Personality of God-head himself."[79] The Bible has a much higher view of Jesus (see John 1:1-5; 14:6; Acts 4:12; Col. 1:15-20).

4. Prabhupada himself is said to have the powers and prerogatives of a god. He can take the "bad karma" of others upon himself, thus becoming a mediator between the god (Krishna) and the Krishna disciple.[80] Compare this with 1 Timothy 2:5, which teaches that Jesus Christ is the only mediator between God and man.

Summary

Although it is a branch of Hinduism, the ISKCON belief in God is essentially monotheistic, and the devotee sees Krishna as his personal savior, just as Christians follow Christ as theirs.[81] The critical difference is that the Krishna devotee tries to fill his karmic bank account with good works by serving God continually with his feet, his eyes or his ears. He gives total devotion of mind, body, soul and senses to the cause of Krishna consciousness but, for all his works, is still caught on the wheel of reincarnation. He is promised that he will someday go to the "supreme eternal atmosphere";[82] but he is never sure if he has done enough. How different for the Christian, who hears Jesus say, "Come to me, all you who are weary and burdened, and I will give you rest" (Matt. 11:28).

THE INTERNATIONAL CHURCHES OF CHRIST (FORMERLY, THE BOSTON CHURCH OF CHRIST)

Origin/Background

The International Churches of Christ (ICC) is a relatively new, fast-growing and controversial church movement that has been accused by its numerous critics (many of them ex-members) of cultic practices, mind control and mental/emotional abuse.[83]

The ICC has roots in the mainline Churches of Christ, one of several nineteenth-century "restoration" movements that sought to return to the original Christianity of the New Testament.[84] The unquestioned leader of ICC is Kip McKean who, as a student at the University of Florida, was converted under the ministry of Chuck Lucas at Crossroads Church of Christ in Gainesville, Florida. Lucas got his ideas from several sources, the foremost of which was Robert Coleman's *The Master Plan of Evangelism*. Out of Lucas's work came the highly intensive evangelistic Multiplying Ministries program, which called for each convert to be put under heavy supervision by an older "discipling partner."[85] Lucas's program was so successful it began to spread across the country, and its popularity actually caused divisions in churches because congregations wanted to be rebuilt along the lines of the Crossroads church.

It was during this intense transitional period that McKean was converted to Christ and discipled by Chuck Lucas. In 1976, McKean, then a graduate of the University of Florida, went on staff at the Heritage Chapel Church of Christ in Charleston, Illinois, and began a campus outreach at nearby Eastern Illinois University. While he had considerable success, he was eventually fired because his discipleship process was accused of being manipulative and controlling.[86] In 1979, McKean moved on to the Boston suburb of Lexington and started ministering at the Lexington Church of Christ. The church went from 30 to 1,000 members in just a few years, outgrew its facilities and finally became the Boston Church of Christ.[87]

With the phenomenal success of the Boston Church, McKean became the undisputed leader of the Multiplying Ministries movement and started adding new doctrines of his own (to be discussed below). In the early 1980s, the Boston movement began planting "pillar churches" in different key cities throughout the world, the first two in Chicago and London. Soon many of these churches, started by disciples from the mother Boston church, had developed into huge ministries, some with thousands of members.[88]

As the Boston church spread and continued to have phenomenal success in acquiring members with its discipleship program,

McKean's new doctrines and attitudes became apparent, including the idea that the BCC was *the* church of God. McKean believed that *all* other churches were poisoned by traditions, compromised or apostate. Using an illogical interpretation of Revelation 2 and 3, he began teaching there should be only "one church in one city." He also taught that churches not affiliated with the Boston church in each city were "not of God."[89]

Because McKean's doctrines were controversial, a great deal of opposition began to form from biblical Christian ministries in various cities. Hoping to stem the criticism, BBC leaders hired an outside church growth research firm headed by Flabil Yeakley to do a study of the BBC and its methods. Instead of showing the BCC to be a wholesome and healthy organization, the study revealed the Boston Church was "producing in its members the very same pattern of unhealthy personality change" that had been observed in studies of other well-known manipulative cults, such as Hare Krishna and the Unification Church (the Moonies).[90]

The study added that the data proved that a group dynamic operating in the Boston Church of Christ "influences members to change their personalities to conform to the group norm."[91] McKean's response to the study was that all the Boston Church of Christ was doing was "making people over after the image of Jesus Christ." Yeakley's reply to McKean was that Christ's divine nature is reflected in individuals whose gifts differ, and their personality types should not change in such a way as to "become a copy of someone else."[92]

In 1990, McKean moved the power center of the Boston movement to Los Angeles. McKean became the lead evangelist of the L.A. Church of Christ, itself a pillar church begun with 25 disciples from Boston and 25 from San Diego and San Francisco.[93] By 1997 the L.A. Church of Christ had nearly 12,000 people attending Sunday services.[94]

Since 1993 the Boston family of churches has called itself the International Churches of Christ (ICC). The movement has grown explosively from 30 members in 1979 to 118,185 members represented by 372 churches located in 158 countries in September 1999. Total Sunday attendance was over 190,000.[95]

Teachings/Practices

The ICC says its main goal is to "seek and save the lost," to fulfill the Great Commission (see Matt. 28:18-20) and to evangelize the world in one generation. McKean sees this one generation distinctive as more evidence that "this marks us as God's true and only modern movement."[96] ICC members seek the "remnant" within other churches and try to recruit them to the ICC, even if they are fully committed within their own fellowship.

In 1994, McKean said, "The opposition greatly intensified when the Bible doctrine of 'one church-one city' was restored" [see Revelation 2-3]. McKean went on to say, "The implication was that if the Boston churches were of God, their own churches were not. They drew this implication themselves which, in retrospect, was true."[97]

ICC elitism comes out in its doctrine that claims the only true salvation is in the ICC and to be saved one must be baptized into the ICC church and then pledge total commitment to the ministry. In fact, even though a new convert to ICC may have been baptized previously, he or she must be rebaptized, because only baptisms within the ICC are recognized as valid. Not only is baptism required for salvation, but discipleship is practiced according to ICC requirements. McKean bases this teaching on Acts 11:26 from which he developed the equation "Saved = Christian = Disciple." McKean said, "I know of no church, no fellowship, no movement that teaches and practices these biblical requirements of obedience to the truth."[98]

The ICC makes the firm demand that all its members express their commitment by total submission to their assigned spiritual superiors. One of the chief authorities in the ICC, Elder Al Baird, has instructed ICC members that "if the leader commands one to do something, even if it is not 'Christlike,' the member must submit."[99] The control extends to everyday affairs, relationships and finances. Not even intimate details between a husband and wife are excluded. The demand for complete obedience is based on verses like Hebrews 13:17: "Obey your leaders and submit to their authority."[100]

The ICC chain of command ends with McKean at the top, who, in so many words, claims to be "God's oracle" and even a mediator between the church and God. Speaking of himself, McKean has declared that, as the lead evangelist of the ICC, he determines "how far a congregation will go in obeying the Scriptures" as he impartially carries out the instructions of God, even when it is not the popular thing to do. McKean believes he knows exactly where the ICC church is, where it is headed and what it will take to get "where God wants it to be."[101]

Most ICC converts become acquainted with the church when they are contacted by a friendly person who seems interested in them. This quickly escalates into being invited to a "Bible study," where the potential convert is exposed to *First Principles: Basic Studies for Making Disciples*, written by McKean.[102] The Bible studies (discussed in some detail below) feed the potential convert the ICC brand of theology that teaches its elitism and its salvation through baptism and discipleship (works) doctrine. Soon the potential convert is assigned a spiritual mentor who continues the discipleship process, with a goal of having the new disciple qualify for baptism in the ICC and declare full commitment to the church. During this period the potential member is "love bombed" with praise and attention.

A major part of the discipling process is to get the potential convert to "confess all sins," not just to God but also to his or her mentor. Numerous cases have been reported that, instead of keeping this information confidential, the mentor simply passes it on up the line to other officials in the church.[103] Rick Bauer, a former high-ranking member of ICC, tells of using embarrassing information against members while part of the organization, and how in one case he found a computer printout of names of a large number of ICC members that listed shocking and private details about their personal sins—"a congregational 'Sin List,' if you will."[104]

Once the new disciple has been baptized and committed to full discipleship in the church, the immediate requirement is to "have no sin in your life." Throughout this entire process, the typical experience for many converts is to be distanced from their old friends and even their families and drawn more and more into ICC church activities, ideas and priorities.

ICC members who tire of the constant pressure, badgering and demands to live up to ICC rules and regulations are told that, if they leave the church, they will go to hell. Members who have doubts or reservations are called in for a session, usually with several church leaders who tell them they are letting God and the church down.

Disenchanted members are compared to a dog returning to its vomit (see Prov. 26:11). The very personal sins they confessed upon joining the church are brought up and rehashed. Then they are accused of not having what it takes to be a disciple—they probably never were Christians in the first place. Often so much pressure is put on a church member who expresses the desire to leave that the member recants the decision out of guilt, fear and confusion.[105] Because of the ICC's oppressive methods, many colleges have banned the ICC from their campuses.[106]

McKean teaches unambiguously that those who oppose or leave the movement leave God. "As for those who continue to oppose us, they are lost—not because their baptism became invalid, but the Scriptures are clear that those who oppose and grumble against God's leaders and divide God's church are, in fact, opposing God" (see Exod. 16:8; Num. 16).[107]

So What's the Difference?

1. Most ICC converts become acquainted with the church by being invited to a Bible study, using the study *First*

Principles: Basic Studies for Making Disciples by McKean. The lesson titled "The Word of God" resembles a conservative evangelical approach, emphasizing verses like 2 Timothy 3:16. However, the slant of this lesson is to discourage "private interpretation," to attack other churches' "traditions or creeds" and to begin limiting critical thinking. See Deuteronomy 17:19; John 5:39; Acts 17:11; Romans 15:4 for clear instructions to "search the Scriptures for yourself." See also 2 Peter 1:20,21 and consult any qualified commentary regarding the phrase "No prophecy of Scripture is a matter of one's own interpretation." What the passage is saying is that prophecy doesn't come from the prophets themselves, it comes from God; it is not forbidding private study and interpretation for oneself.[108]

2. The ICC lesson on the kingdom of God also resembles a standard evangelical approach. The Kingdom that Jesus preached as "at hand" was established through the Church by the apostles in the book of Acts and will be fully established in connection with Christ's Second Coming. But God's kingdom only continues in "true Christian churches," in other words, ICC churches. In contrast, the Bible teaches the unity of the Church and grace for all in the Body of Christ, which is "one in Christ Jesus" (see Gal. 3:26-28; Eph. 4:7-16).

3. An ICC lesson on light and darkness resembles biblical teaching on how sin separates us from God and how only faith in Jesus can save us from God's judgment. However, added to these truths is the doctrine that water baptism actually saves at the time one is baptized! It is baptism that supposedly brings us out of darkness into light and frees us from sins to be totally committed to Christ. In

addition, the ICC maintains that only "disciples," as defined by the ICC, are saved. These doctrines twist Scripture, adding the requirements of the "works" of baptism and "righteous living" to the formula for salvation. The Scriptures clearly teach that faith, not baptism, saves (see John 1:12; 3:16; Eph. 2:8,9). Also see Matthew 16:24 and John 8:31, which describe a disciple as someone who follows Jesus' teachings, not someone who submits to the mandates of a more "mature" Christian. Also, Jesus taught His disciples to serve one another instead of "lording it over each other as the rulers of the Gentiles do" (see Matt. 20:25-28).

4. An ICC lesson on light and darkness denounces common phrases used by evangelicals that are biblically thin, such as the evangelistic appeal to "accept Jesus into your heart." The lesson attacks as completely unbiblical any view of baptism that deviates at all from ICC doctrine, finally insisting that seekers "share" their sins with their assigned spiritual leader. In contrast, the Bible leaves the method and timing of baptism open (see Acts 8:38; 9:18). Also see 1 Peter 3:21, which does not teach that we are saved through baptism but that baptism with water is the vivid symbol of the changed life of a Christian who has peace with God.[109] As for "sharing sins," this practice easily leads to spiritual abuse, especially when confidential information is used later for disciplinary purposes in "breaking sessions," something that many ex-members of the ICC have experienced.[110] The Bible teaches the Christian to confess sins to God, who will cleanse and forgive (see 1 John 1:5-10).

5. An ICC lesson on the Church interprets Hebrews 10:23-25 to mean that all members must attend all the meetings of

the church, whenever and wherever they are held. If an ICC member wants to miss a meeting for any reason, he or she is made to feel guilty and selfish.[111] Hebrews 10:23-25 speaks of spurring one another toward love and good deeds and encouraging one another by meeting together. There is no command to "attend all meetings of a local church."

6. The lesson on discipleship teaches that only disciples of Jesus will be saved, and all true Christians must make disciples. This definition of the word "disciple" turns "salvation by grace through faith" into "salvation by faith plus works," which directly contradicts Ephesians 2:8,9.

Summary

People are attracted to the ICC because the members are highly motivated and committed to practicing what they believe the Bible teaches. Unfortunately, the absolute power the ICC holds over its membership has led to corrupt practices and abuses, which the ICC has admitted and pledged to change. In 1992, McKean and one of his head elders, Al Baird, both wrote articles for the ICC publication *Upside Down*, admitting they were wrong and had made mistakes concerning use of authority. Baird confessed that in ICC discipling relationships, too much emphasis had been put on authority and "too little . . . on motivating out of love for God." He also admitted ICC leaders were wrong in calling for total submission regarding things such as choice of food, cars, clothes and giving money. At the same time, he threw in this qualifying remark: "Leaders should be able to call meetings of the body, call for greater sacrifices, call for specified evangelistic outreach efforts or prayer times, etc."[112]

As the ICC moves into the third millennium, it is hard to say how much "reformation" has gone on regarding abuses of the past, which are thoroughly documented by ICC critics (see appendix A for resources). Even in the late 1990s, some abuses were still going on and Baird's comment about the church still being able to "call for greater sacrifices" and "specified evangelistic outreach efforts, etc.," leaves the door wide open for interpretations that could still lead to abuse. In the words of former ICC leader Rick Bauer: "The system of one-over-one discipling and the control structures employed by Kip McKean are so fundamentally flawed and inherently corrupting that even good people with the best of intentions end up hurting others and being hurt themselves."[113]

SECULAR HUMANISM

Origins/Background

Secular humanism was formally organized as a movement in the first half of the twentieth century, but its roots go back to the explosion of classical learning that occurred during the Renaissance (fourteenth to sixteenth centuries) and even more directly to the Great Enlightenment (seventeenth and eighteenth centuries). Modern science developed through the findings of men like Galileo and Newton. The medieval view of the world and nature was abandoned as people became "enlightened"—in other words, they became "modern" and the age of modernism was born.

As the Enlightenment continued, emphasis began to be placed more on man and less on God. By the eighteenth century, scientists had made such huge strides that it began to appear there was no limit to the power of human reasoning based on scientific fact.

The nineteenth and twentieth centuries have seen an even deeper erosion of belief in a supernatural God who created the universe, as four key movements became all-out enemies of biblical Christianity: the German "higher criticism of the Bible," which overruled any supernatural aspect of the Bible at the outset and reduced it to just another ancient mythological book; the followers of Karl Marx (1818-1883) and his atheistic Communism; those who became enamored with the writings of Charles Darwin (1809-1882), one of the leading exponents of naturalistic evolution—the theory that man evolved from apes, who had in turn evolved from still lower life forms; and those who were taken by the writings of atheistic psychologist Sigmund Freud (1856-1939).

Darwin's theory of natural selection (popularly known as "survival of the fittest") more than strongly suggested the world had not been made by a wise, loving creator with a plan and design. Instead, everything had happened "naturally," which meant God was just an unnecessary hypothesis.[114] That God does not exist became the basic premise of the view that would become secular humanism, although the term did not become widely used until the twentieth century when the American Humanist Association published the *Humanist Manifesto I* in 1933. Ever since that time, secular humanism has been the archenemy of Christianity and any other views that expressed belief in a creator God of any kind.

Teachings/Practices

The *Humanist Manifesto I* included the following basic points:

1. The universe has always existed—it was never created by a "God."
2. In fact, there is no real proof for God; men and women must live as if He does not exist—they must indeed "save themselves."
3. Humankind's chief goal is development of the human personality in this life, which is all there is.
4. There is no objective way to determine morality or what is valuable and useful. The only morality is that which comes out of human experience and experiment. In short, there are no moral absolutes.[115]

Secular humanism's relative ethics and morals are tied to its naive belief in the basic goodness of mankind. Secular humanists assume that everyone—for the most part, anyway—is basically good. Evil doesn't come from within men and women, it comes from without; and if society can be cleaned up and fixed, then evil will disappear.

Secular humanism's predictions of a utopia for mankind suffered severe setbacks when World War II proved (again) how deep mankind can sink into the depths of brutality. By 1973, secular humanists rebounded by publishing *Humanist Manifesto II*, which stubbornly reaffirmed the belief that all moral or ethical truth is relative. Ethics are termed "autonomous and situational," and reason and intelligence are called the most "effective instruments that humankind possesses." *Manifesto II* states that while there is no guarantee that all problems can be answered, critical intelligence, "infused by a sense of human caring," is the best method humanity has for resolving its problems.[116]

Secular humanism is exactly 180 degrees from biblical Christianity. Obviously, the basic difference is that secular humanists say there is no God, while Christians base everything on the existence of a loving Creator who is in charge of the universe and actively involved in running it. When secular humanists say there is no God, all of their conclusions follow, as night has to follow day.

So What's the Difference?

1. Secular humanists are firmly entrenched in a naturalistic/materialist worldview; they flatly state there is no God (atheism). Christians believe in God, the loving supreme creator to whom all mankind is responsible (see Gen. 1:1; Isa. 40:28; Heb. 11:3).

2. Secular humanists claim that man discovers truth by his own reason and logical thinking. Christians respond that

all truth is God's truth and that all of man's discoveries
are only part of what God has created (see Ps. 19:1, Acts
17:24-28; Rom. 1:20).

3. Secular humanists say that in areas that cannot be proved
through human experience or experiment, such as philosophy, religion, ethics and morality, all truth is relative,
that is, truth is a matter of opinion that can differ from
person to person. Christians respond that morals and
ethics are based on God's written Word (see Exod. 21:17)
and His living Word, Jesus Christ (see John 1:1-14).

4. Secular humanists believe that while humans make mistakes, they are not fallen sinners; they must "save themselves" by taking responsibility for their own errors.
Christians contend that humans have fallen because of sin
(see Gen. 3, Rom. 3:23) and their only hope for salvation is
in Christ (see Rom. 8:22-27; 1 Pet. 1:3-7).

Summary

Secular humanism has no set of moral absolutes like the Ten
Commandments. At best, it comes up with numerous "suggestions"
for what people should do, based on their experience in the society in
which they are living and their only court of last resort, which is individual rights. But with no objective and final basis for determining why
anyone should have individual rights, there really is no way to call anything right or wrong. Everything is up for grabs.

Manifesto II trustingly claims that man's goodness will guide him
in using technology for the good of humankind by carefully avoiding
harmful and destructive changes.[117] But again, the humanist faces the
problem of who is to determine what is really good for humankind. In
addition, who will enforce those judgments?[118]

No matter how hard secular humanists try, they cannot avoid arriving at the problem of claiming there are no absolute moral values. Somewhere, someone has to call the shots. The Christian believes God has called the shots and continues to do so. The humanist clings to the belief that human beings can decide what is moral and live peaceful, productive, happy lives. But mankind remains in the same old syndrome. Wars, atrocities, mass shootings and countless other tragedies continue unabated. And secular humanism provides no solution to these problems.

POSTMODERNISM

Origin/Background

The postmodern worldview did not originate with the thinking of any one person or group. Rather, the term emerged during the twentieth century as it began to be used by philosophers, theologians, literary critics, historians and even architects to refer in general to a backlash against the failures of modernism (i.e., secular humanism). Rather than ushering in a predicted Utopia, modernism's scientific wonders and advancements had created institutions and social conditions that were oppressive, burdensome and, at times, tyrannical. Eventually, postmodernism came to the attention of the public through journalists, who used the term to refer to anything from rock videos to the problems of sprawling metropolises plagued with too much crime, decay and overcrowding.[119]

Teachings/Practices

The complex ideas and jargon of postmodernism are not easy to understand, but Christians must try to do so if they are to cope with a foe even more dangerous than secular humanism. Many Christian analysts and observers believe the Church is in the center of a cultural shift that is permeating all of society and that "we are fast becoming a postmodern culture."[120] Basic principles of postmodernism include:

- None of us thinks independently, without bias; we have all been molded by our culture to think in certain ways.
- You cannot judge (pronounce wrong) the thoughts, ideas or actions of another culture or another person because his or her idea of reality is different from yours.
- Each person's reality is in his or her own mind. You construct your own reality. Whatever is real to you is your reality.
- None of us can "prove" anything, whether we use science, history or any other set of facts.[121]

In essence, postmodernism goes beyond modernism, which claims that all moral and ethical truth are relative. Postmodernism says *there is no absolute truth anywhere*. Postmodernists believe that all truth is always changing, whether it is spiritual, moral, political—even scientific truth is suspect.[122] Postmodernists believe all truth is "manufactured," a product of the culture in which we live and the language we use. We are all just "products of our culture, cogs in a social machine."[123]

The postmodern worldview is everywhere today—in the universities, the media, films, TV, even the local PTA. It affects you and your family in a thousand different ways and will increasingly do so in the future. Postmodernism is not easy to understand, but Christians living in the third millennium must learn how to deal with it by recognizing its basic premises and assumptions.

One of the most powerful and dangerous characteristics of the postmodern mind is an absolute dedication to its concept of tolerance. To be tolerant in the traditional sense is to see a difference between what a person thinks or does (which you may not necessarily think is right) and the person himself. While you treat that person with respect, you are also free to say how he thinks, talks or acts is wrong and, in your opinion, should be changed.

Today the new definition of tolerance is spread and promoted by philosophers, educators and other leaders, who give all values and beliefs equal respect and deny categorically there is any such thing as a "hierarchy of truth."[124]

In today's public schools, children and youth are being taught that "what every individual believes or says is equally right, equally valid. So not only does everyone have an equal right to his beliefs, but all beliefs are equal. All values are equal. All lifestyles are equal. All truth claims are equal."[125]

The new definition of tolerance explains why a daughter comes home from college with her new boyfriend and suggests that it will be okay if he sleeps with her in her bedroom; or why a father who says practicing homosexuality is wrong is called a bigot by his teenage son. The new tolerance is why professors find an increasing number of students who know the Holocaust happened but can't bring themselves to say the Nazis were morally wrong. In all of these examples, traditional Christian and biblical morality is questioned and even contradicted. In fact, the new tolerance has proven to be tolerant of everyone except those who say there are objective moral absolutes.[126]

The new tolerance of postmodernism mocks the Christian who says, "Love the sinner, hate the sin." Now you have to love the sinner *and* his sin; or you will be proclaimed a bigot, a racist or a hatemonger. Postmodernists, in short, cannot separate what a person believes or does from who that person is. For the postmodernist, they are one and the same.

So What's the Difference?

1. Postmodernists may or may not admit to the existence of God; but if they do, they usually refer to the "god within" rather than a supreme sovereign creator.[127] Christians

believe God exists outside of His creation and that He is personally and constantly concerned about what and who He has created (see Isa. 40:28-31; Heb. 11:3; Acts 17:24-28).

2. Postmodernists claim society decides what truth is; there is no absolute truth of any kind; not even scientific truth is absolute or trustworthy.[128] In addition, all beliefs and values are "arbitrary social constructs";[129] one set of ideas, no matter how radical or dangerous, is as good as another.[130] Christians believe that ultimate truth is centered in Jesus Christ (see John 14:6) and as they know and abide in that truth they are free to enjoy life to its fullest (see John 8:31,32, 10:7-10).

3. Postmodernism sees "sin" as: (a) intolerance to the views of others (Christian "fundamentalists" excepted); (b) the use of metanarratives (broad explanations of reality) that make the claim of being universal truth but which lead to violence, greed and a thirst for power. Postmodernists see Christianity as just such a metanarrative. In stark contrast, Christians understand sin, which originates in the heart of man, to be mankind's core problem (see Jas. 4:1, Matt. 15:16-20, Ps. 51:5).

Summary

The most compelling argument that Christians can make against postmodernism is to stand on the absolute truth of God's Word. Unfortunately, statistics gathered by Christian and secular pollsters alike more than suggest that not all Christians are sure about absolute truth. Josh McDowell, who has taught biblical principles and apologetics to thousands of teenagers and college students throughout the world, has estimated that 57 percent of *churched* youth do not believe in an objective standard of truth.[131]

According to Christian pollster George Barna, 53 percent of *Bible-believing conservative Christian adults* do not believe in absolute truth.[132] According to a 1997 report in *Christianity Today*, 84 percent of first-year Christian college students find it difficult to adequately defend or explain their beliefs.[133]

From the Gallup poll comes perhaps the most striking statistic of all. Of the 70 percent of Americans who say it is important to follow biblical teachings, *two-thirds of these do not believe in moral absolutes.*[134]

While polls do not necessarily prove anything conclusively, indications are that Christians young and old are being sucked into the postmodern mind-set that all truth is relative and there are no absolutes. They have fallen into this trap, even though they say they believe the Bible and trust Jesus Christ as Savior and Lord.

This lack of commitment to absolute truth has led to a different view of the conscience on the part of many Christians. Right and wrong have been replaced by what "feels right" or praying about some questionable course of action and "feeling at peace about it." As Charles Colson observed, the conscience has become a "barometer of our emotional state" instead of being a strong monitor of moral choices.[135]

What Christians must do above all is make a new commitment to biblical truth and morality. There is absolute truth in the Word of God. There is absolute morality in the teachings of Scripture. And there is the ultimate absolute behind it all—Jesus Christ, who is the way, the truth and the life. (To learn more about postmodernism, see Resources for Further Study, appendix A.)

UNIFICATION CHURCH (THE MOONIES)

Origin/Background

The Holy Spirit Association for the Unification of World Christianity (*Ton-il-Kyo* in Korean, "the Moonies" in popular American usage) is a "new" religion that covers Taoism, Confucianism, occult practices and a messianic figure with a thin veneer of Christianity.

Sun Myung Moon founded the Unification Church in 1954 in Seoul, South Korea. Born in 1920 in what is now North Korea, Moon is the son of Confucian parents who converted to Presbyterianism.[136] However, Moon never fully accepted the Christian faith. From an early age and throughout his life, he was heavily involved in spiritism and the occult.[137]

Moon claims that at age 16 he had a vivid vision of Jesus in which he was told to "complete Jesus' failed mission." Moon says he then spent nine years in the world of the occult, contacting the spirits of Jesus, Confucius, Mohammed and Buddha, all of whom confirmed his evolving knowledge of the truth. During this time, Moon claims to have confronted Satan and forced Satan to reveal the great secret and real cause of the fall of Adam and Eve, namely that Eve had sexual intercourse with Satan and then passed sin on to the human race through sexual relations with Adam. In 1946, Moon found an inspiring theological framework for his occult experiences at the Monastery of Israel (located in North Korea), founded and headed by Baik Moon Kim. Moon's book *The Divine Principle*, which became the authoritative scriptures for the Unification Church, contains teachings very similar to those of Kim.[138]

In a seance conducted by famous spiritist-medium Arthur Ford in 1964, a spirit named "Mr. Fletcher" gave Moon more confirmations of his mission. The Unification Church, realizing that evangelical Christians oppose seances and clairvoyance, has suppressed information about Moon's clairvoyance and medium-inspired "revelations."[139]

Reverend Moon does not consider himself just any spiritual leader; he truly believes he is the Second Coming of the Messiah. In 1960, Moon married for the third time (after two divorces), asserting that this wedding was the "marriage of the Lamb" spoken of in Revelation 21:9 that would usher in "the New Age, the Cosmic Era." In 1972, to reach the entire world with his message, Moon moved from Korea to the United States. He immediately became a media celebrity, mainly due to his public support of President Richard Nixon during the Watergate crisis and his staunch anti-Communism.

A temporary setback happened in 1983 when Moon went to trial for tax evasion. Moon played the suffering innocent, courting the support of numerous church leaders, convincing them he was being persecuted on the basis of his religion and because of racism. He spent 13 months in federal prison.

After his release, on August 29, 1985, Moon revealed for the first time his amazingly grandiose self-image. In a public speech he boasted, "With my emergence as the victorious Lord of the Second Advent for the world, a new order has come into being." These words are obviously a perversion of the biblical promise that Jesus, who came in His first advent as Savior, will come in His second advent as Judge of the world.[140]

Although no official statistics are available, worldwide membership in the Unification Church is estimated at between 1 and 2 million, most of them in Japan and Korea, with perhaps only 10,000 to 30,000 Unification members in "North America."[141]

Teachings/Practices

Two practices by the Unification Church separate it from all other cults: its fund-raising methods and its performance of mass weddings. The Unification Church justifies using deception in fund-raising (called "heavenly deception"), such as having healthy people solicit funds while using wheelchairs. According to Moon, lying to advance the cause of the Unification Church is not a sin because "even God tells lies very often." Moon has boasted in writing about the huge profits he makes on flowers that cost him 80 cents and sell for a $5 "donation." The annual income of the Unification Church of Japan, the United States and Europe in charitable donations is estimated at over $150 million.[142]

The mass weddings performed by Moon and his wife are based on Moon's teachings concerning the fall of mankind. According to Moon's theology, he and his wife are the "true parents" of mankind, and all weddings where they give their blessing will result in "sinless children." A Moon mass wedding involves thousands of couples whose marriages have been arranged by the Unification Church (primarily by Moon himself). Often the bride and groom are total strangers or barely acquainted. In 1995, in one day 300,000 couples were wed in a mass ceremony seen on satellite television in 160 countries. After their wedding, Unification Church couples are required to have 40 days of celibacy, followed by three days of consummation and three years more of celibacy.[143]

So What's the Difference?

1. Unificationists believe that Jesus' real purpose was to save humanity by getting married and having sinless children; that the crucifixion was an unplanned mistake; that salvation through the blood of Christ is ridiculous.[144] The Bible teaches that the central purpose of God in history revolves around the cross, resurrection and ascension of Christ (see Acts 2:23; 1 Pet. 1:19,20; Rev. 13:8).

2. Unificationists believe Rev. Moon united with the perfect bride (wife number three), and in so doing they have become the new "trinity": God, Moon and Mrs. Moon, with their 12 living children beginning a new and perfect race. Unificationists also teach that a thirteenth child, a son whom Moon was grooming to take his place and who died in a car accident in 1984, is the "heavenly Christ" and Moon is the "earthly Christ."[145] The Bible teaches there is only one Lord Jesus Christ, who is not divided between

spirit and body, and that He rose physically from the dead and ascended to the right hand of God (see Mark 16:19; Acts 1:9-11; 2:33; Eph. 1:20; Col. 3:1; Heb. 1:3).

3. Unificationists end their prayers in the name of the True Parents, meaning Reverend and Mrs. Moon, who are said to appear in spirit form to Unification members in various corners of the world. Moonies depend on their works to save them and they believe their spirit ancestors are sent to help them reach their goal of becoming divine.[146] It is in the name of Jesus, not in the name of Moon, that prayers are to be made (see John 15:16; 16:23,24). The Bible also teaches that we are never to go to ancestral spirits, spirit mediums or channelers like Moon for help; we are to rely instead on the guidance of the Word of God and the Holy Spirit (see Deut. 18:9-14; Ps. 19:7-14; John 16:7-15).

4. God is impersonal and dualistic, containing Yang and Yin, positive and negative, white and black, "good" and "evil."[147] In contrast, see 1 John 1:5, which clearly says there is no evil or darkness at all in God, that God is entirely good.

5. The sin in the Garden of Eden was sex. "Eve's eating of the fruit of the knowledge of good and evil denotes that she had consummated a satanic love relationship with the angel (Satan/serpent)." Satan seduced Eve, and then Eve had sex with Adam.[148] The Bible sees sex within marriage as a gift from God, not as a sin; the sin in the garden was disobeying God's clear instructions (see Gen. 3:6,12,13; 1 Cor. 7:5).

6. People are basically good, even divine, but Satan drives them to do evil; people can save themselves through their

own efforts.[149] Compare this with Gal. 2:15; Eph. 2:8,9; Jas. 1:14,15, which show we are not divine (but created by God); we are prone to temptation by our evil desires and our own works cannot save us, but God's grace alone can.

Summary

Sun Myung Moon is a classic example of what sociologist and authority on cults Ronald Enroth describes as being "filled with delusions of messianic grandeur."[150] In Unificationist training materials, Moon is called the "New Messiah, Lord of the Second Advent."[151] But in Matthew 24:5, Jesus has this to say about "new Messiahs": "For many will come in my name, claiming, 'I am the Christ' [or Messiah], and will deceive many."

UNITARIANISM

Origin/Background

The first Unitarians were the Monarchians, a prominent group in the early Church from the middle of the second century to the end of the third, who believed there is no such thing as the Trinity. The Monarchians were soundly refuted, but their Unitarian thinking popped up again in the fourth century in the teachings of the heretic Arius, who claimed Christ was a created being and there was no Trinity. Arius's teachings were condemned at the Council of Nicea in A.D. 325, but Unitarian heresy continued to infect the bloodstream of the Church.

In the sixteenth century, Unitarianism developed among Roman Catholics in Italy and Poland through the teachings of Laelius Socinus and his nephew Faustus Socinus. In the seventeenth century, Unitarian ideas sprang up in England in the teachings of John Biddle (1615-1662). By the eighteenth century, Unitarianism had spread to America through the work of men like Jonathan Mayhew and Charles Chauncey, who helped change Harvard University from its original Christian position to Unitarianism.

One outstanding American Unitarian was William Ellery Channing whose pamphlet on the basic beliefs of Unitarianism became the most well-read pamphlet in America since Thomas Paine wrote *Common Sense* to spark the American Revolution.[152] This led to the formation in 1825 of the American Unitarian Association.

Today all groups with Unitarian beliefs are loosely united as the Unitarian Universalist Association (UUA), which was created in 1961 with the merger of the American Unitarian Association and the Universalist Church of America. According to one estimate, the UUA has just over 200,000 members worldwide, but other surveys show there may be as many as 500,000 Americans who regard themselves as Unitarian/Universalists.[153]

Teachings/Practices

Unitarian thinking formed the basis for liberal theology, which developed rapidly in the eighteenth and nineteenth centuries through the teachings of men like German theologian Friedrich Schleiermacher (1768-1834), who believed there was no transcendent God; instead, man's feelings were his "ground of reality." Jesus was not God but a special man whose feelings of god-consciousness reached the highest perfection.[154] Unitarians and liberals agree, for the most part, on certain key points:

- They do not believe that the Bible is the Word of God, and they reject the Christian doctrines that are derived from it. Some of them say parts of it may contain the Word of God mixed with superstition.
- They do not think of God as a person. They think of Him as a Force, an Oversoul, a Prime Mover or even as being dead.

- They think of Jesus as merely a man, an exceptional man like Moses and Buddha, but no more than a man.
- Their theology constantly changes. Dr. Dana McLean Greeley, a former president of the Unitarians, put it this way, "Actually we Unitarians are changing all the time. And we are not bound by adherence to a particular book—the Bible—or a particular person—even Jesus...."[155]
- They believe that man should not look to God for help, but should be his own savior. Unitarians do not believe that people are sinners; all that is required is to lead a good life and follow the Golden Rule.[156]
- They do not believe there is a heaven or a hell, and there is no need of salvation through Jesus Christ. The very idea of hell is an insult to Unitarians.

Because so much Unitarian thinking puts man above God, it was only natural for Unitarianism to become linked to secular humanism, which became popular during the twentieth century with publication of *The Humanist Manifesto I* and *The Humanist Manifesto II*. Among the many points made in these manifestos are claims that there is no God and that the universe has always existed.

But humanism's blatantly atheistic stance has made Unitarians more and more uncomfortable in recent years, particularly with the rise of many New Age cults embracing Unitarian ideas. The Unitarians have backed away from rationalism and atheistic humanism and moved toward a more "spiritual" position.[157] But by a more "spiritual position," Unitarians hardly mean returning to any kind of biblical belief in God. They have moved instead toward the monistic pantheism of the East, a hallmark of New Age spirituality (see chapter 11).

In moving away from godless humanism and its cold rationalistic approach to making man a "cog in a machine," Unitarians have decided to make the sky the limit in finding spirituality wherever possible, including nature. Neo-pagans are welcome in the UUA.

According to Walter Martin, Unitarians have "warmly embraced the neo-pagan fringe," even accepting Wicca priestesses into their seminaries.[158]

The Unitarian claim that man is basically good and steadily improving is easily refuted, but it remains a source of fundamental concepts found in many of the cults that arose in the nineteenth century, particularly Jehovah's Witnesses and the Mormons.

So What's the Difference?

1. Unitarians claim "the Bible is . . . a myth"[159] and that personal experience, conscience and reason are the final authority.[160] Biblical Christians believe the Bible is the divinely inspired record, not a myth (see Matt. 22:29; 2 Pet. 1:16-21).

2. Unitarians believe "God is one," but by "God" they mean the living processes of nature and conscience at work in mankind; they believe Jesus was special but not God in any Trinitarian sense.[161] Christians believe God is the sovereign creator of everything (see Isa. 64:8; Heb. 11:3) and that Jesus Christ, second person of the Trinity, frequently referred to Himself as God (see John 10:30; 14:9).

3. Unitarians do not believe mankind is born in sin and that God forgives our imperfections.[162] Christians believe man is a sinner, fallen in Adam (see Rom. 3:23; 5:19).

4. Unitarians reject the idea that God sacrificed Jesus "His Son" to atone for human sin, believing instead in salvation by character.[163] Christians believe only Christ's shed blood can atone for sins (see Rom. 3:24,25; Heb. 9:22).

5. Unitarians do not concern themselves with heaven or hell, but concentrate instead on this life only.[164] Christians believe heaven and hell are real, not imaginary (see 2 Thess. 1:7-9; Heb. 9:27).

Summary

While Unitarianism is at odds with biblical Christianity at every point, its weakest link is its claim that man is basically good and steadily improving. There is no doubt that humans are in a moral predicament from which they cannot escape. We want to change, but how can we? We are offered on one hand the answer of the Unitarians (which is the same answer offered by the liberals and the secular humanists). On the other hand, we have the well-known words of Paul the apostle: "Therefore, if anyone is in Christ, he is a new creation; the old is gone, the new has come!" (2 Cor. 5:17). Now that *is* a difference!

WICCA (WITCHCRAFT AND NEO-PAGANISM)

Origin/Background.

The modern religion of Wicca, otherwise known as Old Religion, Magick, Witchcraft, the Craft and the Mysteries, is part of the neo-pagan movement. All branches of the neo-pagan movement attempt to revive the ancient gods and goddesses, mystery cults and nature religions of the Celts, Druids, Egyptians, Greeks, Romans, Sumerians and other peoples.[165] Wiccan and neo-pagan groups draw from many sources, including Gnosticism, occult writings, Freemasonry, Native American religions, shamanism, spiritism and even science fiction.[166]

During the Middle Ages and up through the seventeenth century, witches and satanists were hunted down and killed by Catholics and

Protestants alike.[167] However, Wicca and satanism are very different religions. Modern Wiccans see satanism as a distortion of the relatively new religion of Christianity, while Wicca, with its roots in ancient occult religions such as Druidism, is viewed as a viable worldview in its own right.[168]

The rise of the modern witchcraft movement can be traced to Gerald Gardner (1884-1964), a British archeologist who, in his early career, went to Southeast Asia and studied occult practices. Upon his return to England, he was initiated into European witchcraft. Gardner wrote the novel *High Magic's Aid* (1949) and a descriptive work, *Witchcraft Today* (1954), in which he combined his Asian occult experiences with Western magical texts and developed a new religion with worship of a Mother Goddess as its focus.[169]

Estimates on the number of witches and neo-pagans range from 50,000 to 400,000 worldwide.[170] Wicca is now recognized in the United States as a legitimate religion, protected by law and given tax-exempt status.[171] Wicca is practiced in some branches of the military and has also become popular among teenagers in recent years due to increased media and entertainment attention. In addition, Wicca has infiltrated many mainline Christian denominations, particularly among women influenced by the feminist movement.[172]

Teachings/Practices

Wicca is essentially a nature religion, grounded in reverence for planet Earth, which is seen as a manifestation of the Goddess or "Great Mother." Wicca and neo-paganism are similar in many ways to the nature religions mentioned in the Bible, where many gods were worshiped and religions mixed. For example, the fertility religions of Canaan led many Israelites astray and brought God's wrath upon them (see 1 Kings 14:22-24).[173]

Because there is tremendous diversity among neo-pagans, of which witchcraft is a part, it is hard to say specifically what all witches and other neo-pagans believe. In general, they are anti-authoritarian, refusing to have any centralized authority. They are also against religious dogma; but in creating their own beliefs, neo-pagans mix and match various views and practices to build their own religion. Witchcraft and other kinds of neo-paganism draw heavily from personal experience. Neo-pagans see truth as subjective or relative; the only way you can know any kind of "truth" is through feelings or intuition.[174]

The key ethical principle taught by neo-pagans is called the Wiccan Rede, which can be stated, "Do what thou will, but harm none." Wiccans believe they must "follow their conscience."[175]

Tolerance is possibly the greatest virtue for neo-pagans and witches. They hold animosity toward Christianity for its exclusive claims to be the "only way to God."

Many neo-pagans believe in animism—the idea that the entire Earth is a living organism. The view of some witches is that animism is "the heart and soul" of ancient witchcraft.

Some neo-pagans even believe that inanimate matter is alive (e.g., rocks) and that all objects in the entire universe have some kind of inner or psychological consciousness. Polytheism, pantheism and monism are also worldviews held by many neo-pagans.

Witches celebrate eight primary holidays annually, called *sabbats*, all of which are centered around the solar cycles. Regular coven meetings of witches are called *esbats*. Activities include initiating new members into the coven, training and teaching in witchcraft (divination and magic) and practice of rituals. The esbat is often held during the full or new moon. Witches also practice going into altered states of consciousness and trances. When in a trance, a witch believes he or she is possessed by the Goddess. Common trance states are described as "drawing down the moon" or "drawing down the sun."

Divination, magic and sorcery in psychic abilities are also part of the practices of many neo-pagans and witches. Many of them are also involved in spiritism—interaction with spirits.[176]

So What's the Difference?

1. Regarding revelation, experience is more important than dogma; metaphor and myth more important than doctrine. "In Witchcraft each of us must reveal our own truth" (Starhawk).[177] Compare this idea with Psalm 119:47,72,97,140; 2 Timothy 3:16; Hebrews 4:12.

2. Deity for most neo-pagans is found by recognizing "the divinity of nature and of all living things."[178] Christians worship the creator, not His creation (see Deut. 4:39; Rom. 1:25; Jude 25).

3. Regarding Jesus Christ, witches reject that He was God incarnate or creator of the universe. A typical neo-pagan view of Jesus is that "He was a great white witch and knew the secret of the Coven of Thirteen."[179] In contrast, Christians believe that one of Jesus' names is Emmanuel, which means "God with us" (see Matt. 1:18-22; John 1:1,14,18; 8:24; 14:6; Phil. 2:5,6).

4. Regarding mankind, witches believe in their own divine nature. "Thou art Goddess, thou art God."[180] Christians believe that, although created in God's image (see Gen. 1:26,27) man is fallen and sinful (see Rom. 5:12). Jesus taught that all kinds of evil come from within man, not divinity (see Mark 7:14-23).

5. "Most witches do believe in some form of reincarnation" (Starhawk);[181] however, reincarnation for witches is not the Eastern view but, instead, is seen as something positive that takes the soul upward in its advancement toward godhood.[182] Reincarnation is

anti-biblical and anti-Christian (see 2 Cor. 5:8; Heb. 9:26-28; 2 Pet. 2:9).

6. Some Wiccans balance worship of the Goddess with her consort, the horned god (i.e., Pan). Sex is seen as a gift to be enjoyed without moral guilt. Compare this with 1 Corinthians 6:18-20; 1 Thessalonians 4:3-8.

7. Wiccans have a magical worldview, in which practitioners attempt to influence reality through invoking invisible spirits or powers. "Magic is the craft of witchcraft" (Starhawk).[183] For what God thinks of "magic," see Deuteronomy 18:9-13; Isaiah 8:19.

8. The witch Starhawk sums up the Wiccan view of salvation when she says, "We can open new eyes and see that there is nothing to be saved *from*, no struggle of life *against* the universe, no God outside the world to be feared and obeyed."[184] Of the hundreds of verses Christians could offer in return, John 3:16 may be the best response: "For God so loved the world that he gave his one and only Son, that whoever believes in him shall not perish but have eternal life."

Summary

Witchcraft is only one of several forms of the occult that has a considerable appeal to teenagers. Films and TV shows are built around witchcraft, which is on the increase, particularly among high school and college-age girls and women. The book *Teen Witch: Wicca for a New Generation* by Silver Ravenwolf, is popular among teenagers. Its opening section tells parents that the book is "okay for your children to read" and that the book will explain why witchcraft is one of the "fastest growing religions in America."[185]

Teen Witch promises its young readers that they can explore what it's like to "be a real witch," as they discover how Wiccan mysteries can enhance their lives. The book also tells them how they can make their own magical formulas out of common herbs, create their own sacred space and learn craft techniques for gaining love, money, health, protection and wisdom.[186]

Other forms of occult activity popular among youth today include the Gothic (or Goth) movement and vampirism. (To find sources of more information on witches and other forms of the occult, see appendix A.)

RESOURCES FOR FURTHER STUDY

WORLDVIEWS AND BIBLICAL THEOLOGY

Colson, Charles, and Pearcey, Nancy. *How Now Shall We Live?* Wheaton, IL: Tyndale House Publishers, 1999. Why the Christian worldview is the only rational approach to life today.

Grudem, Wayne. *Systematic Theology: An Introduction to Biblical Doctrine.* Downers Grove, IL: InterVarsity Press, 1994. A "reader friendly" introduction to theology with a strong emphasis on Scripture; nontechnical and practical.

Sire, James. *The Universe Next Door: A Basic Worldview Catalogue*, 3d ed. Downers Grove, IL: InterVarsity Press, 1997. Includes discussions of Christian theism, deism, naturalism, nihilism, existentialism, Eastern pantheistic monism, the New Age and postmodernism.

ROMAN CATHOLICISM AND EASTERN ORTHODOXY

Clendenin, Daniel B. *Eastern Orthodox Christianity: A Western Perspective*. Grand Rapids, MI: Baker Books, 1994. An evangelical scholar's assessment of orthodoxy's pros and cons.

Colson, Charles, and Neuhaus, Richard John. *Evangelicals and Catholics Together: Toward a Common Mission*. Dallas, TX: Word Publishing, 1995. Three leading evangelicals—Charles Colson, Mark Noll and J. I. Packer—exchange views with three leading Catholics, outlining differences and commonalities. Includes the original ECT statement issued in 1994.

Sproul, R. C. *Faith Alone, the Evangelical Doctrine of Justification*. Grand Rapids, MI: Baker Books, 1995. A strong critic of ECT, Sproul explains what the reformers really meant by *sola fide* (faith alone) and *sola gratia* (grace alone).

Ware, Timothy. *The Orthodox Church*, new edition. New York: Penguin Books, 1997. A detailed introduction to the Orthodox Church by an Orthodox bishop.

White, James R. *The Roman Catholic Controversy*. Minneapolis, MN: Bethany House Publishers, 1996. Excellent insights on the differences between Catholics and evangelical Protestants.

For more information on the Orthodox Church, contact the Conciliar Press, P.O. Box 76, Ben Lomond, CA, 95005-0076.

JUDAISM, ISLAM, HINDUISM AND BUDDHISM

Farah, Caesar E. *Islam*. Minneapolis, MN: Barron's Educational Series, 1994.

Langley, Myrtle. *World Religions*. Oxford, England: Lyon Publishing, 1993, chaps. 2, 3, 9, 11.

Martin, Walter. *The Kingdom of the Cults*. Revised, updated, and expanded. Edited by Hank Hanegraaff. Minneapolis, MN: Bethany House, 1997. See chapter 9, "Buddhism"; chapter 14, "Eastern Religions"; and appendix D, "Islam: The Message of Mohammed."

McDowell Josh, and Stewart, Don. *Handbook of Today's Religions*. Nashville, TN: Thomas Nelson Publishers, 1983. Part III, chaps. 1, 3, 8, 9.

Nazir-Ali, Michael. *Islam, A Christian Perspective*. Philadelphia, PA: The Westminster Press, 1983.

Yamamoto, J. Isamu. *Hinduism, TM, & Hare Krishna*. Zondervan Guide to Cults and Religious Movements. Series ed. Alan W. Gomes. Grand Rapids, MI: Zondervan Publishing House, 1998. One of a 16-volume series.

Yamamoto, J. Isamu. *Buddhism, Taoism, & Other Far Eastern Religions*. Zondervan Guide to Cults and Religious Movements.

Series ed. Alan W. Gomes. Grand Rapids, MI: Zondervan Publishing House, 1998.

SECULAR HUMANISM, POSTMODERNISM AND THE NEW AGE

Colson, Charles, and Pearcey, Nancy. *How Now Shall We Live?* Wheaton, IL: Tyndale House Publishers, 1999. Part I, "Worldview: Why It Matters."

Colson, Charles. *Answers to Your Kids' Questions.* Wheaton, IL: Tyndale House Publishers, 2000. "Must" reading for parents and youth leaders on the questions that young people are asking about God's existence, the origin of evil, creation, evolution, biblical accuracy, Jesus' deity, sex, abortion, and mercy killing. The book covers 100 questions in all and is written in language that helps make sense of how to deal with the current secular postmodern culture.

Groothuis, Douglas. *Confronting the New Age.* Downers Grove, IL: InterVarsity Press, 1988. How to understand and witness to those caught up in the New Age movement.

_____. *Unmasking the New Age.* Downers Grove, IL: InterVarsity Press, 1986. How to understand and witness to those caught up in the New Age movement.

_____. *Truth Decay.* Downers Grove, IL: InterVarsity Press, 2000. A powerful, logical defense of Christianity against the challenges of postmodernism. Demanding reading but very worthwhile.

McCallum, Dennis, gen. ed. *The Death of Truth*. Minneapolis, MN: Bethany House Publishers, 1996. An excellent comparison of modernism (secular humanism) and postmodernism with biblical Christianity.

McDowell, Josh, and Hostetler, Bob. *The New Tolerance*. Wheaton, IL: Tyndale House Publishers, 1998. Current illustrations of how postmodernism pressures Christians in every walk of life.

JEHOVAH'S WITNESSES AND MORMONS

Abanes, Richard. *Cults, New Religious Movements and Your Family*. Wheaton, IL: Crossway Books, 1998. See chap. 9, "Mormonism Through the Looking Glass," an excellent overall discussion featuring Joseph Smith's scrying activities and strong critiques of Smith's writings that are considered scripture by Mormons; also see chap. 10, "Jehovah's False Witnesses." Especially strong sections on their continued failure to predict Armageddon.

Blomberg, Craig L., and Robinson, Stephen E. *How Wide the Divide?* Downers Grove, IL: InterVaristy Press, 1997. A good example of the "new Mormonism." Blomberg could have put many issues in sharper contrast rather than allow conclusions by Robinson that suggest Mormons and Christians aren't that far apart.

Bowman Jr., Robert M. *Jehovah's Witnesses*. Zondervan Guide to Cults and Religious Movements. Series ed. Alan W. Gomes. Grand Rapids, MI: Zondervan Publishing House, 1995. An excellent overview of the JWs in succinct outline form, with thorough refutations of JW doctrine from Scripture.

Martin, Walter. *The Kingdom of the Cults*. Revised, updated, and expanded. Edited by Hank Hanegraaff. Minneapolis, MN: Bethany House, 1997. See chap. 6. An exhaustive discussion of all Mormon doctrinal errors by an authority who spent much of his life debating Mormons and helping many of them find the truth in Scripture alone.

Rhodes, Ron. *Reasoning from the Scriptures with the Jehovah's Witnesses*. Eugene, OR: Harvest House Publishers, 1993. Answers virtually every question on JWs.

Scott, Latayne Colvette. *The Mormon Mirage*. Grand Rapids, MI: Zondervan Publishing House, 1979. An eye-opening inside look at Mormonism by a former Mormon, who discusses many topics not covered in this book due to lack of space, including baptism for the dead; the Adam God; blood atonement; temple work; temple garments; the connection between Mormonism and Freemasonry (Joseph Smith was a Mason); the curse of inferiority on those born Black, which barred them from the Mormon priesthood until 1978; the Mormon views of the end times and the true Church.

BAHA'I

Martin, Walter. *The Kingdom of the Cults*. Revised, updated, and expanded. Edited by Hank Hanegraaff. Minneapolis, MN: Bethany House, 1997. See chap. 10, "The Baha'i Faith," updated and edited by Gretchen Passantino. See especially pp. 330, 331 for a summary of how Baha'i operates in the United States.

CHRISTIAN SCIENCE

Ehrenborg, Todd. *Mind Sciences: Christian Science, Religious Science, Unity School of Christianity.* Zondervan Guide to Cults and Religious Movements. Series ed. Alan W. Gomes. Grand Rapids, MI: Zondervan Publishing House, 1995. A thorough treatment of the mind sciences, with copious references.

Martin, Walter. *The Kingdom of the Cults.* Revised, updated, and expanded. Edited by Hank Hanegraaff. Minneapolis, MN: Bethany House, 1997. See chap. 7, "Christian Science." Besides giving extensive quotes from science and health and refutations from Scripture, Martin includes a strong section on the history of Christian Science and where Mary Baker Eddy got her ideas.

EVOLUTIONISM

Johnson, Philip E. *Darwin on Trial.* Downer's Grove, IL: InterVarsity Press, 1991. This book stung the evolutionist community and caused a great deal of discussion among evolutionists and creationists alike. See chaps. 3-7 for devastating reasoning against macro-evolution.

_____. *Reason in the Balance.* Downer's Grove, IL: InterVarsity Press, 1995. This book zeroes in on naturalism as the predominant view in science, law and education. See especially chap. 4, "Is There a Blind Watch Maker?"

_____. *Defeating Darwinism by Opening Minds.* Downer's Grove, IL: InterVarsity Press, 1997. This book offers a good high school education in how to think about evolution—also excellent for college students, parents, teachers, youth workers and pastors.

Colson, Charles, and Pearcey, Nancy. *How Now Shall We Live?* Wheaton, IL: Tyndale House Publishers, 1999. See chaps. 5-14 for excellent discussions of the fallacies of evolutionism.

FREEMASONRY

Campbell, Ron. *Free from Freemasonry*. Ventura, CA: Regal Books, 1999. An in-depth look at the secret society of Freemasonry, extensively documented with Masonic sources.

Mather, George A., and Nichols, Larry. *Masonic Lodge*, Zondervan Guide to Cults and Religious Movements. Series ed. Alan W. Gomes. Grand Rapids: Zondervan Publishing House, 1995. Covers the historical background of Freemasonry and all its theological differences with biblical Christianity.

HARE KRISHNA

Martin, Walter. *The Kingdom of the Cults*. Revised, updated, and expanded. Edited by Hank Hanegraaff. Minneapolis, MN: Bethany House, 1997. See chap. 14, "Eastern Religions," a discussion of ISKCON, Transcendental Meditation and Rajneeshism.

THE INTERNATIONAL CHURCHES OF CHRIST

Branch, Rick. *Watchman Fellowship Profile*. "Boston Church of Christ," Watchman Fellowship, P.O. Box 530842, Birmingham, AL 35253; tel. (205) 871-2858; e-mail: vantagewfi@aol.com.

The Quarterly Journal. Published by Personal Freedom Outreach, P.O. Box 26062, St. Louis, MO 63136; tel. (314) 921-9800. Ask for articles by Stephen Cannon.

The Christian Research Journal, 30162 Tomas, Rancho Santa Marguerita, CA 92688; http://www.equip.org. Ask for articles by Joanne Ruhland or James Bjornstad. Ruhland is in countercult ministry and specializes in ICC. Contact her at Here's Life San Antonio, P.O. Box 12472, San Antonio, TX 78212.

Bauer, Rick. *Toxic Christianity—the International Churches of Christ/Boston Movement Cult.* Bowie, MD: Freedom House Ministries, 1994. An excellent book on the ICC and an inside look at ICC doctrines and methods of intimidation by a former top leader in the organization.

UNIFICATION CHURCH

Abanes, Richard. *Cults, New Religious Movements and Your Family.* Wheaton, IL: Crossway Books, 1998. See chap. 7, "Moonies." Extensive documentation of Moon's warped theology, including his teaching on Jesus Christ's failure to provide salvation, something Moon claims he can do.

Martin, Walter. *The Kingdom of the Cults.* Revised, updated, and expanded. Edited by Hank Hanegraaff. Minneapolis, MN: Bethany House, 1997. See chap. on "Unification Church," Kurt Van Gorden, which thoroughly documents from primary sources the Unification Church's roots and practices.

Yamamoto, J. Isamu. *Unification Church,* Zondervan Guide to Cults and Religious Movements. Series ed. Alan W. Gomes.

Grand Rapids, MI: Zondervan Publishing House, 1995. Covers everything concerning the Unification Church from its history and practices to Moon's theology, which directly contradicts biblical Christianity.

UNITARIANISM

Gomes, Alan W. *Unitarian Universalism*, Zondervan Guide to Cults and Religious Movements. Series ed. Alan W. Gomes. Grand Rapids, MI: Zondervan Publishing House, 1998. Packed with information in brief outline form. The history of Unitarians, plus a complete analysis of their doctrines, with refutations from Scripture.

Martin, Walter. *The Kingdom of the Cults*. Revised, updated, and expanded. Edited by Hank Hanegraaff. Minneapolis, MN: Bethany House, 1997. See appendix E, "Unitarian Universalism," pp. 633ff. A good overall view of Unitarians and Universalists and how they have switched strategies and become quite aggressive in reaction to the so-called "religious right." (See also chaps. on "Scaling the Language Barrier," "The Psychological Structure of Cultism," and "Critiquing Cult Mind Control Model," pp. 27-78.)

WICCA/WITCHCRAFT

Hawkins, Craig S. *Goddess Worship, Witchcraft and Neo-Paganism,* Zondervan Guide to Cults and Religious Movements. Series ed. Alan W. Gomes. Grand Rapids, MI: Zondervan Publishing House, 1995. Presents the history, core beliefs, practices and theology of contemporary witchcraft and other forms of neo-paganism.

For excellent, up-to-date information on how the world of the occult is attracting youth, see *The Watchman Expositor* magazine, vol. 15, No. 6, 1998. To obtain back issues of *The Watchman Expositor*, contact Watchman Fellowship, Inc., P. O. Box 530842, Birmingham, AL 35253; phone: (205) 871-2858; http://www.watchman.org/al.

MINISTRIES FOR INFORMATION ON CULTS

INFORMATION ON CULTS, NEW RELIGIONS, THE OCCULT AND NEW AGE

Religious Information Center
Richard Abanes, President/Founder
P.O. Box 80961, Rancho Santa Margarita, CA 92688
Phone/Fax: (714) 858-8936; E-mail: raric@aol.com

Watchman Fellowship
James Walker, National Director
P.O. Box 13340, Arlington, TX 76094
Phone: (817) 277-0023; Fax: (817) 277-8098; http://www.watchman.org

Spiritual Counterfeits Project
Publications, Journal, Newsletter, Audio and Video Resources
Tal Brooke, President
P.O. Box 4308, Berkeley, CA 94704
Business Phone: (510) 540-0300
Hotline Phone: (510) 540-5767
E-mail: scp@scp-inc.org
Hotmail: access@scp-inc.org
Website: www.scp-inc.org

Personal Freedom Outreach
Kurt Goedelman, President
P.O. Box 26062, St. Louis, MO 63136
Phone: (314) 921-9800

Jude 3 Missions
Kurt Van Gorden, Founder/Director
P.O. Box 1901, Orange, CA 92668
Phone: (714) 247-1850

INFORMATION ON JEHOVAH'S WITNESSES

Witness, Inc.
Duane Magnani, National Director
P.O. Box 597, Clayton, CA 94517
Phone: (510) 672-5979

Reasoning from the Scriptures Ministries
Ron Rhodes, Director
P.O. Box 80087, Rancho Santa Margarita, CA 92688
Phone/Fax: (949) 888-8848; E-mail: ronrhodes@earthlink.net

INFORMATION ON MORMONISM

Utah Lighthouse Ministry
Jerald and Sandra Tanner, Founders/Directors
P.O. Box 1884, Salt Lake City, UT 84110
Phone: (801) 485-8894, Fax: (801) 485-0312
E-mail: ulm@utah-inter.net; http://www.alphamin.org/catalog.html

Mormonism Research Ministries
Bill McKeever, Founder/Director
P.O. Box 20705, El Cajon, CA 92021
Phone/Fax: (619) 447-3873; http://www.mrm.org

ENDNOTES

Introduction

1. George Barna, *Virtual America* (Ventura, CA: Regal Books, 1994), pp. 81-85, 283.
2. See, for example, Episcopalian bishop John S. Spong's "A Call for a New Reformation," available at http://www.dioceseofnewark.org/jsspong.
3. Ronald H. Nash, *Worldviews in Conflict: Choosing Christianity in a World of Ideas* (Grand Rapids, MI: Zondervan Publishing House, 1992), p. 16.
4. For different descriptions of the questions a worldview should answer, see James W. Sire, *The Universe Next Door*, 3rd ed. (Downers Grove, IL: InterVarsity Press, 1997), pp. 17, 18. Also see Nash, *Worldviews In Conflict*, pp. 26-31.
5. Charles Colson and Nancy Pearcey, *How Now Shall We Live?* (Wheaton, IL: Tyndale House Publishers, Inc., 1999), p. 22.
6. For a good discussion of how basic Christian theism answers life's big questions and issues, see James W. Sire, *The Universe Next Door*, pp. 23-38.
7. Wayne Grudem, *Systematic Theology: An Introduction to Biblical Doctrine* (Grand Rapids, MI: Zondervan Publishing House, 1994), p. 857.
8. Ibid., p. 856.
9. Ibid., p. 855.
10. In chapters 2 and 3, we will look at the claims of the Roman Catholic and Roman Orthodox Churches to be the "one true church," descended from the apostles through an "apostolic succession" of a line of bishops.
11. See David B. Barrett and Todd M. Johnson, "Annual Statistical Table of Global Missions: 2000," *International Bulletin of Missionary Research*, vol. 24,

no. 1 (January 2000), p. 25. Among the nearly two billion people Barrett and Johnson put under the label "Christian" are seven ecclesiastical blocs or groups: Roman Catholics (1,056,920,000); Eastern Orthodox (Greek Orthodox and Russian Orthodox, 215,129,000); Protestants (342,035,000); Anglicans (the Church of England and its extensions, including Episcopalians in the U.S., 79,650,000); non-Roman Catholics (groups that separated from the Catholic [universal] Church of the early centuries, including the Copts, the Armenians, the Syrians and the Maronites, 6,688,000); non-white indigenous Christians (including Black or non-White denominations, churches, or movements in the third world, as well as Black evangelicals and Black neo-Pentecostals in the U.S., 379,054,000); Marginal Christians (26,054,000). See David B. Barrett, ed., *World Christian Encyclopedia, A Comparative Study of Churches and Religions in the Modern World, A.D. 1900-2000* (Oxford University Press, 1982), p. 125.

12. Grudem, *Systematic Theology*, p. 853. As theologians have pointed out over the centuries, not all members of visible churches are in the Body of Christ. For example, Marginal Christians, as identified in David Barrett's survey, would not be considered part of the Body of Christ as defined in this book. Barrett defines "Marginal Christians" as followers of para-Christian or quasi-Christian western movements or deviations out of mainline Protestantism, which include pseudo-Christians and New Age cults that do not profess mainstream Protestant christo-centric doctrine, but claim a second or supplementary or ongoing source of divine revelation in addition to the Bible. See Barrett, *World Christian Encyclopedia*, p. 125.

Chapter 1

1. Readers who are sensitive to the use of gender-based terms to describe both genders may prefer the word "humankind" to "mankind." Throughout this revised edition, effort is made to be generically up-to-date, but in some instances the word "man," "men" or "mankind" is used in reference to all of humanity, both men and women. See Gen. 5:2: "He created them male and female, and He blessed them and named them Man in the day when they were created" (*NASB*).

2. See Luke 22:66-70.

3. See C.S. Lewis, "Rival Conceptions of God," in *Mere Christianity* (1943; reprint, New York: Macmillan Press, 1980), p. 56.

4. Wayne Grudem, *Systematic Theology: An Introduction to Biblical Doctrine* (Grand Rapids, MI: Zondervan Publishing House, 1994), p. 530.

5. Ibid.

6. James Strong, *The New Strong's Concordance of the Bible* (Nashville, TN: Thomas Nelson Publishers, 1984).

7. For two more examples, see Matt 28:19; 2 Cor. 13:14.

8. In Acts 1:1, the author recaps what Jesus "began to do" during His earthly ministry, how Jesus' work was continued through the Holy Spirit (see Acts 1:6-8 and the rest of the book). For other passages stating that the Holy Spirit is God or equal to God, see Acts 5:3-4; 1 Cor. 2:10-11; 12:4-6; 2 Cor. 13:14; 1 Pet. 1:2; Jude 20-21.

9. Grudem, *Systematic Theology*, p. 255. For a thorough discussion of the doctrine of the Trinity, see Grudem's entire chapter, pp. 226-261.

10. Everett F. Harrison, Geoffrey W. Bromiley, Carl F. H. Henry, eds., *Baker Dictionary of Theology* (Grand Rapids, MI: Baker Book House, 1960), p. 532.

11. Ibid., p. 450.

12. For more on the hope the Christian has because of the Resurrection, see all of 1 Cor. 15; also see 2 Cor. 4:14.

13. J. D. Douglas, ed., *The New International Dictionary of the Christian Church* (Grand Rapids, MI: Zondervan Publishing House, 1978), p. 840.

14. While all three major branches agree that Adam acted as "federal head," Eastern Orthodox theologians hold a different view of the result of the Fall, claiming that it got man "off the path to deification" rather than plunging him into total depravity (see chapter 4).

15. Grudem, "The Doctrine of Inherited Sin," section C in *Systematic Theology*, pp. 494-498.

16. Ibid., p. 497.

17. J. B. Phillips, *Letters to Young Churches* (New York: The Macmillan Company, 1950), p. xii.

18. Peter Stoner, *Science Speaks* (Chicago: Moody Press, 1963), quoted in Josh McDowell, *Evidence That Demands a Verdict*, vol. 1 (San Bernardino: Here's Life Publishers, Inc., 1979, 1991), pp. 166, 167. For many more examples of fulfilled Bible prophecy, see all of chapter 9, which covers messianic prophecies, as well as chapter 11, "Prophecy Fulfilled in History."

19. McDowell, *Evidence*. p. 65.

20. McDowell, *Evidence*, p. 65. Also see all of "Part II—Confirmation by Archaeology" in *Evidence*.

21. Phillips, *Letters*, p. xii.

22. For other references to what Jesus said about Scriptures, see Matt 4:4; 5:18.

Chapter 2

1. In this chapter, the terms "evangelical Protestant," "evangelical" and "Protestant" refer only to Christians who follow the teachings of the sixteenth-century Reformers who tried to get the Roman Catholic Church to return to the biblical Christianity of the first century.

2. "The Council of Trent Documents, Fourth Session," *Decree Concerning the Canonical Scriptures.*

3. Among the scriptural proof texts Rome uses for its teachings concerning Sacred Tradition is 2 Thessalonians 2:15, where Paul told the Thessalonians to hold to the traditions which they had been taught. Evangelical Protestants believe Paul was clearly referring to traditions that had already been delivered to believing Christians—the gospel message. Much of what Rome calls Sacred Tradition (150 volumes of material) developed well after the first century, but it is still put on a par with Scripture because Catholic scholars claim that "the Church is always advancing towards . . . divine truth." See Austin Flannery, ed. *Vatican Council II, The Conciliar and Post Conciliar Documents, Dei Verbum* (1975; reprint, North Port, NY: Costello Publishing Co., 1996), p. 754.

4. For more on the Catholic view of Scripture plus tradition, see the *Catechism of the Catholic Church (CCC)* (New York: Doubleday, 1995), paragraphs 74-83.

5. For a thorough discussion of what *sola scriptura* is and is not, see James R. White, *The Roman Catholic Controversy* (Minneapolis, MN: Bethany House Publishers, 1996), pp. 55-67.

6. Flannery, *Vatican Council II*, p. 758.

7. *CCC*, paragraphs 881, 882. In addition, since the decree of Vatican Council I in 1870, the pope enjoys infallibility "in virtue of his office, when as supreme pastor and teacher of all the faithful . . . he proclaims by a definitive act a doctrine pertaining to faith and morals," see paragraph 891.

8. For one of the best discussions of claims of the papacy concerning the primacy of Peter, see White, *Controversy*, chapter 8.

9. Ibid., pp. 78, 79.

10. *CCC*, paragraph 405.

11. Ibid., paragraph 1519.

12. Ibid., pararaphs 1590-1600; see also Anthony Wilhelm, *Christ Among Us* (New York: Paulist Press, 1973), pp. 348, 349.

13. *CCC*, paragraph 1374, which also notes the Council of Trent (A.D. 1551).

14. Ibid., paragraphs 1365-1367.

15. Wilhelm, *Christ Among Us*, p. 249.

16. *CCC*, paragraphs 1857-1861.

17. Wilhelm, *Christ Among Us*, pp. 298-307.

18. *CCC*, paragraphs 1862, 1863.

19. Wilhelm, *Christ Among Us*, pp. 284, 285.

20. *CCC*, paragraph 1863.

21. Ibid., paragraph 1459.

22. Ibid., paragraph 1460.

23. Wilhelm, *Christ Among Us*, pp. 306, 307.

24. CCC, paragraph 1992.

25. In direct refutation of Protestant teaching, the Council of Trent proclaimed that anyone believing the sacraments of the Roman Catholic Church were not necessary for salvation and they could obtain justification through faith alone was *anathema* (see Council of Trent, canons 9, 12, 14). See also CCC, paragraph 1993.

26. Mario Colacci, *The Doctrinal Conflict Between Roman Catholic and Protestant Christianity* (Minneapolis, MN: T. S. Denison and Company, Inc., 1962), pp. 140-142.

27. Karl Keating, *Catholicism and Fundamentalism* (San Francisco: Ignatius Press, 1988), pp. 167, 168.

28. Everett F. Harrison, Geoffrey Harrison, Geoffrey Bromiley and Carl F. H. Henry, eds., *Biblical Dictionary of Theology* (Grand Rapids, MI: Baker Book House, 1960), p. 282.

29. A key passage on sanctification is Romans 6:11-14. Christians consider themselves dead to sin and alive to God; sin need never again be the Christian's master.

30. Wayne Grudem, *Systematic Theology: An Introduction to Biblical Doctrine* (Grand Rapids, MI: Zondervan Publishing House, 1994), p. 748. Grudem points out that the view of sanctification as a lifelong process generally is held among most Christians today. There are groups, particularly in the Wesleyan/Holiness tradition, who believe in achieving "entire sanctification" or "sinless perfection." For a good discussion of why most of the Christian Church believes sanctification cannot be completed in this life, see pp. 748-753.

31. Wilhelm, *Christ Among Us*, p. 420.

32. CCC, paragraphs 1479, 1498.

33. Ibid., paragraphs 1476, 1477.

34. Colacci, *Conflict*, p. 157.

35. Luke 1:28, *(KJV)*.

36. Colacci, *Conflict*, pp. 188, 189.

37. Mary's lifelong virginity was proclaimed official Church doctrine at the Fifth Ecumenical Council in 553.

38. In his encyclical of September 22, 1891, Pope Leo said, "Mary is this glorious intermediary" to whom were directed the prayers and praises of "many hundreds of thousands of pious people . . . saluting Mary, invoking Mary, hoping everything through Mary." Other encyclicals released by Pope Leo—in 1892 and 1894—also spoke of Mary in Mediatrix terms. In 1904, Pope Pius X spoke of how Mary "has been associated by Jesus Christ and the work of redemption," and in 1954 Pope Pius XII described Mary as Christ's "associate in the redemption." See White, *Controversy*, pp. 212-216.

39. Flannery, *Vatican Council II*, pp. 418, 419.
40. Charles Colson and Richard John Neuhaus, *Evangelicals and Catholics Together Toward a Common Mission* (Dallas, TX: Word Publishing, 1995), p. xviii.
41. "The Gift of Salvation," *Christianity Today* (December 8, 1997), p. 36.
42. Ibid., p. 38.
43. Douglas A. Sweeney, "Reformation Day Celebrations Ain't What They Used to Be," *Christianity Today* (November 1, 1999). Available on the Internet at *www.christianityToday.com*. Also available on the site is the entire Joint Declaration on the Doctrine of Justification.
44. David W. Cloud, "Liberal Lutherans and Roman Catholics Agree to Deny the Gospel," (Oak Harbor, WA: Fundamental Baptist News Service, 1997). Available on the Internet at http://wayoflife.org/—dcloud.
45. Flannery, *Vatican Council II*, paragraph 755.
46. Ibid., paragraphs 755, 756.

Chapter 3

1. The 6 million estimate is from Thomas Doulis, ed., *Journeys to Orthodoxy: A Collection of Essays by Converts to Orthodox Christianity* (Minneapolis, MN: Light and Life, 1986), p. 7, quoted in Daniel Clendenin, *Eastern Orthodox Christianity: A Western Perspective* (Grand Rapids, MI: Baker Books, 1994), p. 17. In 1997 Clendenin, a Protestant scholar and writer who has studied Orthodoxy extensively, estimated that the number of Orthodox believers in the United States was 3 million—see Daniel Clendenin, "Why I'm Not Orthodox," *Christianity Today* (Jan. 6, 1997), p. 34.
2. Nine other autocephalous Orthodox churches can also be found in Russia, Serbia, Romania, Bulgaria, Georgia, Cyprus, Greece, Poland and Albania. In addition, Orthodox churches exist throughout the world—particularly in Western Europe, North and South America and Australia.
3. Orthodox theologian and historian Timothy Ware has estimated that there could be over 200 million Orthodox believers—see Ware's estimates for different Orthodox churches on pp. 6, 7 of his book *The Orthodox Church* (London: Penguin Books, 1997). Daniel Clendenin estimates the number of Orthodox believers worldwide at 185 million—see Clendenin, *Eastern Orthodox Christianity*, p. 7. David B. Barrett, research professor of Missiometrics, Regent University, Virginia Beach, gives the figure of 215,129,000 Orthodox believers worldwide in the year 2000 (see *International Bulletin of Missionary Research*, vol. 24, no. 1 [January 2000], p. 25).
4. Ware, *Orthodox Church*, p. 7.
5. Ibid., p. 246.
6. Clendenin, *Eastern Orthodox*, p. 32.

7. Ware, *Orthodox Church*, p. 27.

8. For more on how Catholics, Orthodox and Protestants see apostolic succession and the early history of the Church, see Mark A. Noll, *Turning Points* (Grand Rapids, MI: Baker Books, 1997), pp. 33, 34; see also Richard E. Higginson, "Apostolic Succession," in Harrison, Bromiley, and Henry, eds., *Baker's Dictionary of Theology*, p. 60.

9. Clendenin, *Eastern Orthodox*, pp. 106, 107.

10. Ware, *Orthodox Church*, p. 199.

11. Ibid., p. 199.

12. Clendenin, *Eastern Orthodox*, p. 105.

13. This is a statement by Orthodox theologian Georgii Florovsky, quoted in Clendenin, *Eastern Orthodox*, p. 105.

14. Don Fairbairn, "Partakers of the Divine Nature: An Introduction to Eastern Orthodox Thought," an unpublished paper prepared for Christian workers doing evangelism and discipleship in the former Soviet Union, March 1993, pp. 4, 5.

15. Reverend Thomas Fitzgerald, "The Holy Eucharist" (Brookline, MA: Greek Orthodox Archdiocese of America, department of Religoius Education, n.d.), n.p.

16. Ware, *Orthodox Church*, p. 286.

17. Ibid., pp. 285-287.

18. Ibid., pp. 289, 290.

19. When an Orthodox believer once asked his priest why the Church did not do more teaching of doctrine, he responded, "Icons teach us all that we need to know." See Daniel Clendenin, "Why I'm Not Orthodox," *Christianity Today* (January 6, 1997), p. 37.

20. Clendenin, *Eastern Orthodox*, p. 132.

21. Fairbairn, "Partakers," p. 32.

22. Ware, *Orthodox Church*, p. 231.

23. Orthodoxy contends that, while Christians might become "gods," they still have a human nature. Becoming a partaker of the divine nature does not mean you become a divine being. See Clendenin, *Eastern Orthodox*, p. 130.

24. Fairbairn, "Partakers," p. 46.

25. Ibid.

26. Ibid., p. 47.

27. Clendenin, *Eastern Orthodox*, p. 18.

28. Ware, *Orthodox Church*, p. 308.

29. See, for example, James S. Cutsinger, ed., *Reclaiming the Great Tradition: Evangelicals, Catholics, and Orthodox in Dialogue* (Downers Grove, IL: InterVarsity Press, 1997).

30. Clendenin, "A Hermeneutic of Love," chap. 7 in *Eastern Orthodox*, pp. 139-159.

31. C. S. Lewis, *Mere Christianity* (New York: Macmillan, 1943), p. viii.

32. Archimandrite Chrysostomos, *Contemporary Eastern Orthodox Thought: The Traditionalist Voice* (Belmont, MA: Duechervertriesbanstalt, 1982), p. 104.
33. The Orthodox particularly stress Early Church father Irenaeus, *Against Heresies*, 324.
34. Panagiotes Chrestou, *Partakers of God* (Brookline, MA: Holy Cross Orthodox, 1984), pp. 19, 20, 28.

Chapter 4

1. Rabbi Morris N. Kertzer, revised by Lawrence A. Hoffman, *What Is a Jew?* (New York: Collier Books, McMillan Publishing Co., 1993). After the death of King Solomon about 922 B.C., the Israelites were divided into two kingdoms: the northern part called Israel, the southern part called Judah. In 721 B.C., the Assyrians swept down on the northern kingdom (Israel) and scattered its people. The only Hebrew people left were Judeans, who lived in the southern kingdom of Judah. From that time on, those who had been known as Hebrews were called Jews, an abbreviation of Judeans.
2. A. Cohen, *Everyman's Talmud* (New York: Schoken Books, 1949), p. xvi.
3. Mordell Klein, comp., *Passover* (New York: Leon Amiel, Publishers, 1973).
4. David Chernoff, *Messianic Judaism: Questions and Answers* (Havertown, PA: MMI Publishing Co., 1990), p. 8.
5. Gary Thomas, "The Lord Is Gathering His People," *Charisma Magazine* (April 1997), p. 54.

Chapter 5

1. Caesar E. Farah, *Islam* (Minneapolis, MN: Barron's Educational Series, Inc., 1994), pp. 5, 6.
2. Myrtle Langley, *World Religions* (Oxford: Lion Publishing, 1993), p. 84.
3. Farah, *Islam*, p. 41.
4. See, for example, Surah 4.171 in the Qur'an. See also Michael Nazir-Ali, *Islam, A Christian Perspective* (Philadelphia: The Westminster Press, 1983), p. 15.
5. Surah 96:1-5, quoted in Farah, *Islam*, p. 39.
6. Farah, *Islam*, pp. 39, 40.
7. Ibid., p. 38.
8. Kenneth Boa, *Cults, World Religions, and You* (Wheaton, IL: Victor Books, 1977), p. 52, quoted in Josh McDowell and Don Stewart, *Handbook of Today's Religions* (Nashville, TN: Thomas Nelson Publishers, 1983), p. 387.
9. Farah, *Islam*, p. 157.
10. Boa, *Cults*, p. 52, quoted in McDowell and Stewart, *Handbook*, p. 387.

11. McDowell and Stewart, *Handbook*, p. 386.
12. Ibid., pp. 389, 390.
13. Langley, *World Religions*, p. 89.
14. McDowell and Stewart, *Handbook*, pp. 390-392.
15. Ibid., p. 393.
16. The theories on Judas replacing Christ on the Cross, Jesus' translation to heaven before the Crucifixion and Jesus' return to Earth to comfort His mother and the Apostles are found in most approved Muslim commentaries. See, for example, George Sale, *The Koran, With Preliminary Discourse* (London: F. Warne and Co., n.d.), pp. 38, 39.
17. Nazir-Ali, *Islam, a Christian Perspective*, pp. 17, 18.
18. For extensive documentation of this fact, see Bat Ye'or, trans. Miriam Kochan and David Littman, *The Decline of Eastern Christianity Under Islam: From Jihad to Dhimmitude, Seventh-Twentieth Century* (Cranbury, NJ: Associated University Presses, 1996, first published in French in 1991).
19. Muslim leaders living in the United States claim they have to deal constantly with correcting "misinformation and stereotypes" about Islam. See, for example, Brad Bonhal, "In the Name of Islam, in the Name of Love," *Los Angeles Times* , August 11, 1996, p. E1. Other reports clearly document that persecution of Christians by Muslims does go on, especially in Muslim countries. See Ralph Kinney Bennett, "The Global War on Christians," *Reader's Digest*, August 1997, p. 51; John Daniszewski, "Mideast Christians Feel Persecuted," *Los Angeles Times*, August 14, 1997, p. 1.
20. Marcus Mabry, "The Price Tag of Freedom," *Newsweek* (May 3, 1999), pp. 50, 51.
21. "The New Religious Movements page on the Nation of Islam," part of the *Religious Movements Homepage of the University of Virginia* located at http://virginia.edu/^jkh8x/soc257/nrms/islm.html.

Chapter 6

1. The Western world includes Europe, North and South America, Australia and New Zealand.
2. Donald A. McGavran, *Ethnic Realities in the Church: Lessons From India* (South Pasadena, CA: William Carey Library, 1978), chap. 1.
3. Joseph Padinjarekara, *Christ in Ancient Vedas* (Burlington, Ontario, Canada: Welch Publishing Co., 1991), p. 34.
4. Swami Prabhavananda and Frederick Manchester, *The Upanishads, Breath of the Eternal* (New York: Mentor Books, New American Library, 1975), p. 9, quoted in Joseph Padinjarekara, *Christ in Ancient Vedas* (Burlington, Ontario, Canada: Welch Publishing Co., 1991), p. 35.

5. Vishal Mangalwadi, "Can Hindutva Survive the Persecution of Christians in India?" *Mission Frontiers* (March-April 1999), p. 24.
6. *Funk and Wagnall's New Encyclopedia*, 1971, s. v. "Hinduism."
7. See Washington State University's website, which gives a brief description of Brahman and atman, http://www.wsu.edu:8080/~dee/GLOSSARY/BRAH-MAN.HTM (accessed 11/21/00).
8. *Funk and Wagnalls New Encyclopedia*, 1971, s.v. "Hinduism."
9. *Funk and Wagnalls New Encyclopedia*, 1971, s.v. "Puranas."
10. The Canaanite religion was corrupt and brutal, including prostitution practiced by both sexes and infant sacrifice. For these and other evils God commanded the Israelites to exterminate the inhabitants of Canaan, and because they did not completely do so, they paid the price in later years. See Charles Caldwell Ryrie, "Introduction to the Book of Joshua," *The Ryrie Study Bible* (Chicago, IL: Moody Press, 1978), p. 326.
11. J. Isamu Yamamoto, *Hinduism, TM and Hare Krishna*, Zondervan Guide to Cults and Religious Movements, series ed. Alan W. Gomes (Grand Rapids, MI: Zondervan Publishing House, 1998), p. 13.
12. Swami Prabhavananda, *The Sermon on the Mount According to Vedanta* (Hollywood, CA: Vedanta Press, 1972).
13. Ibid.
14. *Mahatma Gandhi Autobiography* (Washington, DC: Public Affairs Press, 1948), p. 170.
15. Ibid.
16. These incarnations (avatars) included a fish, a tortoise, a boar and a man-lion, as well as different human forms, including Siddhartha Gautama, the founder of Buddhism Kalki; the tenth *avatar* is yet to come. See Myrtle Langley, *World Religions: A Guide to Faiths That Shaped the World* (West Oxford: Lyon Publishing plc, 1993), p. 22.
17. Cited by S. H. Kellogg, *A Handbook of Comparative Religions* (Philadelphia, PA: Westminster, 1899), p. 30.
18. Yamamoto, *Hinduism, TM and Hare Krishna*, pp. 55, 85.
19. Yogananda, Paramahansa, *Autobiography of a Yogi* (Los Angeles, CA: Self-Realization Fellowship, 1972), pp. 195, 196.
20. Ibid.

Chapter 7

1. Josh McDowell and Don Stewart, *Handbook of Today's Religions* (Nashville, TN: Thomas Nelson Publishers, 1983), pp. 304-306.
2. David B. Barrett and Tom M. Johnson, "Annual Statistical Table on Global Missions: 2000," *International Bulletin of Missionary Research*, vol. 24,

no. 1 (January 2000). The estimated number of Buddhists in the world by Barrett and Johnson in 2000 is 359,982,000.

3. Myrtle Langley, *World Religions: A Guide to the Faiths That Shape the World*, p. 30.
4. Ibid.
5. Yamamoto, *Buddhism, Taoism & Other Far Eastern Religions*, p. 15.
6. McDowell and Stewart, *Handbook*, p. 318.
7. Walter Martin, *Kingdom of the Cults, Revised, Updated and Expanded*, ed. Hank Hanagraaff (Minneapolis, MN: Bethany House Publishers, 1997), p. 302.
8. For more on Buddhism, see *Funk and Wagnalls New Encyclopedia*, 1971, s.v. "Buddha," "Buddhism."
9. George A. Mather and Larry A. Nichols, *Dictionary of Cults, Sects, Religions and the Occult* (Grand Rapids, MI: Zondervan Publishing House, 1993), p. 45.
10. Ibid., p. 46.

Chapter 8

1. Walter Martin, *The Rise of the Cults* (Grand Rapids, MI: Zondervan Publishing House, 1955), pp. 11, 12.
2. Martin, *Kingdom of the Cults, Revised, Updated and Expanded*, ed. Hank Hanagraaff (Minneapolis, MN: Bethany House Publishers, 1997), p. 17.

Chapter 9

1. Latest statistics are taken from the "1998 Report of Jehovah's Witnesses Worldwide," posted on the official Watchtower Society internet web site, http://www.watchtower.org.statistics.
2. Ibid.
3. For quotations from JW publications, see Ronald Enroth, ed., *Evangelizing the Cults* (Ann Arbor, MI: Servant Publications, 1990), p. 121.
4. Richard Abanes, *Cults, New Religious Movements and Your Family* (Wheaton, IL: Crossway Books, 1998), pp. 229-231.
5. Martin, *Kingdom of the Cults*, p. 80; also see Mather and Nichols, *Dictionary of Cults*, p. 148.
6. Martin, *Kingdom of the Cults*, pp. 83-87.
7. For Russell's complete quote, see Martin, *Kingdom of the Cults*, p. 87.
8. Abanes, *Cults*, pp. 235, 237.
9. The name Jehovah does not actually appear in the Bible; it is the anglicization of the Hebrew consonants JHVH (referred to as the Tetragramaton), which writers of Old Testament Hebrew used when referring to the Lord God.
10. The Jehovah Witness's teaching that only 144,000 will go to heaven is based on an erroneous interpretation of Rev. 7:4-8. The passage clearly refers to the twelve tribes of Israel, 12,000 from each tribe, which are clearly named and listed.

11. Ron Carlson and Ed Decker, *Fast Facts on False Teachings* (Eugene, OR: Harvest House Publishers, 1994), p. 126.

12. For example, in 1938, the WTBTS advised all JWs not to marry or have children. Instead, they should spend all their time working for the coming kingdom, which they would enjoy after surviving Armageddon. See Abanes, *Cults*, p. 239.

13. For citations of various Watchtower publications that began teaching the 1975 date for Armageddon, see Abanes, *Cults*, pp. 240, 241.

14. For quotes from Watchtower publications pushing the 1975 date for Armageddon and again advising JWs not to marry, have children or even pursue careers, see Abanes, *Cults*, pp. 240, 241.

15. For the verbatim transcript of Franz's admission, which amounted to perjury, see Martin, *Kingdom of the Cults*, p. 124.

16. Abanes, *Cults*, pp. 241, 242.

17. Ibid., pp. 242, 243.

18. For just a few references, see Deut 13:5; 18:22; Isa. 9:15; Jer. 2:8; Hos. 9:7; Matt. 7:15; 24:11; Mark 13:22.

19. Abanes, *Cults*, pp. 243-252, especially the famous JW analogy concerning "tacking into the wind," which they use to excuse their many mistakes on prophecy as well as their doctrinal flip flops on any number of subjects, including vaccinations and organ transplants.

20. *Awake!* (May 8, 1951), p. 26.

21. For a side-by-side comparison of Russell's teachings with the Watchtower's teachings today, see Martin, *Kingdom*, pp. 107-110.

22. James Bjornstad, *Counterfeits at Your Door* (Ventura, CA: Regal Books, 1979), p. 78.

23. Ibid., pp. 80, 81.

24. Abanes, *Cults*, p. 253ff. Also see Abanes' excellent discussion of "blessed Trinity," appendix A, pp. 265-268.

25. The JW version of the Virgin birth is taught in the Watchtower book *The Kingdom Is At Hand*, p. 49. See also Bjornstad, *Counterfeits*, p. 66.

26. Bjornstad, *Counterfeits*, pp. 66, 67.

27. For a thorough discussion of the claim by Jehovah's Witnesses claim that Jesus is Michael the archangel, see Bjornstad, chap. 6, "What Do They Say About Jesus?" *Counterfeits*, pp. 65-76.

28. Walter Martin observes that JWs like to point out that the New English Bible also refers to the word as "a god," thereby giving their translation some credence. Martin joins any other number of Greek scholars in saying, however, that the *NEB* simply mistranslates the passage. See Martin, *Kingdom of the Cults*, p. 141.

29. See Ron Rhodes, *Reasoning from the Scriptures with the Jehovah's Witnesses* (Eugene, OR: Harvest House Publishers, 1993), p. 103-104. Walter Martin's

interview of Dr. Mantey appeared in Christian Research Newsletter, 3:3, p. 5.

30. Ibid., p. 129. See also Robert M. Bowman, Jr., *Jehovah's Witnesses*, Zondervan Guide to Cults and Religious Movements, series ed. Alan Gomes (Grand Rapids, MI: Zondervan Publishing House, 1995), pp. 24, 25, for a thorough discussion of why, in the Greek, the presence or absence of the definite article does not alter the fundamental meaning of a noun.

31. For another classic example of an *NWT* mistranslation to try to make Christ less than God, see Martin, *Kingdom*, pp. 118, 119, where he discusses Phil. 2:5-11. The correct translation of Phil. 2:6 says Christ, "being in very nature God, did not consider equality with God something to be grasped." The NWT changes the Greek to read "was not ambitious to become equal with His Father."

32. For a comparison of Russell's teachings with current JW doctrine on the Resurrection, see Martin, *Kingdom of the Cults*, pp. 108, 109.

33. Bjornstad, "What Is Re-Creation?" chap. 9 in *Counterfeits*, pp. 93, 94.

34. Passantino, "Jehovah's Witnesses," *Evangelizing*, p. 133.

35. For five examples of Watchtower errors regarding the Holy Spirit, see Martin, *Kingdom*, pp. 102, 103.

36. Wesley Walters and Kurt Goedelman, "Jehovah's Witnesses," quoted in *A Guide to Cults and New Religions* (Downers Grove, IL: InterVarsity Press, 1983) p. 109. For more references, see Robert M. Bowman, Jr., *Jehovah's Witnesses*, pp. 29, 30.

37. Bjornstad, *Counterfeits*, p. 87.

38. For examples of Jehovah's Witness erroneous teaching on the atonement, see Martin, *Kingdom of the Cults*, pp. 103, 104. Also see Bjornstad, *Counterfeits*, pp. 85-87.

39. *The Watchtower* (October 15, 1958), pp. 614, 615, quoted in "Jehovah's Witnesses Good News," http://home.sol.no/~norhov/Incredib.htm.

40. Anthony A. Hoekema, *Jehovah's Witnesses* (Grand Rapids, MI: Wm. B. Eerdmans Publishing Co., 1963), p. 107.

41. The events of the Last Days, according to JWs, are discussed at length with proper citations from Watchtower publications by Anthony Hoekema, *Jehovah's Witnesses*, pp. 108-121.

42. Description of the JWs' five-meeting-a-week schedule taken from *Jehovah's Witnesses in the Twentieth Century*, quoted in Martin, *Kingdom of the Cults*, p. 96.

43. Martin, *Kingdom*, p. 165.

44. *The Watchtower* (January 15, 1983), pp. 22, 27.

45. *The Watchtower* (May 1, 1972), p. 272.

46. *Let God Be True*, rev. ed. (Brooklyn, NY: Watchtower Society, 1952). Presents a summary of doctrines taught by Jehovah's Witnesses.

47. *The Truth Shall Make You Free* (Brooklyn, NY: Watchtower Society, 1943).
48. *Let God*, p. 276.
49. Abanes, *Cults*, p. 253; see also appendix A, "Blessed Trinity," pp. 265-268.
50. *The Watchtower* (July 1, 1947), p. 204.
51. Charles Taze Russell, *Studies in the Scriptures*, vol. 2 (Brooklyn, NY: Watchtower Bible and Tract Society, 1886-1917), p. 191.
52. *Let God*, p. 68.
53. *You Can Live Forever in Paradise on Earth* (Brooklyn, NY: Watchtower Bible and Tract Society, 1982), p. 77.

Chapter 10

1. Statistics published by Adherents.com, "Religious Bodies of the World with at Least 1 Million Adherents," http://www.adherents.com/adh_rb.-html, which lists the LDS Church at 10,600,000 as of September 14, 1999.
2. Carlson and Decker, *Fast Facts on False Teachings*, pp. 163, 164.
3. For Smith's own account, see Joseph Smith, *Pearl of Great Price* (Salt Lake City, UT: Church of Jesus Christ of Latter Day Saints, 1968), pp. 46-48.
4. George A. Mather and Larry A. Nichols, *Dictionary of Cults, Sects, Religions and the Occult* (Grand Rapids, MI: Zondervan Publishing House, 1993), pp. 186-188; also see Daniel H. Ludlow, ed., *Encyclopedia of Mormonism*, vol. 2, "History of the Church" (New York: Macmillan Publishing Co., 1992), pp. 598-601.
5. Mather and Nichols, *Dictionary of Cults*, p. 188.
6. For a detailed account of Smith's use of peep stones for scrying and participating in other occult activities, such as carrying a magic Jupiter talisman, see Abanes, *Cults*, pp. 190-197. See also *Encyclopedia of Mormonism*, vol. 2, p. 601, where Smith's conviction in court is admitted but explained as an experience that "helped him learn to discern between good and evil." See also Smith, *Pearl of Great Price*, p. 54, for Smith's own explanation for his reputation as a "money digger." He does not mention, however, his conviction for scrying.
7. Smith, "History," in *Pearl of Great Price*, pp. 55, 56.
8. E. D. Howe, *Mormonism Unveiled* (Painsville, OH: E. D. Howe, 1834). For a copy of the entire letter, see Martin, *Kingdom of the Cults*, pp. 197-199.
9. Mather and Nichols, *Dictionary of Cults*, pp. 189, 190.
10. Ibid., p. 48. See also Joseph Smith, *Doctrine and Covenants* (Salt Lake City, UT: The Church of Jesus Christ of Latter Day Saints, 1982), section 132:54. Evidently Smith had been practicing polygamy long before he issued his revelation. *Doctrine and Covenants*, section 132:52 has God telling Emma to "receive all those who *have been given* unto my servant, Joseph" (emphasis added).

11. For one version of what happened when Joseph Smith was killed, see Daniel H. Ludlow, *The Encyclopedia of Mormonism*, vol. 2 (New York: Macmillan Publishing Co., 1992), pp. 613, 860-862. For another account, see Kurt Van Gorden, *Mormonism*, Zondervan Guide to Cults and Religious Movements, p. 11, which notes that Smith shot three men and killed two, information based on the Mormon publication *Documentary History of the Church of Jesus Christ of Latter-day Saints*, 6 vols., B. H. Roberts, ed. (Salt Lake City: Deseret Book Co., 1976), 7:102.

12. *Encyclopedia of Mormonism*, vol. 2, pp. 613-622; also vol. 4, p. 1609.

13. "Excerpts from three addresses by President Wilford Woodruff regarding the Manifesto," in *Doctrine and Covenants*, pp. 292, 293.

14. Brigham Young, *Journal of Discourses*, 10:110 and 8:115, quoted in Abanes, *Cults*, pp. 205, 207.

15. Bruce McConkie, *Mormon Doctrine* (Salt Lake City, UT: Bookcraft, 1966), p. 513.

16. This brief account of the two great civilizations that produced the *Book of Mormon* is based on material in the Introduction to the *Book of Mormon*, quoted in Abanes, *Cults*, p. 211.

17. For a detailed discussion of the *Book of Mormon*, its lack of archaeological evidence, anachronisms, contradictions, plagiarisms, etc., see Martin, *Kingdom of the Cults*, pp. 192-212. See also Floyd C. McElveen, *The Mormon Illusion* (Ventura, CA: Regal Books, 1984), p. 61.

18. Harry Ropp, *The Mormon Papers* (Downer's Grove, IL: InterVarsity Press, 1977), pp. 51-54. Ropp quotes, among others, John L. Sorenson, a Mormon elder and assistant professor of anthropology and sociology at Brigham Young University; and D. Green, former assistant professor of anthropology, who holds an M.A. in archaeology from BYU.

19. Joseph Smith, documented in *History of the Church* (Salt Lake City, UT: Desert Book Co, 1978), 4:461.

20. Joseph Smith, "The Articles of Faith of the Church of Jesus Christ of Latter Day Saints," *The Pearl of Great Price* (Salt Lake City, UT: The Church of Jesus Christ of Latter-day Saints, 1968), p. 60.

21. Orson Pratt, *Orson Pratt's Works* (Salt Lake City, UT: Deseret News Press, 1945), p. 196, quoted in Marvin W. Cowan, *Mormon Claims Answered*, rev. ed. (Salt Lake City, UT: Utah Christian Publications, 1989).

22. In stark comparison to the *Book of Mormon*, the Bible continues to be authenticated and proven correct. For example, in 1993 archaeologists discovered a basalt stone with an inscription referring to "the house of David." This was the first real proof of the existence of King David to be found in the records of antiquity outside the pages of Scripture. See Jeffrey L. Sheler, "Is the Bible True?" *U.S. News and World Report* (October 25, 1999), pp. 50-52. Also, for an excellent book on the veracity of the

Bible, see F. F. Bruce, *The New Testament Documents: Are They Reliable?* (Downers Grove, IL: InterVarsity Press, 1973).

23. For a complete list of what Smith included in *Doctrine and Covenants* that is not taught in the *Book of Mormon*, see Ropp, *Mormon Papers*, p. 55.

24. Cowan, *Mormon Claims*, pp. 68-72; see also pp. 72-76 for examples of more false Mormon prophets. See also Martin, *Kingdom of the Cults*, pp. 207, 208.

25. When Smith began putting together his revelations in addition to the *Book of Mormon*, the first 65 were published as "The Book of Commandments" in 1833. In 1835, more revelations were added, and the entire collection was retitled *Doctrine and Covenants*. For a good discussion of the many changes in *Doctrine and Covenants*, see Ropp, *Mormon Papers*, pp. 56-62.

26. Ropp, *Mormon Papers*, pp. 67, 68.

27. Abanes, *Cults*, pp. 216-220, which includes examples of the correct translation of various Egyptian hieroglyphics and Joseph Smith's *Book of Abraham* translation.

28. *Encyclopedia of Mormonism*, vol. 1, p. 136.

29. James Talmadge, *A Study of the Articles of Faith* (Salt Lake City, UT: The Church of Jesus Christ of Latter Day Saints, 1952), p. 430.

30. Pratt, *The Seer*, p. 132.

31. Latayne Colvette Scott, *The Mormon Mirage* (Grand Rapids, MI: Zondervan Publishing Co., 1979), pp. 167-171. In *Journal of Discourses*, 6:3, Joseph Smith taught "that God the Father of us all dwelt on an earth the same as Jesus Christ Himself did." Joseph Fielding Smith, 10th president/prophet of the Mormon Church, taught that "our Father in heaven at one time passed through a life and death and is an exalted man" (see Joseph Fielding Smith, *Doctrines of Salvation* (Salt Lake City, UT: Bookcraft, 1956), 1:10.

32. *Encyclopedia of Mormonism*, vol. 2, pp. 868, 869. Joseph Smith first taught this idea in *Doctrine and Covenants* when he said, "The elements are eternal" (93:33). See also Sterling McMurrin, *The Philosophical Foundations of Mormon Theology* (Salt Lake City: University of Utah Press, 1959), pp. 12, 29, quoted in James Bjornstad, *Counterfeits*, p. 117.

33. Bjornstad, *Counterfeits*, pp. 110, 111; see also *Encyclopedia of Mormonism*, vol. 2, p. 379.

34. For a thorough discussion of the racism Mormons have perpetrated for nearly 150 years, see Abanes, *Cults*, pp. 205-208.

35. Ezra Taft Benson, *Teachings of the Prophet Ezra Taft Benson* (Salt Lake City, UT: Bookcraft, 1988), p. 7.

36. For a more complete discussion of how Jesus was begotten by God as a spirit being, conceived by the Virgin Mary after God had intercourse with her, and later was married and had children, see: Abanes, *Cults*, pp. 204,

205; Bjornstad, *Counterfeits*, pp. 110-112; Scott, *Mirage*, pp. 173-176; Van Gorden, *Mormonism*, Zondervan Guide, pp. 44-51; Cowan, *Mormon Claims*, pp. 21-23.

37. *Journal of Discourses*, 6:4, quoted in Van Gorden, *Mormonism*, Zondervan Guide, pp. 48, 49.

38. These ideas are taught by Joseph Fielding Smith, tenth president of the Mormon Church, in *Doctrines of Salvation*, 2:48; and by Heber C. Kimball, first counselor to Brigham Young, in *Journal of Discourses*, 1:356. See Van Gorden, *Mormonism*, Zondervan Guide, pp. 56, 57. See also *Encyclopedia of Mormonism*, vol. 2, pp. 465-466, 479, 554, 555.

39. Technically, Mormonism is not polytheism (belief in or worship of many gods). It is more accurate to say Mormonism is henotheism (worship of one God while believing in the existence of many others). See Bill McKeever and Eric Johnson of Mormonism Research Ministry, "How Wide Is the Divide?" (September 1977), available on the Internet at http://www.mrm.org/articles/divide.html.

40. Joseph Smith, *Journal of Discourses*, 6:4

41. For another set of Scriptures concerning the oneness and eternality of God, see Isa. 44:6; 45:5,14,21,22; 46:5; and especially 46:9: "I am God, and there is no other; I am God, and there is none like me."

42. Joseph Smith, *Documentary History*, 6:476.

43. Van Gorden, *Mormonism*, Zondervan Guide, pp. 51, 52.

44. *Encyclopedia of Mormonism*, vol. 2, s.v. "Godhead," pp. 552, 553. For thorough discussions of the difference between the Mormon trinity and biblical Trinity, see Van Gorden, *Mormonism*, Zondervan Guide, pp. 39-44; Cowen, *Mormon Claims*, pp. 13, 14; and Scott, *Mirage*, pp. 167-169, for a discussion of how Smith moved from monotheism and Trinitarian concepts to the idea of three gods in the godhead.

45. Joseph Smith, "Articles of Faith" no. 3, *Pearl of Great Price*.

46. Cowan, *Mormon Claims*, p. 102, for teachings by Joseph Fielding Smith, prophet of the church, and James Talmadge, an apostle, concerning the two kinds of salvation.

47. Bjornstad, *Counterfeits*, pp. 133, 134. For an extensive discussion of all eight requirements, see Cowan, *Mormon Claims*, pp. 104-131.

48. Craig L. Blomberg and Stephen E. Robinson, *How Wide the Divide?* (Downers Grove, IL: InterVarsity Press, 1997).

49. Ibid., p. 18.

50. Ibid., p. 20.

51. Ibid, p. 20.

52. Ibid., p. 163.

53. The most extensive review (and one of the best) is McKeever and Eric Johnson, "How Wide Is the Divide?" http://www.mrm.org/articles/divide.html. Also

excellent is James R. White, "How Wide the Divide? A Mormon and Evangelical in Conversation," *Christian Research Journal* (November/December 1997), pp. 48-51; and Eric Pement, "Is Mormonism Christian?" *Cornerstone Magazine*, vol. 26, no. 112, (1997), pp. 43, 44, 46, 47. Also available on the Internet at http://www.cornerstonemag.com/archives/index/iss112.htm. One other review of great interest is "Sizing Up the Divide: Reviews and Replies," which appears in the *BYU Studies* 38, no. 3 (1999). BYU editors give a summary of various reviews, books, etc., done on *How Wide the Divide?* since its publication in 1997, citing pro and con comments by Mormons and evangelicals. The review also includes replies by Robinson and Blomberg to the various assessments of the book.

54. Robinson, *How Wide the Divide?* p. 15.
55. See http://www.mrm.org/articles/divide.html (accessed 11/8/00).
56. See http://www.mrm.org/articles/divide.html (accessed 11/8/00).
57. Jospeh F. Smith, *Gospel Doctrine* (Salt Lake City, UT: Deseret Book Company, 1977), p. 36.
58. Daniel H. Ludlow, ed., *Encyclopedia of Mormonism*, vol. 1 (New York: Macmillan Publishing Co., 1992), pp. 106, 107.
59. Joseph Smith, *Doctrine and Covenants*, 130:22
60. Talmadge, *A Study of the Articles of Faith*, p. 430.
61. Ibid., pp. 47, 48.
62. Joseph Fielding Smith, *Teachings of the Prophet, Joseph Smith*, (Salt Lake City, UT: Desert Book Co., 1949), p. 370.
63. Grudem, *Systematic Theology*, p. 226. Also see all of chapter 14, pp. 226-261.
64. Joseph Smith, "The Articles of Faith of the Church of Jesus Christ of Latter Day Saints," *Pearl of Great Price*, p. 60.
65. Bruce McConkie, *What Mormons Think of Christ* (Salt Lake City, UT: Bookcraft), p. 28.
66. Bruce McConkie, *Mormon Doctrine* (Salt Lake City, UT: Bookcraft, 1966), p. 670.
67. Ibid.

Chapter 11

1. Russell Chandler, *Understanding the New Age* (Dallas, TX: Word Publishing, 1988), p. 17.
2. J. Gordon Melton, *Encyclopedic Handbook of Cults in America* (New York and London: Garland Publishing, 1986), p. 113, quoted in Chandler, *Understanding*, p. 27.
3. Mary Ann Lind, *From Nirvana to the New Age* (Grand Rapids, MI: Fleming H. Revell Co. Publishers, 1991), pp. 34-42.
4. For why "New Age" is an "umbrella term," see Chandler, *Understanding*, p. 17.

5. These statistics are based on research done by Chandler, *Understanding*, pp. 20, 21.

6. Lind, *From Nirvana to the New Age*, p. 51.

7. Douglas R. Groothuis, "The New Age Movement" (Downers Grove, IL: InterVarsity Christian Fellowship, 1986), p. 9.

8. Shirley MacLaine, *Dancing in the Light* (New York: Bantam Books, 1985), p. 420.

9. Douglas Groothuis, *Confronting the New Age* (Downers Grove, IL: InterVarsity Press, 1988), p. 24.

10. Groothuis, "The New Age Movement," p. 15.

11. MacLaine, *Dancing*, p. 420.

12. Gene Edward Veith, *Post-Modern Times* (Wheaton, IL: Crossway Books, a division of Good News Publishers, 1994), p. 199.

13. Chandler, *Understanding*, p. 206. Spiritism was also popularly known as "Spiritualism," but "spiritism" is the more accurate word. See J. K. Van Baalen, *The Chaos of Cults* (Grand Rapids, MI: W. B. Eerdmans Publishing Co., 1956), p. 20.

14. Groothuis, *Confronting*, p. 27.

15. Van Baalen, *Chaos*, p. 20.

16. Chandler, *Understanding*, p. 83.

17. Groothuis, *Confronting*, p. 28.

18. Quoted in Martin Gardner, "Is-ness Is Her Business," *New York Review* (April 9, 1987), p. 18.

19. Chandler, *Understanding*, pp. 210-212.

20. Dean Halverson, "A Course in Miracles: Seeing Yourself As Sinless," *Spiritual Counterfeits Project Journal*, vol. 7, no. 1 (1987), pp. 18-29.

21. Chandler, *Understanding*, p. 264.

22. MacLaine, *Out On a Limb* (New York: Bantam, 1983), p. 249.

23. For a discussion of what Origen taught and why he was condemned at the Fifth Ecumenical Council, see John Hick, *Death and Eternal Life* (San Francisco: Harper & Row, 1980), pp. 392-394. Also, for a full discussion of reincarnation and the twisting of Scripture done by New Age proponents such as Shirley MacLaine, see Groothuis, *Confronting*, pp. 94-103.

24. James Redfield, *The Celestine Vision* (New York: Warner Books, 1997), pp. 138-140, and especially chap. 12.

25. Constance Cumbey, *Hidden Dangers of the Rainbow* (Layfayette, LA: Huntington House, 1983), p. 90.

26. Alice A. Bailey, *Discipleship in the New Age II* (New York: Lucius Publishing Co., 1955), p. vi.

27. Marilyn Ferguson, *The Aquarian Conspiracy* (Los Angeles, CA: J P. Tarcher, Inc., 1990), pp. 213-221.

28. Lind, *From Nirvana to the New Age*, pp. 52, 53. For other examples of Christian analyzers of the New Age who do not see it as a conspiracy but

Christian analyzers of the New Age who do not see it as a conspiracy but as a movement that must be confronted and combated, see Ron Rhodes, *New Age Movement,* Zondervan Guide to Cults and Religious Movements, series ed. Alan W. Gomes (Grand Rapids, MI: Zondervan Publishing House, 1995), pp. 11, 12; Douglas R. Groothuis, *Unmasking the New Age* (Downers Grove, IL: InterVarsity Press, 1986), pp. 33-36.

29. Carrie D. McRoberts, *New Age or Old Lie?* (Peabody, MA: Henrickson Publishers, Inc., 1989), p. 49.

30. Groothuis, *Confronting,* pp. 190-195.

31. For a more thorough discussion of the entertainment industry, particularly films, television, video games and music, see Lind, *From Nirvana to the New Age,* pp. 119-127.

32. Berit Kjos, "The Dangers of Role Playing Games: How Pokemon and Magic Cards Affect the Minds and Values of Children," http://www.crossroad.to/text/articles/pokemon5-99.html (accessed 11/18/00).

33. MacLaine, *Dancing,* p. 354.

34. David Spangler, *Reflections on the Christ* (Forres, Scotland: Findhorn Publishers, 1981), p. 28.

35. See Levi Dowling, *The Aquarian Gospel of Jesus the Christ* (London: L. N. Fowler and Co., 1947), p. 56.

36. Ferguson, *Aquarian,* p. 29.

37. Julius J. Finegold and William M. Thetford, eds., *Choose Once Again: Selections from A Course in Miracles* (Millbrae, CA: Celestial Arts, 1981), pp. 2, 3.

38. MacLaine, *Limb,* p. 233.

Chapter 12

1. John Boykin, "The Baha'i Faith," chap. 2 in Ronald Enroth and Others, *A Guide to Cults and New Religions,* (Downers Grove, IL: InterVarsity Press, 1983), p. 26; see also Walter Martin, *The Kingdom of the Cults, Updated, and Expanded,* gen. ed. Hank Hanagraaff (Minneapolis: Bethany House Publishers, 1997), p. 321.

2. George A. Mather and Larry A. Nichols, *Dictionary of Cults, Sects, Religions and the Occult* (Grand Rapids, MI: Zondervan Publishing House, 1993), p. 32.

3. This number of Baha'i adherents—6,500,000—obtained from "Major Branches of Religions Ranked by Number of Adherents," http://www.Adherents.com.

4. Enroth and Others, *A Guide to Cults,* p. 28.

5. According to Baha'i teachings, there were nine manifestations in all. In addition to the seven named in the text, Mirza Ali Mohammed (The Bab) was the eighth manifestation, followed 13 years after his death by Baha'u'llah, considered the last and greatest manifestation of all.

6. Shoghi Effendi, *World Order Of Baha'u'llah* (Wilmette, IL: Baha'I Publishing Trust, 1955), pp. 40, 41, quoted in Enroth and Others, *A Guide to Cults,* pp. 30, 31.

7. Grudem, *Systematic Theology*, pp. 226-230, which includes discussion of many other passages referring to the plurality of God.

8. Enroth and Others, *A Guide*, pp. 31, 32.

9. See the account of an interview of a Baha'i teacher by Gretchen Passantino in Martin, *Kingdom of the Cults*, pp. 325-327.

10. For a thorough discussion of differences between Baha'i and Christianity, particularly Baha'u'llah's claims regarding the Holy Spirit, see Enroth and Others, *A Guide*, pp. 32-36.

11. Effendi, *Baha'u'llah*, p. 133, quoted in Enroth and Others, *A Guide*, p. 28.

12. For a graphic example of Baha'i displeasure with the exclusive claims of Christianity, see Martin, *Kingdom of the Cults*, pp. 329, 330.

13. Martin, *Kingdom of the Cults*, p. 245.

14. Todd Ehrenborg, *Mind Sciences: Christian Science, Religious Science, Unity School of Christianity*, Zondervan Guide to Cults and Religious Movements, series ed. Alan W Gomes (Grand Rapids, MI: Zondervan Publishing House, 1995), pp. 7, 8.

15. Martin, *Kingdom of the Cults*, p. 248.

16. Ibid., p. 249.

17. Ibid., pp. 249, 250.

18. For comparisons of specific passages from Eddy's and others' writings, see Martin, *Kingdom*, pp. 250-253.

19. Martin, *Kingdom of the Cults*, pp. 254, 255.

20. Ehrenborg, *Mind Sciences*, p. 10.

21. Ibid., p. 12.

22. *Science and Health* (1881 edition), p. 169, quoted in Martin, *Kingdom of the Cults*, p. 250.

23. Ibid., (p. 468), p. 252.

24. Martin, *Kingdom of the Cults,* p. 262.

25. Ehrenborg, *Mind Sciences*, p. 12.

26. Ibid., pp. 15, 16.

27. *Science and Health*, pp. 256, 361, quoted in Martin, *Kingdom of the Cults*, p. 259.

28. Ibid., (p. 466), p. 250.

29. Ibid., (pp. 25, 45, 46), p. 260.

30. *Science and Health*, p. 266, quoted in Martin, *Kingdom*, p. 261

31. Mary Baker Eddy, *Miscellaneous Writings*, p. 261, quoted in Martin, *Kingdom*, p. 261.

32. Ehrenborg, *Mind Sciences*, p. 20, where he summarizes the teachings of *Science and Health* concerning the Trinity, which appear on pp. 588:7, 8; 55:27-29.

33. *Science and Health*, p. 2, quoted in Martin, *Kingdom*, p. 277.

34. *Science and Health*, p. 447, quoted in Martin, *Kingdom*, p. 260.

35. Colson and Pearcey, *How Now Shall We Live?*, p. 54.

36. Colin Brown, "A World Come of Age," *Introduction to the History of Christianity*, ed. Tim Dowley (Minneapolis, MN: Fortress Press, 1995), pp. 548, 549.

37. George M. Marsden, index references under "Evolution" in *The Soul of the American University: From Protestant Establishment to Established Nonbelief*, (New York: Oxford University Press, 1994).

38. Douglas Futuyma, *Evolutionary Biology* (Sunderland, MA: Sinauer, 1986), p. 3.

39. "NABT Unveils New Statement on Teaching Evolution," *The American Biology Teacher*, 68, no. 1 (January 1996), p. 61, quoted in Colson and Pearcey, *How Now*, p. 82. Due to widespread protests, the NABT dropped the words "unsupervised and impersonal" from their statement, but the words "unpredictable and natural" were understood to mean the same thing.

40. William B. Provine and Philip E. Johnson, "Darwinism: Science or Naturalistic Philosophy?", videotape of debate held at Stanford University, April 30, 1994, quoted in Colson and Pearcey, *How Now*, p. 92. The videotape is available through Access Research Network, P. O. Box 38069, Colorado Springs, CO 80937-8069.

41. Charles Darwin, *The Origin of Species* (New American Library, 1958), p. 450.

42. David A. Noebel, *Understanding the Times* (Eugene, OR: Harvest House Publishers, 1991), p. 266.

43. For excellent discussions of how the fossil record, gene mutation and the complexity of the cell all disprove Darwinian evolution, see the following: Colson and Pearcey, "Darwin In the Dock," chap. 9 in *How Now*, esp. pp. 83-90; Philip Johnson, *Darwin On Trial* (Downers Grove, IL: InterVarsity Press, 1993); Philip Johnson, chap. 5, "Intelligent Design," esp. pp. 75ff, "Opening the Black Boxes of Biology," in *Defeating Darwinism By Opening Minds* (Downers Grove, IL: InterVarsity Press, 1997). Also see Tom Woodward's excellent article, "Meeting Darwin's Wager," *Christianity Today* (April 28, 1997), pp. 15-21, for a thorough discussion of Michael Behe's work and how it virtually destroys the theory of Darwinian macro-evolution.

44. For refutation of the various efforts to explain the gap in the fossil records, see Johnson, *Trial*, pp. 50-62.

45. Stephen Jay Gould, "This View of Life," *Natural History* (July 1995), quoted in Dave Foreman "Abiologism," *Wild Earth* (Richmond, VT: The Cenozoic Society, Summer 1997), p. 3.

46. Reverend John Selby Spong, Episcopal Bishop of New Jersey, in "A Call for a New Reformation" in *The Voice: The Official Newspaper for the Newark Diocese* (May 1998). Also available at the website of the Diocese of Newark, www.dioceseofnewark.org/jsspong/reform.html.

47. Professor Louis Bounoure, director of the Strasbourg Zoological Museum, director of research at the French National Center of Scientific Research, writing in *The Advocate* (March 8, 1984), p. 17.

48. Isaac Asimov, *In Science and Creationism*, ed. Ashley Montagu (Oxford: Oxford University Press, 1984), p. 182.

49. Source unknown.

50. John Ankerberg and John Weldon, *The Secret Teachings of the Masonic Lodge: A Christian Perspective* (Chicago, IL: Moody Press, 1989, 1990), p. 10.

51. For a thorough discussion of the many lodges, orders, rites and other organizations in Freemasonry, including those for women, see George A. Mather and Larry A. Nichols, *Masonic Lodge*, Zondervan Guide to Cults and Religious Movements , series ed. Alan W. Gomes (Grand Rapids, MI: Zondervan Publishing House, 1995), pp. 10-24.

52. None of these claims is supported by historical evidence. See Mather and Nichols, *Masonic Lodge*, pp. 7, 8.

53. Mather and Nichols, *Masonic Lodge*, pp. 8, 9.

54. Ibid., p. 9.

55. Ibid., p. 27.

56. *Webster's New World Dictionary* (New Jersey: Prentice Hall, 1970, 1988).

57. Mather and Nichols, *Masonic Lodge*, p. 40.

58. John J Robinson, *Born in Blood: The Lost Secrets of Freemasonry* (New York: M. Evans & Company, 1989), p. 177. See also Ankerberg and Weldon, *Secret Teachings*, pp. 244-253.

59. Mather and Nichols, *Masonic Lodge*, pp. 24, 25.

60. Ibid., p. 42.

61. Ibid., pp. 33-36.

62. Ankerberg and Weldon, *Secret Teachings*, pp. 168-177, 215-243, 254-263. See also Ron Campbell, *Free From Freemasonry* (Ventura, CA: Regal Books, 1999).

63. Ankerberg and Weldon, *Secret Teachings*, p. 97, quoting Albert Mackey's *Revised Encyclopedia of Freemasonry*, revised and enlarged by Robert I. Clegg, 3 vols. (Richmond, VA: Macoy, 1966), vol. 1, p. 133.

64. *Coil's Masonic Encyclopedia* quoted in and *Mackey's Revised Encyclopedia of Freemasonry*, vol. 2, pp. 735, 746, referenced in Ankerberg and Weldon, *Secret Teachings*, pp. 119, 120.

65. Thirty-third Degree Masonic leader Jim Shaw, Past Worshipful Master of the Blue Lodge, Past Master of all Scottish Rite Bodies and Knight Commander of the Court of Honor, quoted in Ankerberg and Weldon, *Secret Teachings*, p. 131. See also Jim Shaw and Tom McKenney, *The Deadly Deception: Freemasonry Exposed By One of Its Top Leaders* (Lafayette, LA: Huntington House, 1988), pp. 126, 127.

66. Carl H. Claudy, *Little Masonic Library*, 4 (Richmond, VA: Macoy Publishers and Supply Company, 1946), p. 51.

67. Ankerberg and Weldon, *Secret Teachings*, pp. 126-129.

68. Albert Pike, *Morals and Dogma of the Ancient and Accepted Scottish Rite of Freemasonry* (Charleston, SC: The Supreme Council of the 33rd Degree for the Southern Jurisdiction of the United States, 1906), pp. 219, 161, quoted in Ankerberg and Weldon, *Secret Teachings*, p. 200.

69. J. Isamu Yamamoto, "Hare Krishna (ISKCON)," chap. 6 in Enroth and Others, *A Guide*, p. 94.

70. Ibid., p. 94.

71. Mather and Nichols, *Dictionary of Cults*, pp. 117, 137. See also Yamamoto in Enroth and others, *A Guide*, pp. 92-93. The three significant gods that came out of the Hindu pantheon of India included Brahma, Shiva and Vishnu.

72. Yamamoto, in Enroth and Others, *A Guide*, p. 97.

73. Ibid., p. 93.

74. Mather and Nichols, *Dictionary of Cults*, p. 139.

75. Ibid., p. 138.

76. For the account of one young girl who was caught up in Krishna and later freed from the cult through the work of her parents, see Ron Enroth, "The Hare Krishna Movement," chap. 1 in *Youth Brainwashing and the Extremist Cults* (Grand Rapids, MI: Zondervan Publishing House, 1977), pp. 19-34.

77. Enroth, *Brainwashing*, pp. 23, 24.

78. A. C. Bhaktivedanta Swami Prabhupada, *Bhagavad Gita As It Is* (Los Angeles, CA: ISKCON, 1975), p. 168.

79. Siddha Swarup Ananda Goswam, *Jesus Loves Krsna* (Los Angeles, CA: Vedic Christian Committee and Life Force, Krsan Yoga Viewpoint, 1975), p. 14, quoted in Martin, *Kingdom of the Cults*, p. 400.

80. Yamamoto, in Enroth and Others, *A Guide, p.* 96.

81. Ibid., pp. 96, 97.

82. Prabhupada, *Bhagavad Gita*, p. 81.

83. Randy Frame, "The Cost of Discipleship?: Despite Allegations of Abuse of Authority, the International Churches of Christ Expands Rapidly," *Christianity Today* (September 1, 1997), pp. 64-66, 88; Charles Anzalone, "That New Time Religion," Buffalo Magazine section of the *Buffalo News* (March 26, 1995).

84. For a good description, see Frank S. Mead, *Handbook of Denominations in the United States*, 6th ed. (Nashville: Abingdon Press,1975), pp. 79, 107, 108.

85. Stephen F. Cannon, "History of the Boston Church of Christ—Has Mind Control Come to Bean Town?" *The Quarterly Journal*, vol. 9, no. 2 (April-June 1989).

86. Frame, "Cost," pp. 64-68; also see Rick Branch, Watchman Fellowship Profile, "Boston Church of Christ," 1993, available at Watchman Fellowship, P. O. Box 530842, Birmingham, AL, 35253, or contact at www.watchman.org/al/.

87. James Bjornstad, "At What Price Success? The Boston (Church of Christ) Movement," *Christian Research Journal* (Winter 1993), p. 27.

88. For McKean's autobiographical account of how he developed the Boston movement into a "worldwide outreach," see his paper "Revolution Through Restoration," available on the ICC home page: *www.icoc.org* (accessed 11-16-00). Also available in the ICC publication *Upside Down Magazine*, issue no. 2 (April 1992).

89. McKean, subsections "Introduction," "Restoration in Boston," "The Twentieth Century Church" and "The Movement of God" in "Revolution." Also see *Upside Down Magazine* (April 1994).

90. Flabil Yeakley, Jr, ed., *The Discipling Dilemma* (Nashville, TN: Gospel Advocate Pub. Co., 1988), p. 37.

91. Yeakley, *Dilemma*, p. 37. See also Cannon, "Bean Town."

92. Ibid., p. 27.

93. McKean, subsection "Boston to Moscow" in "Revolution."

94. Frame, "Cost," p. 66.

95. Statistics from the ICC webpage at www.icoc.org.

96. McKean, subsection "The Evidence of Grace: Growth" in "Revolution Through Restoration, Part 2."

97. Ibid., subsection "The Movement of God."

98. Ibid.

99. Jerry Jones, *What Does the Boston Movement Teach?*, p. 104, quoted in Branch, "Boston Church," p. 2.

100. For good discussions of ICC discipleship practices, see Bjornstad, "Boston Movement," p. 31.

101. Kip McKean, "The Role of the Evangelist," *BBC Bulletin* (Aug 9, 1987).

102. Available at the ICC webpage at www.icoc.org.

103. Rick Bauer, *Toxic Christianity—The International Churches of Christ/Boston Movement Cult* (Bowie, MD: Freedom House Ministries, 1994). n.p.

104. Ibid.

105. Joanne Ruhland, "Effective Evangelism: Witnessing to Disciples of the International Church of Christ (ak.a., The Boston Movement), *Christian Research Journal* (Fall 1996), p. 43.

106. Reported in the *Miami Herald*, 25 March 1992, p. 1A, 15A, quoted in Branch, subsection "Other Doctrines in Boston Church."
107. McKean, subsection "The Ultimate Challenge: Unity" in "Revolution Through Restoration Part 2."
108. Charles Caldwell Ryrie, *Ryrie Study Bible* (Chicago: Moody Press, 1978), p. 1874, for further commentary on 2 Pet. 1:20 and how prophecy should be interpreted.
109. Ibid., p. 1869.
110. Frame, "Cost,"p. 66. Also see Julianna Gittler, "Church or Cult? A Look at the Controversial Los Angeles Church of Christ," *The Long Beach Union*, Cal State University, Long Beach, student newspaper, Nov. 29, 1993; Olaina Gupta, "A Question of Faith," *Daily Nexus*, University of Santa Barbara student newspaper, Wed., Nov. 30, 1994.
111. Bjornstad, "The Boston Movement," p. 26.
112. McKean, "Revolution," pp. 5-16; also see Al Baird, "A New Look At Authority," *Upside Down Magazine* (April 1992), pp. 18, 19.
113. Bauer, *Toxic Christianity*, p. 18.
114. Tim Dowley, *Introduction to the History of Christianity* (Minneapolis, MN: Fortress Press, 1995), p. 548.
115. Paul Kurtz and Edwin Wilson, *Humanist Manifestos I and II* (Buffalo, NY: Prometheus Books, 1973). Also see James Hitchcock, *What Is Secular Humanism?* (Ann Arbor, MI: Servant Books, 1982), pp. 11,13.
116. Ibid., pp. 17, 18.
117. Kurtz and Wilson, *Humanist Manifesto II*, statement 6, p. 22
118. For a thoughtful critique of *Humanist Manifesto II*, see McDowell and Stewart, *Handbook*, pp. 462-477.
119. For books discussing Postmodernism's emergence, see Margaret Rose, *The Post-Modern and the Post-Industrial: A Critical Analysis* (Cambridge: Cambridge University Press, 1991); Bernard Iddings Bell, *Religion for Living: A Book for Post-Modernists* (London: The Religious Book Club, 1939); Arnold Toynbee, *A Study of History* (London: Oxford University Press, 1939), vol 5, p. 43; vol. 8 (published 1954), p. 338.
120. Jim Leffel, "Post-Modernism and 'The Myth of Progress": Two Visions," in Dennis McCallum, ed., *The Death of Truth* (Minneapolis: Bethan House Publishers, 1996), p. 50.
121. Ibid., p. 50.
122. Jim Leffel, "Our New Challenge: Post-Modernism," *The Death of Truth*, Dennis McCallum, ed. (Minneapolis, MN: Bethany House Publishers, 1996), p. 31.
123. Ibid., p. 32.
124. McDowell and Hostetler, *New Tolerance*, p. 19.
125. Ibid., p. 20.

126. For documentation of how the "new tolerance" challenges and oppresses those with Christian values and morals, see McDowell and Hostetler, *The New Tolerance*, pp. 26, 27.

127. McCallum, *Death of Truth*, pp. 199-212.

128. McCallum, *Death of Truth*, p. 31. Also see Lee Campbell, "Post-Modern Impact: Science," chap. 11 in *Death of Truth*.

129. Ibid., p. 35.

130. Ibid., pp. 34, 35, 99.

131. Josh McDowell and Bob Hostetler, *Right from Wrong* (Dallas: Word Publishing, 1994), p. 15.

132. George Barna, *What America Believes: An Annual Survey of Values and Religious Views in the United States* (Ventura, CA: Regal Books, 1991), p. 85.

133. Ted Olson, "Many College Students Do Not Probe Beliefs," *Christianity Today*, vol. 41, no. 2-3 (Feb. 1997), p. 88.

134. Gallup poll, *PRRC Emerging Trends* (February 1992), p. 3.

135. Chuck Colson, "The Searing of the Conscience," *Jubilee* (Summer 2000), 23.

136. Kurt Van Gorden, "The Unification Church," in Walter Martin, *Kingdom of the Cults*, p. 352.

137. Martin, *Kingdom of the Cults*, pp. 352, 353.

138. Ibid., p. 353. See also Abanes, *Cults*, pp. 138-140.

139. Martin, *Kingdom of the Cults*, p. 355.

140. Martin, *Kingdom of the Cults*, p. 359.

141. J. Isamu Yamamoto, *Unification Church*, Zondervan Guide to Cults and Religious Movements, series ed. Alan W. Gomes (Grand Rapids, MI: Zondervan Publishing House, 1995), p. 17

142. Martin, *Kingdom of the Cults*, p. 357.

143. Ibid., p. 358.

144. Ibid., pp. 364, 365.

145. Yamamoto, *Unification Church*, p. 33.

146. Walter Martin, *Kingdom of the Cults*, p. 367.

147. Walter Martin, *Kingdom of the Cults*, pp. 361, 362.

148. Sun Myung Moon, *Exposition of the Divine Principle* (New York: The Holy Spirit Association for the Unification of World Christianity, 1996), quoted in Abanes, *Cults*, p. 148, xxii. See also Yamamoto, *Unification Church*, p. 25.

149. Yamamoto, *Unification Church*, p. 25.

150. Ronald Enroth, *Youth Brainwashing and Extremist Cults* (Grand Rapids: Zondervan Publishing House, 1977), p. 110.

151. Walter Martin, *Kingdom of the Cults*, p. 359.

152. Ibid., pp. 639, 640.

153. Ibid.

154. Sinclair B. Ferguson and David Wright, *New Dictionary of Theology* (Downers Grove, IL: InterVarsity Press, 1988), pp. 386, 619.

155. Dana McLean Greeley, "Spry Downgarder of Divinity," *Life* (July 28, 1967), p. 31.

156. "What Is a Unitarian?" *Look* (March 8, 1955), n.p.

157. Martin, *Kingdom of the Cults*, p. 642.

158. Ibid., p. 644.

159. Arvid Straube, "The Bible in Unitarian Universalist Theology," *Unitarian Universalist Christian*, vol. 44, no. 1 (1989), p. 23.

160. *We Are Unitarian Universalists* (Boston: Unitarian Universalist Association, 1992).

161. Paul Trudinger, "St. Paul: A Unitarian Universalist Christian?" *Faith and Freedom*, 43 (Spring/Summer 1990), p. 57.

162. John A. Buehrens and F. Forester Church, eds., *Our Chosen Faith: An Introduction to Unitarian Universalism* (Boston: Beacon, 1989), p. 134.

163. Carl M. Chworowsky and Christopher Gist Raible, "What Is a Unitarian Universalist?" *Religions in America*, ed. Leo Rosten (New York: Simon and Schuster, 1975), pp. 267, 268.

164. George N. Marshall, *Challenge of a Liberal Faith, Revised and Enlarged Edition* (New Canaan, CT: Keats, 1980), p. 237.

165. Craig S. Hawkins, *Goddess Worship, Witchcraft and Neo-Paganism*, Zondervan Guide to Cults and Religious Movements, series ed. Alan W. Gomes (Grand Rapids, MI: Zondervan Publishing House, 1998), p. 7.

166. Alan W. Gomes, *Truth and Error: Comparative Charts on Cults and Christianity*, Zondervan Guide to Cults and Religious Movements, series ed. Alan W. Gomes (Grand Rapids, MI: Zondervan Publishing House, 1998), p. 68.

167. Mather and Nichols, *Dictionary of Cults*, pp. 312, 314.

168. Craig S. Hawkins, *Goddess Worship, Witchcraft and Neo-Paganism*, p. 23.

169. Mather and Nichols, pp. 314, 315.

170. Hawkins, p. 26.

171. Robinson, "Excerpts from a U.S. District Court Decision Recognizing Wicca as a Religion" at the Wicca and Witchcraft website, www.religioustolerance.org.

172. Catherine Edwards, "Wicca Infiltrates the Churches," *Prayer Net Newsletter, U.S. Prayer Tract*, Nov. 24, 1999, http://www.usprayertract.org.

173. Hawkins, pp. 8-11.

174. Hawkins, pp. 9, 10.

175. For more on Neo-pagan ethics, see Hawkins, pp. 10, 11.

176. For a more complete discussion of Wiccan core beliefs and practices, see Hawkins, pp. 11-22.

177. Starhawk (Miriam Simos), *The Spiral Dance: A Rebirth of the Ancient Religion of the Great Goddess* (San Francisco: Harper & Row, 1979), p. 9.

178. Prudence Jones and Caitlin Matthews, eds., *Voices From the Circle: The Heritage of Western Paganism* (Wellingborough, Northamptonshire, England: The Aquarian Press, 1990), p. 40.

179. Doreen Valiente, *An ABC of Witchcraft: Past and Present* (New York: St. Martin's Press, 1973), p. 14.

180. Margot Adler, *Drawing Down the Moon: Witches, Druids, Goddess-Worshippers, and Other Pagans In America Today, Revised and Expanded Edition* (Boston, MA: Beacon Press, 1986), p. ix.

181. Starhawk, *Spiral Dance*, p. 84.

182. Ceisiwr Serith, *The Pagan Family: Handing the Old Ways Down* (St. Paul, MN: Llewellyn, 1994), p. 198.

183. Starhawk, *Spiral Dance*, pp. 13, 109.

184. Starhawk, *Spiral Dance*, p. 14.

185. Silver Ravenwolf, *Teen Witch: Wicca For a New Generation* (St. Paul, MN: Llewellyn, 1998), p. xiii.

186. Ravenwolf, frontispiece.